HOUSE OF COMMONS LIBRARY	
LOCATION	R Newspaper
AUTHOR	BARKER
Acc DATE	

ACCESSION NUMBER

15 DEC 1972

HOUSE OF COMMONS LIBRARY

TO BE
DISPOSED
BY
AUTHORITY

D0295712

One for sorrow,
Two for joy

One for sorrow, Two for joy

ten years of NEW SOCIETY

edited by Paul Barker

London · George Allen & Unwin Ltd
Ruskin House   Museum Street

First published in 1972

This book is copyright under the Berne Convention. All
rights are reserved. Apart from any fair dealing for the
purpose of private study, research, criticism or review, as
permitted under the Copyright Act, 1956, no part of this
publication may be reproduced, stored in a retrieval
system, or transmitted, in any form or by any means,
electronic, electrical, chemical, mechanical, optical,
photocopying, recording or otherwise, without the
prior permission of the copyright owner. Enquiries should
be addressed to the publishers.

© New Society 1972

ISBN 0 04 300040 1 hardback
0 04 300041 x paper

Printed in Great Britain
in 11 point Times Roman type
by Cox & Wyman Ltd
London, Fakenham and Reading

CONTENTS

Contents

ONE FOR SORROW, TWO FOR JOY

"The way we tell our furtune is to keep our bus
tickets and add up the numbers at the top,
see how many times seven gos into the number,
see how many you have over. Say this little ryhmn
and that is your furture. The ryhmn is—
    One for sorrow,
    Two for joy,
    Three for a letter,
    Four for a boy,
    Five for silver,
    Six for gold,
    Seven for a secret, that's never been told."

Ten year old Birmingham girl in THE LORE AND
LANGUAGE OF SCHOOLCHILDREN *by Iona and
Peter Opie*

INTRODUCTION

All magazines, probably, have some sort of inner tension—a conflict that keeps them going. They have two aims, two subject-matters, which the magazine tries to reconcile. Much of its dynamic comes from that tension. In the case of *New Society*, the two aspects are what might be called anthropological (ie, the way the world is) and administrative (ie, what you can do about it).

The starting point for *New Society* was, of course, the social sciences. The first issue, on 4 October 1962, ran an editorial that said: "It is in the belief that the human sciences must come into their own that *New Society* is now launched." If they have since come into their own in Britain, if social scientific research is more heeded, it may be not too much like self-praise to see *New Society* as having had a lot to do with it.

Within the social sciences, the point of *New Society* has always been to cross-pollinate. It also cross-pollinates between these sciences and people working outside them. "We shall not ignore ideas or theories," that editorial said, ". . . but we aim above all to link the study of society with practice: to tell the manager what the psychologist has to say, to make the town planner aware of what the social anthropologist is revealing . . . and—in each case, equally important—vice versa. The experience of the practitioner and the research of the academic are complementary, and our contributors will be drawn from both groups."

Fortunately, nothing important in social science is yet at the stage where it cannot be put in reasonably plain language for the non-specialist; and that has been an aim, too, even if beauty of phrase is not always possible. If behaviour, or policy, is to be influenced, laymen must be able to get the point.

New Society has never been stuffy about what it contained. Rigorous research is crucial, but so are imagination and diversity. Some of our more interesting articles have contained the least hard data. Social journalism has also always been given space in our pages; often there are subjects which research has not yet come to. But our journalism has been respectful of facts—and, come to that, of ordinary people. With the shrinking definition of what "serious" journalism means, in what used to be known as quality papers, this may have become, with time, a more important function than in 1962.

From the start, *New Society*, which remains the only weekly of its kind in the world, distinguished itself from the more traditional London-based weeklies (preoccupied with "news", politics and literature) by its attempt at objectivity. It has never given general support to any party; never tried to tell its readers how to vote. (A pointless exercise, in any case: rather like trying to tell the Chancellor of the Exchequer, on budget eve, what to put in his budget.) *New Society* has been concerned to improve the life of the underprivileged; so its readers have not generally come from the hard right of any party. But it has not been all that easily defined as of the left, with the characteristic (especially far-left) problem of distinguishing verbal aspiration from achievement. Neither has *New Society* really been a campaigning magazine—unless you could say that its campaign is to set out facts with neo-Victorian passion. No one, of course, can be totally objective. But at least one can try to find out what facts there are, and form as honest a conclusion as one can.

Social science itself is often—perhaps excessively—concerned with the underprivileged, the unsuccessful, the deviant. (They are easier to intrude on and to get to talk.) But one cannot understand the world, or even set wrongs right, without understanding what moves the mass of the people most of the time. *New Society* tries to keep this in mind—as when John Barr once wrote for us an inquiry into the homes that people *want*, as opposed to those that others think they should want.

New Society tries to avoid the trap of conspiracy theory, too. It has, I suppose, kept as close a watch on the activities of central and local government as any magazine; but on the basis that one should, among other things, try to discover what the administrators themselves were hoping to do. Few professions are manned by demons. Most members of most professions are simply run-of-the-mill, which is not a crime. Miracles have been rare, for some centuries now.

By and large, *New Society* covers an area of interest that, in H. J. Eysenck's terminology, one might call "tender-minded."

But within that area, it has tried to be relatively tough. There is little point in saying: let all social services have more money; they are not all going to get it. Nor is there much point in saying: let everyone forswear materialism, or aggression, or elitism, or whatever; they are not going to. *New Society* attempts, first, to understand the underlying forces, motives and aspirations; and, second, to pin down what the practical alternatives are. One of the more informative opinion surveys that the magazine itself commissioned was on attitudes towards Europe. It showed how, even among people who said they were pro-Marketeers, there was much more human sympathy with Americans (or with Nigerians) than with the French. This kind of complexity is worth having. This same survey, though centrally about British society, was also an example of the way in which we have tried to avoid parochialism. We have regularly run long, informed pieces about other parts of the world: ideally, those *not* in the news. . . .

The original idea for *New Society* sprang indirectly from a conversation over lunch between Tim Raison, who was to become the first editor, and Michael Young. It was reinforced later by a conversation he had with anthropologists on the need for a new journal about man. At his father's request, he was at that point on the lookout for new magazine projects, to follow up the success of *New Scientist*.

Maxwell Raison had been managing director of *Picture Post*. He left it to found, with Nicholas Harrison, an independent company, and to start up *New Scientist*. Tim Raison also moved from the staff of *Picture Post* to that of the new magazine. Begun in 1956, *New Scientist* rode on the wave of a government desire to encourage more people to become scientists and technologists. *New Society*, however, was a much more speculative enterprise. No such drive for social scientists existed then. A good book creates its own audience, and this was what *New Society* needed to do. While it did so, the company sustained it through a money-losing three years. Anyone who was on it during that time (as I was myself) retains, I think, a feeling of crusade, of seeking to establish a magazine which, whatever you felt about it, was unmistakably different from the other magazines around.

Tim Raison was not by training a social scientist; at Oxford

13

he read modern history. But it may be generally right for the editor of *New Society* not to be over-committed to any of the specialisms it covers. In any event, he was an excellent editor: he knew what he wanted. He established the magazine well. He launched it with a small, politically balanced team (he himself had been editor of the Bow Group's *Crossbow* while he was still on *New Scientist*). When the first issue came out, it even *looked* different from other magazines, because it had been decided to carry more illustrations than was then usual; these helped to give statistics a human face.

Sales moved forward, after the launch, in two main stages: 1964–66 and 1968–70. The first helped to make us viable, in the upper 20,000s a year; the second carried us into the upper 30,000s. Besides sales, the other component in *New Society's* (commercial) success was classified advertising. Careful calculations had been made—especially by Collin Shepherd, later our publisher—about what we could attract. Gradually the advertisers came. Just as the magazine created a new audience, so it created a new marketplace. Many jobs in (roughly) social work came to be advertised in *New Society*. Partly as a result of the changes brought about by the Seebohm report on local authority social services, these advertisements have, so far, continued to grow.

I know that this marketplace has been useful for those working, or hoping to work, in the professions it serves. It has also been very useful for *New Society*. Through the glummer stretches of recent economic history, *New Society* was never squeezed for space because of a lack of advertising. It is useful, too, that such advertisements do not exert the pressure, editorially, that other kinds have been known to do elsewhere—either in terms of the look of the magazine, or in terms of its content. The social services—and, in particular, social work—have always remained *part* of our subject-matter. Here, too, we have cross-pollinated, rather than over-specialised. And *New Society* has been able to be freer in what it has said about many things (including about segments of the advertising industry) than almost any other magazine.

In 1966, at about the time that *New Society* began to break even, it and *New Scientist* became part of the International Publishing Corporation. They are now published with *The*

Geographical Magazine (a later addition) as a separate unit. On the whole, magazines like *New Society* are best run and owned by companies whose entire purpose revolves around them. But the editorial policy has at no point changed; and there has never been any attempt to curb that "editorial discretion which (to quote Lord Devlin from memory) lies at the heart of the freedom of the press."

Tim Raison was editor until 1968. At that date, after having been gradually more and more involved in the editing of the magazine, I succeeded him. In the general election of June 1970, he entered the House of Commons as a Conservative MP. In fact, all the members of that first editorial team have now moved on. *New Society* often recruits people at a fairly early stage in their career. This prevents ossification; and it has always been good to see writers coming on. Most have gone into other branches of journalism, often combined with authorship. For several, I think that being on *New Society* was crucial to their growth as writers. To one of the most talented, John Barr—the quietest of quiet Americans—tribute must, alas, be posthumous.

New Society's approach has always been (to use Iain Macleod's bitter phrase) non-Magic-Circle. It has not taken people on its staff because of any "connexions." In the same way, *all* articles that come in to *New Society* are considered for publication. Some of our best have come out of the blue, in this way; often they have been a good antidote to metropolitan-ness; too much is written about London. The sole test has been whether an article had something new to say.

It has always been important for *New Society* to move onto new ground. (R. D. Laing, for example, made a very early appearance in its pages.) The magazine lives by the quality of its ideas and information—its intelligence in both senses. It has tried never to be obsessed by news, as opposed to events (to make the distinction that Talleyrand drew, on being told of the death of Napoleon). But it responded directly to, for example, a local disaster like Aberfan (about which Dennis Potter wrote a moving article), at one end of the spectrum, and to the crises of 1968 in France and Czechoslovakia (about which we had a whole clutch of pieces), at the other.

New Society tries to handle intelligently what always comes hard to journalists, and to many social scientists—positive

15

events, rather than negative ones. Good news may be no news; but it is at least as central to the way the mass of the population lives. This is one reason why the magazine attempts to assess proposals for change fairly and at length, calling on experts. Thus, we had several pieces on both the Robbins and the Plowden reports. On the Roskill commission on the third London airport, we had a number of articles, at various times— notably, close analysis of the actual hearings by Professor Peter Hall, and a brilliant demolition of the whole method (before the commission reported) by Professor Peter Self. There is a vast wealth of material in the *public* arena which much journalism, through its concern with what's hidden, what's being kept quiet, can miss. To use it needs time, patience and expertise. The growth of specialist journalists has not always yet removed this reproach.

Occasionally, perhaps, the magazine has overdone its search for the underlying. There was the time when, as an election series, it ran a week-by-week set of articles actually called "non-issues." Yet, even here, the idea was right, and the articles were thorough; and I am sure that generally the search, too, has been right. Anyone who wants the instant response has plenty of other sources for it. In *New Society* there is a continuing debate. I mentioned France and Czechoslovakia. The magazine had, for example, kept a close watch on the early stirrings that led to this. In fact, a thoughtful piece by Professor Nathan Glazer in April 1965, on the Berkeley Free Speech Movement, made *New Society* (I think) the first "overground" paper to print the now-common-place *fuck*. This was partly a sort of gesture; partly, it seemed something to get out of the way.

Education and urban/countryside planning are two subjects which, crosscutting most of our other themes, have been of special interest to *New Society*. There were education corres-pondents before *New Society* was launched, but I don't think there were any planning ones. Well before the disaster of Ronan Point, we were printing Robin Best, of Wye College, "Against high density." Early in 1969, we ran a *jeu d'esprit* called "Non-plan." It was amusing to see attacks on it crop up in architecture paper after architecture paper, only to find that some of the thoughts it contained risked becoming received ideas a year or so later. (A more welcoming, but similar, fate overtook the Open

Group pamphlet, *Social Reform in the Centrifugal Society*, which we printed later in 1969.)

New Society is obviously, in a sense, weekly journalism; but, because of the quality of the social science, and of the social scientists, we have been able to draw on, it is not strictly ephemeral. It gives me minor pleasure when I see the magazine's name bob up, as it often does, in academic footnotes. *That* must have been an article that said something fresh. And the value of our bound back-numbers is revealed almost every time a newspaper or television runs an in-depth study of a social issue.

From the start, *New Society* established a special link with its readers. Many of those who began to read it at the beginning, I am sure, "recognised it" when it appeared. They continue to feel it as "theirs," even though much has changed in these last ten years, not least within the kinds of subject we discuss in the magazine. It was characteristic that, when *New Society* ran a questionnaire in early 1963 to ask readers about social issues, we got the very high response of 7,000 questionnaires returned.

Those who return questionnaires are those who return questionnaires. But it may be relevant to recall that 72 per cent of those who did return them were under 40. As to jobs: 41 per cent were "practitioners" in some branch of welfare work or administration; 38 per cent were academics. I suspect that the number of "general" readers has grown from its 21 per cent proportion then. Certainly I myself have always tried to extend our readership in that direction, without losing our central purpose. But one needs to define "general" fairly carefully. One needs, for example, to know what the other people in the household do, besides the person who buys the copy of *New Society*. Often, I would guess, the wife or husband or son or daughter of a "general" reader has a "particular" reason for reading the magazine—especially now that both welfare work and the universities have expanded so much.

That questionnaire's results were widely reported (as they were intended to be). Already in 1963, it was clearly felt that *New Society*, and its readers, were a voice worth listening to. Those were very introspective years in Britain. A *New Society* comment in 1964 said: "1962 and 1963 can be seen in retrospect as the years when we discovered that we were not so good as we thought we were: 1964 looks likely to stand as the year in which

we started to do something about it." The second half of that
sentence reads rather hollowly now, though the achievements of
the Labour government's years (especially some humanitarian
ones) are now too easily denigrated. But the first half is true
enough. Almost 80 per cent of the *New Society* sample saw
Britain as no longer "great"; over 70 per cent saw future great-
ness as largely dependent on education, and on the arts and
sciences. Interestingly, 79 per cent felt, though often with regret,
that no classless society was in prospect.

Almost ten years after that, it seems as though the British are
once again at a period of self-questioning. I do not propose,
here, to do a brisk trot through the social history of the past
decade. Britain has changed in many ways, not least because
wealth has, despite everything, continued to grow. New injus-
tices have been discovered, to replace those that have been partly
overcome. The class structure may be much the same, but there
do appear to have been some permanent shifts in status, and
even marginally in power. Our social commentators, however,
are very liable to "American flu" (as literary gents once got
French flu): Britain's problems do often follow America's, after
a time lag, but with so many cultural differences that easy comparisons, especially about remedies, don't help much.

Acheson's reproach about Britain's lack of a role has not yet
been finally answered. With the Beatles a tide of pop culture
rose, which has since subsided. At around 1965, it reached the
point where *this* was what Britain was about. I remember, rather
sadly, my time in Canada that year, helping to make a television
film about mentally handicapped children. Especially as my
name was Paul, and my hair wasn't all that short, many of the
children were convinced that my colleagues and I were, in fact,
the Beatles; or if we weren't, that we *must* know them.

You didn't have to be handicapped to feel that way about
Britain then. To people outside the country, it seemed an
astonishing turn-around. To some inside Britain, it all seemed,
for a while, like the answer to the lack of political change.
There was cultural change, instead. It hasn't quite worked out
like that, though; and a new concern with politics has emerged.
There has been cultural change; but it has not, so far, gone all
that deep. A much-quoted survey by *New Society* on religious
education showed, in its way, how mixed people's views can be

—how far from congruent with a straight liberal or straight radical ticket.

I rather regret the elan of those mid-sixties years, even if the price was the sidestepping of certain issues. That spirit was probably an improvement on the galloping parochialism which has often succeeded it. And there has been an air of options closing, not opening. All the same, one of the encouraging things I found, in going back through ten years' of *New Society* in order to compile this book, has been the continuity of what may now seem very new preoccupations.

New Society has not given a direct mirror-image of the past ten years, as, in its day, *Picture Post* might have done (though our illustrations have sometimes had this quality). Indeed, some of our best issues have appeared at times of year when the pressure of hard news, of government documents and ministerial pronouncements, tends to diminish. In a farewell article as editor, Tim Raison cited an August issue as perhaps the best we had had till then. And it was in a December (1963) that Claude Lévi-Strauss first appeared in our pages—asking, "Where does Father Christmas come from?" (Fortunately, social science does not have to mean solemnity.)

Series of articles, which can hardly be all that topical, have been fairly steadily characteristic of *New Society*. Often, they have had a didactic function, like the *Founding Fathers of Social Science* series. (This was also, however, a way to tackle some fairly abstract ideas.) A variant was the important series in 1967, based on a special survey of the social services.

Sometimes these series have been reprinted, for wider use. *Founding Fathers* became a Penguin, as did the 1971 series called *A Sociological Portrait*. We have ourselves republished as book-lets a series on human development, *The Seven Ages of Man*, and a social-historical series, *The Origins of the Social Services*. *New Society* has brought out pamphlet-guides to various changes in social administration: the Seebohm report, the Maud report on local government, the Children and Young Persons Act, the Courts Act. Recently, we have offprinted collections of *New Society* articles on linked subjects (on race, say, or on the environment), especially for colleges and schools. In 1966, a book of our articles on young people came out, *Youth in New Society*. Since 1971, there has been some direct origination of

19

books, with the series, *Towards a New Society*, brought out by Maurice Temple Smith in a publishing association with *New Society*.

Indeed, much of the material which has appeared in *New Society* at article-length has appeared in book form, in one way or another. Often, of course, it drew originally on academic work which was destined for a book, or which had just come out as one. Sometimes, too, contributors have themselves brought out their *New Society* articles as a book. Thus, much of John Berger's recent *Selected Essays and Articles: The Look of Things* first appeared in *New Society*. And publishers themselves read *New Society* keenly for the new names and new work it carries.

Again this emphasises our (relative) lack of ephemerality. Within its general framework of objectivity, *New Society* can offer an author space, freedom and seriousness; and that is a great deal. It can offer other authors (who may prefer this) less space, more frivolity, but nonetheless freedom. I like to think that, with *New Society*, we have established a magazine which is not just one of the many that come and go, but one that will last, as a voice with something individual to say, as long as any great weekly. The study of human behaviour seems unlikely to cease to be relevant; there is, unfortunately, no sign of any early end to social injustice; and what has been described as "the sociological imagination" has been called by some the prime form of imagination of our time, in succession to other images of reality. I am not certain about this latter point. The power of art, philosophy, ideology and religion remains enormous. But if "sociological" is stretched to include "social anthropological" and "social psychological," I think (recollecting innumerable bad novels I've reviewed for the *TLS* and *The Times*) it may yet turn out to be so.

In this collection, I have tried to put together pieces of article-length which would give a fair representation of what *New Society* has printed during its first ten years. But I hope it is more than a *Festschrift*: I have tried to give the book a valid theme of its own, by concentrating on developing patterns of behaviour. I do not say that *all* these articles are among the best *New Society* has printed. Many of them are; others are here to "cover" a point. And I felt that some subjects should get good individual showing, even at the cost of less space for others.

I hope that my title and epigraph, from the Opies' delightful and original book, gives something of the feel of what I have tried to convey. There is a nice mixture of continuity and change in a rhyme, which was once used for working out the deeper meaning of groups of magpies, being urbanised into bus-ticket fortune-telling. And the Opies', like much social science, is a book —as I would want to think this is—in which the reader recognises himself, at either a general or an anecdotal level. (At the latter level, I remember collecting Halifax Corporation tickets myself, for a related purpose: to get serial numbers that totalled a lucky twenty one.) That rhyme conveys, also, something of the verve of "ordinary," un-elite, working people—what E. P. Thompson once called their "stubbornness of being." If, in *"One for sorrow, Two for joy," one* and *two* are scores (as in Forster's *Two Cheers for Democracy*), they show the right order of priorities.

I have tried to avoid articles that can be got in book form elsewhere. That has cut out several which I might otherwise have included, particularly some of the "hard" social science pieces. There is not so much on the social services as one would find in any given issue of *New Society*. This is not because I myself incline, in the tension I mentioned at the start, to the "anthropological" rather than to the "administrative" (though I often do). It is because such articles, however excellent, are often very time-specific. Despite my own strong interest in them, I have included little on the arts, either mass or elite. And the focus I have chosen means that, to my regret, much which is not about Britain has had to be excluded.

Articles by many writers I value highly are not here, either. The only way to avoid that would have been simply to reprint ten years' issues. So let me end by dedicating this book to all those—among its readers, its contributors, and its editorial and publishing staff—who have made *New Society* what it is. For me, it has been a form of further education. I hope that others, too, have enjoyed it, and have found it useful.

Paul Barker, London, 1972

Symbols die,

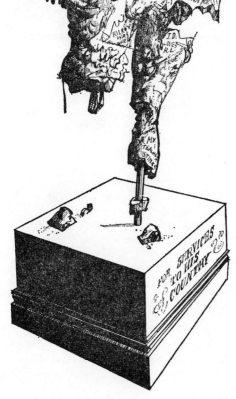

WINSTON'S WAKE

Ray Gosling

When I was small I did believe John Bull was really Churchill. He has always been as dead as Pickwick or King Henry v. Yet I've often thought—what a day it's going to be when that man dies. What a funeral. *Our flags on Saturday won't be at half mast. No, sir. They'll be right out at the top of the pole. We'll have clubs open all night and dancing in the streets if we could. Because, I'll tell you, here we are glad he's gone.*

Tonypandy and the valleys, Fife, Don valley: all must have echoed what I heard Thursday night in North Notts.

It was '21 or '26 when Churchill said, "I shall not rest until the miner is on his knees and eating grass". . . . He wanted two men chasing every job . . . He killed my mother. Indirectly, but he killed her.

To these men who in The Finest Hours were digging the same coal seams they had in '25 and '35: coal to keep the home fires burning: to these men working in the same factories, then turned over to full employment munitions: to these men who won no medals or glory Churchill was as the chairman of one council actually said in public last week: *He was Public Enemy No. 1.*

In the big provincial towns, councils planned tributes, and cinemas announced later opening times for Saturday as tokens of respect. On the buses and the bars, remembering Kennedy:

Heard they're changing the name to Churchill University . . .

I never thought he'd die. Thought he was immortal . . .

They're going to call Straits of Dover Straits of Churchill and them White Cliffs the Winston Cliffs.

But life went on. You opened the paper and flipped straight to begin on page two.

London: Friday. And the very first words I overheard coming onto Euston Road were: *Down to a four hour queue now, I believe.* And I wasn't listening for stuff. I'd only just got in, and it wasn't until I got the other side I realised what they were on about. Then the newspaper placards—NEW REHEARSAL—like they were code words in a telegram—200,000 PASS THROUGH.

That heading to the black London Transport poster—LYING IN STATE. However I read it on the poster I wanted to laugh. LYING IN STATE. The Underground will run to 2 am. Takes a funeral to keep London open after midnight.

In the Underground I saw a large number of black ties—and most odd and eerie—people were reading the front page word by word. Like the Cuba Crisis. A little man, boiler suit, Andy cap, took from Monument to Victoria on the *Evening News* front page.

Interesting about the papers. As He was dying, while the French papers spoke of His last hours, English papers printed prayers for His speedy recovery. After He died solemn faces at first came down the steps at the airport. Sarah Churchill became Lady Audley.

At Victoria, homegoing commuters were snapping up the Churchill souvenir editions like they were five pound notes. Bankers and brokers and jobbers were off to Bromley and Haywards Heath to hold hands with their wives and watching TV re-live their own finest hour in civil defence, the home guard, or the RAF.

It was London's wake. Shop windows—"shall not open on Saturday"—had busts: Harrods. Black crepe round the Karsh photo appeared in the most incongruous windows.

Victoria Street was running away from Churchill. Parliament Square was deserted but for police wagons. Not until we crossed Whitehall did we meet the mourners. The Empire had gathered in St Stephen's Tavern. An old man stood between the bar and his walking stick. On his chest were pinned the silver heads of Victoria, Edward Seven, George Five and more.

Ninety-five I am ... met them all ... when I shook hands with the Queen Mother I showed her the box of chocolates I got given by Queen Victoria and she said—you mean you haven't given any away to all the young ladies in your life? ... Boer ... Shrapnel ... Aldershot ... I don't mind if I do. A whisky, if it's all right with you, sir ... 1s 1d a day we had ...

He turns to us and says: "have you been over yet," and it read like "promoted to glory" in the *War Cry.*

A drink, sir? I don't mind if I do. Whisky, sir, I went over and the sergeant comes up to me and says—do you want to go round— and he led me right to the front of the queue ... Mafeking ...

*the gee-gees . . . France . . . You come from South America then,
do you? . . . I was a steward on the Mauretania once, but that
might have been before you were born . . . No, I don't mind if I do.
Can you make it Scotch . . . best of health, sir . . . ninety-five, yes
. . . No, that's the Big One, the Boer War. I was wounded. All
here it was. Great scars. I'd show you but . . . Queen Victoria she
gave me a box of chocolates and when I saw the Queen Mother,
this Queen Mother she said to me: have you kept them all that
time? Haven't you given them to your young ladies? . . . Young
ladies I said Ma'am, when I come back to this earth again I want
to be a young lady and if I touched his pocket and heard it jingle
I'd say come on then my darling. Queensway, that's it . . . I'd re-
enlist tomorrow if I could . . . the best life for any young man . . .
not the same though . . . gee-gees . . . 1s 1d a day. I remember when
we were in France . . . I don't mind if I do, sir. Scotch . . . Cold. You
don't know what cold is. You should have seen it—Black Tuesday
of Eighty One. Cold. Don't know what cold is . . . that's it,
boy.*

And as we leave he looks at his stout for the first time in 20
minutes of Haig, takes a wee sip and looks around the room for
the rest of the Empire. It was 6.30.

A copper outside with a loudhailer bawls in a Halifax accent:
*Do not cross the road until told to do so . . . Cross now. Cross now.
The queue begins over Westminster Bridge.*

Briskly, like commuters sweeping into the City we cross to the
Albert Embankment. More loudhailers. Caught in the flood of
people to escalate down between the Thames and St Thomas.
Crowd thickens into queue. Man in knitted yachting cap plus
wife plus friend at 6ft 2in and a bowler. Queue stiffens to
shuffle. Sign on a lampost: *Public Conveniences open all night.*
Why not the pubs? This is Winston's wake. *He was a commoner
and more people have come than came for Queen Mary.* He can
only die once was the theme, but no one was quite that blunt.
Paris Match was there in a white coat and a cockney voice.
*The last three left. Souvenir edition. All the photos of the great
man.* It could be the Rolling Stones.

Ahead stands a van and beefy Hattie Jaques women, shouting:
*Bovril. Hot Bovril, Tea or Bovril. All free. Tea this side. Bovril
that and don't take the spoons away. No—it's all free. Just put
whatever you can in the jam jar for a cause to be named by Lady*

Churchill. Lady Churchill's special fund. Please don't take the spoons away. Bring that spoon back, son. Bring it back.

And I was thinking of what the pitmen said of Him; of His slogan in the '51 campaign, "Set the People Free"; of His paintings; of Lady Churchill who had lost her man; of 1940 when I was one. Was everyone thinking behind the chitchat. Keeping their thoughts to themselves. Maybe theirs like mine bordered on the unutterable. What a wonderful war it must have been, and what a tame, tepid peace the years of MacWonder and Harold from Huddersfield.

We'd been at it an hour when we came on to the Westminster side and saw the queue take a cunning great s-bend around the park. *If I'd have known that, I'd have had second thoughts about this.* But the wvs, in a second wave of Bovril and tea, confronted us. St John's Ambulance men stood with police—just in case. *Tatta*, I said to the Bovril lady. *Bye*, her shrill voice sailed back.

We wound around the park. Through the mud. A tired army, so desperate for a pee we jumped the queue and ran across a no-man's-land to the translucent tent and jet-plane-style bowl latrines. British and gentlemen we waited to rejoin the queue at the spot we came from. On to Millbank and cold wet paving slabs and we began halting so they could let the toffs through. Hot dog floats tempted you to run across the road. *Save my place, will you.* But few crossed. This was Memory Mile: Bovril and tea.

We trod the black sodden mat into Westminster Hall. It isn't true we didn't look at the toff's platform. We did, the moment all talk ceased as we caught the whiff of candles and history. After all, we'd given two hours for the whole circus, not just the clown. But there were no toffs I could name.

The RAF stood guard by the catafalque. I bowed my head. He was a great man. He had a great life. But as we came out into Palace Yard I looked up at this ordinary Protestant, suburban crowd chattering away . . . *You'll remember that, children, all your lives, won't you . . . It's a very large coffin . . . such a wonderful hall . . . there wasn't anyone famous was there, did you see? . . .*

Let's eat. Let's go east. I tell you I cried and was not alone the night Stalin died: the day Bevan went. Out in the sticks in a small town at a Kennedy memorial service the aisles were a river of tears. I asked one man why he'd come to mourn Churchill

28

and he said: *I'm a Jew. Do I have to have another reason?* But he was the exception. Most of us, I'm sure, came not just to mourn or say thank you, but to live again those few short days in our lives when we had meaning and glory and fulfilment.

Out east, life went on. The landlord said, *He was a great man in the war*; but there was no extension. Aldgate. Back in the City, the faithful, the ardent and the once-in-a-lifetime were gathering: good people from the corners of the earth, just as they had when London married Alexander to Ogilvy; Margaret to Jones.

But Fleet Street—it looked like Old Elvet the night before the Durham Miners' Gala: barricaded up to the eyebrows.

In Soho the teen scene raved. The Establishment was open. But the strippers and girlies were a bit slack and where had all the fairies gone?

11.30 pm, back at Westminster, and everywhere "Morning papers," "Morning papers," Special Souvenir Edition—and still *Paris Match. Is it all in French? Yes, my darling, it's all in French, but very lovely pictures.*

I thought I'd go to church, to say a prayer and light a candle, but they were closed. Westminster Cathedral locked as tight as the Bank of England. Only the public conveniences were open all night.

Took a little sleep and then it was dawn. Coming into SE across the SWs, as deserted as at Christmas Dinner time. Like there'd been an evacuation. Lambeth council were making up convoys to fight the litter of the Embankment, and we were there just before them, in time to salvage one ten bob note, 25 gloves (no pairs), bottles of whisky (empty) and thousands of plastic beakers.

A solitary policeman says: *You know, he was a cunning old man. When he was big in the war, he had it agreed how he'd go when it came. Past all his glories: the House and Whitehall; Fleet Street and the City—you notice he nearly gets to Aldgate, but not quite.*

On the other side, the shops are shut, but the diggers and levellers pound furiously at the building sites. Caxton Hall was open. The guns began to boom, and we're running like it was 6.4 and we want to catch the 6.5, and in time to join the thousands clicking cameras as the procession that was everything the

Sunday papers said it was leaves Westminster. Then we're off, bevies of us, trotting round over Horseguards Parade. Nearly knocked down by De Gaulle as he comes from somewhere, and we reach Trafalgar Square in time to see the procession all over again. We chased it right into the city. At the Law Courts in the Strand a copper said to me—*Don't stand on that wall please sir. I've got my instructions to obey just like you sir.* We could have been bit actors in *The Dam Busters.*

You notice familiar faces in every chase. There was a little man on a bicycle, who near Covent Garden asked me to share his cucumber sandwich and a flask of coffee. He'd come from Devon. Churchill he told me was "the greatest man of all time" and he nearly went into a trance every time he said it which was often.

At the back of St Paul's, while the sovereign was for the first time in history attending the funeral of a commoner, I came across the strangest sight I'd seen all day. I was walking around the big cars, flanked by the police motor bikes, looking at the flags, hoping to find a few provincial lord mayors, but couldn't find any; all the nations: none of the cities, when I saw a trickle going into an underground car park. I followed. They came out the other side, teenagers and city gents and into a big hole in the ground: a building site not being worked. They crossed this on planks, only to find the scoop spot came to a dead end with high wire fencing and wooden boards. Then city gents were helping to lift teenage girls over. Old men; women in flat shoes, all ardent and no lipstick, near-polevaulted over. When I got over, I spend a happy ten minutes holding people's umbrellas and briefcases while they jumped. It was quite exciting. More fruitless chasing to find a good position to watch the procession leave the cathedral. Give up. Join the crowd: doing the mirror and periscope trick. Turning your back on the procession, you hold up a mirror and see a fraction of a fraction and wish you'd come earlier, or stayed at home to see it all on TV.

As the coffin passed, a postman came to attention and saluted. The crowds were more cosmopolitan, but still no emotion. Cold eyes. Bare heads. It was a good day for the pipes. You couldn't tell if they were real or from someone's transistor. I was on the South Bank again, near Hay's Wharf, in a tobacconist's and there were two nippers and one said, *Mister, he was the greatest man wasn't he?* I said, *Yes*—and he turned on his mate and started belting him. *There y'are I told you*—and just then the screams of the flypast came.

The Great Commoner, Son of a Lord, Born in a Palace, was sailing down a Thames the colour of whisky and ginger laced with fog ash on a freezing day to a train hauled by a steam engine to Oxon, the most feudal of the midland counties. Walking on to London Bridge, thousands were streaming to the station. In the bar of the Steampacket, Lower Thames Street, the TV men and wvs and St John's were cooling off. In the spit and sawdust were two Irishmen, two Cockneys, a Potteries man and then myself. *He never got to Aldgate, did he? I could have medals and stand up there with them getting my mush on the telly, but what did he do? I lost all my mates. I don't blame Churchill, but I stayed here all morning. He goes to glory on the blood and sweat of millions—and what good did it do us ... ?*

In peace we haven't been able to love one another: we've given life little magic. "Out of the depths of sorrow and sacrifice will be born again the glory of mankind." Is there no other way?

Just before the Steampacket closed, he pushed his face up to mine and said—*You know what. There's a lot of people who long for another war.*

[*4 February 1965*]

TELEVISION AND THE KENNEDY ASSASSINATION

Ruth Leeds Love

The social contexts in which news organisations cover and report the news often intervene between a subject for news and the kind of coverage it receives. Thus the policies of a news medium owner, reinforced by his membership of various social groups, mean that his news organisation will give heavy emphasis to some news subjects while virtually ignoring others. The characteristics of a reporter's contacts and his regular beat also lead to differential emphasis on and treatment of different news subjects. In addition, there are three other factors that help determine the kind of coverage a news subject is likely to receive. These are the newsman's *news judgments*, normative dimensions of *situational appropriateness* (in other words, the right mood or tone), and the exercise of *other-party controls* (or outside influences and authority). To examine these factors I shall use incidents that arose during the networks' three and a half day continuous television coverage of President Kennedy's assassination.

The data to be used here come from 91 lengthy qualitative interviews conducted shortly after the assassination with personnel in the news division of ABC (American Broadcasting Company) and NBC (National Broadcasting Company), the news staffs of the networks' affiliate stations and several independent stations in Dallas, some Dallas newspaper editors, and several wire service newsmen.

The news division broadcasters at all levels identify themselves as professional newsmen, many having worked previously in other news media. As with their newspaper counterparts, reporting is an ultimate value for them. They feel their job communicating news is important and gratifying, preferring it to other work. An NBC editor's comments are illustrative:

I am very proud to be in the business. I am happy to be a newsman, and I can't think of anything I would rather have been doing when [the assassination] happened. We had a part in history, and

32

*it is a little different from the people I know and live with. I think
we all feel that way down deep inside. It was self-fulfilment, personally and professionally.*

At the outset of the assassination period, which became known
as the Black Weekend, news executives established the basic
policy that the assassination would be covered like any other
news story, for it was a momentous and shocking event that
raised many questions. As much news as possible would be
broadcast in the time that became available through the cancellation of all commercial broadcasting.

Had the President died naturally, commercial broadcasting
would have been cancelled anyway, for this action was premised
on the idea that cancellation is the only appropriate response to
the death of the head of state, not on news values. Had the
President died naturally, however, there would have been no
policy to cover the event like a news story. Whatever news there
was about the President's death would have been reported, and
the long interludes between news would have been filled with
appropriate memorial programmes, as was done when President
Roosevelt died in 1945. As professional newsmen, the broadcasters preferred covering Kennedy's assassination to Roosevelt's death. Some news executives explained:

*It wasn't like Roosevelt's death . . . with Roosevelt everything
went according to the book. Foreign nations sent the proper con-
dolences; it was all done with the proper pomp and dignity. You
knew what was going to happen. But it's different with the assassination. It's not all cut and dry. We were cops and robbers.
Who did it? Was there a bomb?* (NBC executive.)

In FDR's *case it was much harder. In Kennedy's case there was
more news, the assassination, Oswald's death. With* FDR *it was a
natural death, and the funeral train moving up from Warm Springs,
stopping at each place, and covering Truman who was very reticent
and then the funeral.* (NBC executive.)

The policy of staying with the story placed heavy demands on
news material, for it meant that only a minimum of non-hard
news programming would be prepared to fill air time. In this
way a producer would not find himself trapped in a discussion
on the presidency when he wanted to switch to a news site.
Virtually all available news was aired, and what became
available was largely determined by the articulation of the

broadcasters' news judgments, their perceptions of what news was appropriate to the situation, and the exercise of other-party controls.

News judgment means determining what events are news-worthy and involves criteria of immediacy, relevancy and importance. The baselines for the criteria are perceptions of what affects the national interest and what interests the audience. During the Black Weekend, news worth was determined largely by what was of immediate relevance to the assassination. Unrelated news events occurred at the time but they received scant attention, although on an ordinary weekend they would have been covered extensively. The broadcasters were totally involved with the assassination, both personally and professionally, so did not care to cover other news, claiming lack of audience interest in it. Moreover, they felt that switching from the sacred ceremonies in Washington to other profane news would be in bad taste, disrupting the mourning mood. Only news that could affect American values as profoundly as did the assassination could be legitimately reported. An ABC producer explained:

The news editor came to me and said: "[Aldous] Huxley died and there's a plane crash, do we want to do other news?" I said, "We'll programme the death of the President." I felt unless it was an outstanding piece of news, we shouldn't do it. The problem was this—it's much more difficult to come from the scene in the Rotunda and have an announcer say, ". . . Huxley also died." You can't equate the two. Now if communist China had declared war on Russia, we would have figured out a way to programme it but it would have had to be something that monumental.

News subjects or persons who control access to them exercise other-party controls by saying yes or no to press requests for news and camera coverage. Because the broadcasters stress live television, they may be more at the mercy of other parties than are other members of the press. If a news subject holds aloof from television cameras, the broadcasters have little to show. The articulation between the broadcasters' newsgathering efforts and other-party controls may determine whether a particular news story has led to the invasion of privacy, or the infringement of civil rights, or the abridgement of freedom of the press.

The third factor, perception of situational appropriateness,

34

focuses on actions that can be interjected into a situation without disrupting its mood and tone. Following the assassination, the broadcasters were most concerned about not airing material that might disrupt the national mood of sorrow and mourning, like news unrelated to the assassination. Several considerations of situational appropriateness guided the broadcasters in televising news.

One entailed concentrating on the culturally appropriate and expected responses of shock and horror to the assassination. The broadcasters added to the legitimacy of these responses by reporting mainly on appropriate reactions, both at home and abroad, to the assassination. Thus, on the day of Kennedy's funeral a cameraman did not film the people along the funeral route who were laughing *en passant*.

I avoided taking shots of people laughing and smiling. I didn't think it was proper. There wasn't any bad behaviour but people do laugh.

Deviations from the appropriate responses, if televised, would detract from the mood that broadcasters wished to convey.

Like most newsmen, the broadcasters are on the alert for the unusual so they are not enthusiastic about covering expected, appropriate responses unless they are particularly apt, symbolising the main news event. An NBC editor said:

We went after the anti-Kennedy people ... Welch ... Wallace ... Barnett and General Walker to get a balanced judgment, but I wouldn't have cared if we didn't get ... them, either professionally or personally ... all they could say was, "I'm sorry he is dead" or "I am glad he is dead." And it wasn't necessary to say the latter, no matter how much anybody hated him.

An ABC executive said:

I would have done more man-in-the-street interviews ... there were people huddling along the curb in blankets on ... the day of the funeral in that biting cold. We did a few ... and some of them were really beyond hoping for. They asked an eight year old boy why he came and he said, "My mother and father didn't like Kennedy, but he was our President and that's why I'm here." Someone in New York called ... to say that he summed it up better than anyone yet.

A second consideration focused on cultural standards of taste.

35

News material that the broad middle class might deem offensive is consistently kept off the air, particularly if it is judged to have little news value. Correspondents refrained from describing President Kennedy's wounds and the fact that Mrs Kennedy was heard to say that she had her husband's brains on her hands.

A third consideration involved not marring the public images of public figures with incidental news reporting. If a person is popular, has a good public image, the broadcasters tend not to air material that contradicts the image, particularly in the context of live coverage of national events. An NBC producer said he would not have used the pictures immediately of Mrs Kennedy climbing onto the deck of the presidential limousine even if these had been available:

I would have used [the pictures] considerably after the fact, not Friday . . . a sense of taste . . . it was a little too close to grief . . . Taste is a peculiar animal. I would have thought it was too soon to show it right afterwards . . . This is all hindsight on my part . . . Crawling out of the car was the kind of . . . you know, it left the wrong impression. I thought when I first saw it that not very great dignity was involved . . . [I don't think] she was fleeing . . . but that's the impression it left.

These three considerations all relate to the elusive concept of taste. To broadcast material that deviates from expected behaviour, does not accord with prevalent standards of taste and morality, or puts favoured persons in a bad light, is to detract from the overall tastefulness and appropriateness of coverage. Such material would not only be offensive to public sentiment but to professional satisfaction, for the broadcasters pride themselves almost as much on producing a tasteful coverage as they do a comprehensive news coverage. An NBC executive said:

Technical flaws are quickly overcome. I assume that almost anything is possible technically. But more than most people, certainly more than the critics, I have a higher opinion not of the talents— that's assumed—but of the taste of the people in the business . . . the news departments of all the networkers are as tasteful as anything there is . . . In terms of taste, of course, it's what you leave out—assuming that anything is technically possible.

Although the broadcasters cannot define what they mean by taste there is general but not universal agreement on what material can be broadcast. Another NBC producer indicated that he would have used the pictures of Mrs Kennedy even though members of the audience might have objected to the network.

About Mrs Kennedy, that wouldn't have bothered me. If we had used it we probably would have gotten calls but I wouldn't have hesitated because of that. I don't do things because of calls or no calls.

A fourth consideration bearing on situational appropriateness is how the audience will respond to broadcast material. Viewers can reward and sanction broadcasters by communicating with the networks, and some broadcasters take this into account. An ABC correspondent said that for trivial matters he considered potential audience sanctions:

I'm glad that there was no breach of taste . . . we were so exhausted and tempers were flaring . . . I was always afraid . . . that we might say something accidentally . . . another correspondent was very tired after 24 hours and then there were some pictures of Kennedy's furniture being moved out of his office. He began to say something like they might have waited at least until the President's body was cold. And then he collected himself at the last minute to say they might have waited until the President was buried . . . the idea of the President's body being cold might have been . . . bad taste and we would have gotten letters.

The audience's capacity to sanction is a much less important control source, however, than its capacity to react emotionally and to be interested in what is broadcast. This form of control operates like an alter ego, reinforcing the broadcasters' commitment to professional norms and reminding them of norms and expectations held by the larger society. The audience *qua* alter ego is vague, for the broadcasters have no sharp image of the viewers, ascribing no specific social qualities to them. If they do ascribe characteristics they are their own, so the broadcasters feel they can use their own concerns as guides to what concerns the audience.

At the same time the broadcasters feel they should not play on the audience's feelings by evoking responses in it beyond those already stimulated by the news itself. An NBC correspondent said:

Suddenly I found myself talking for [a few minutes] about John-John. I felt I had to. I recall saying that I will try not to get maudlin; I didn't want to arouse any sympathy in the audience by talking about a little child. I just had to talk about it; it may have been an emotional cathartic for myself.

The desire not to arouse the audience's feelings derives partially from and reinforces the broadcasters' professionalism. In broadcasting a statement that might evoke audience feelings, the broadcasters might also arouse their own feelings and portray emotion on the air which would be unprofessional. An NBC correspondent explained:

Everybody wanted to be careful, to be calm, not to permit emotion to show . . . It's just unprofessional . . . you don't have the right to impose your own feelings on any viewer . . . In . . . a tight situation you must keep a stiff upper lip . . . if you didn't panic might result: . . . you must preserve a calm appearance, it's a matter of taste . . . and professionalism.

The desire not to evoke feelings in the audience is also a control source operating independently of professional norms. One producer said that if the decision had been his he would not have permitted the interview with Officer Tippit's widow to go out.

I was damn mad they befouled themselves by interviewing Mrs Tippit, making her answer inane questions. The interview with her was an invasion of privacy, not only hers but mine too, it made my flesh crawl. Not [because of] what we were doing to her, but to the audience. The impact of television is much greater than of newspapers so things that were standard in newspaper days are much more repulsive on television, when you see them as moving pictures.

The broadcasters, then, attribute rights to the audience beyond the democratic right of being informed.

In addition, the broadcasters wish to dampen negative audience feelings like fear or panic. An NBC producer did not cover the story that Strategic Air Command was alerted after the assassination for it might have contributed to potential panic in a time of crisis.

The broadcasters' efforts to dampen negative feelings in the audience was in part an effort to dampen their own fears. A correspondent who broadcast soon after news broke that shots were fired at Kennedy stressed that this was no time for speculation.

All I could do at this point was to offer caution. I guess I was reading a set of directions to our people as much as to the outside, let's not speculate . . . we will get the information to you as fast as we can . . . There is a great tendency to speculate when the President is shot, you can create pandemonium . . . I was concerned that this could have been a plot on the part of our adversaries . . .

The projection of the broadcasters' own fears onto the audience was also apparent in their coverage of Lyndon Johnson. The day after the assassination a producer felt it was time to tell who he was and what he stood for.

This was very important because we were frightened . . . and we wanted to get this to the audience, dampen this fright in the audience. We didn't know [the audience was frightened] but there are not that many different types in the audience. We were frightened so we assumed they were, not the majority perhaps, but some of them . . . I believe the country is run by the President, all its crises are at least so we have to ask who is this man? I didn't mention on Friday that LBJ *had had a heart attack, and that if he had another we'd get McCormick—then we'd all go to the storm cellars.*

An ABC correspondent said:

I thought of how to ease the mind of the general public . . . We literally had the public in our power . . . An important part of our work was the coverage of Lyndon Johnson. Without exception the reports about [him] were highly favourable, but honest and it was the truth. We played up . . . his favourable qualities, Johnson as a man of strength, Johnson's ability to carry on. It needed to be said . . . at that time, and it was said.

The broadcasters could go only so far in reassuring the audience about governmental continuity and Johnson's abilities. Too much emphasis would detract from mourning for Kennedy and give the impression that the nation might be better off with a new president. One correspondent believed that since Johnson knew Congress better than Kennedy, he would succeed in having Kennedy's programme passed, yet this point could not be made easily without giving the wrong impression.

In sum, nothing should be broadcast which would violate the audience's expectations and definitions about a situation, or exacerbate the public's feelings about the news. The broadcasters' commitment to news norms, the reactions to broadcast material that they attribute to the audience and the possibility of audience sanctions combine to maintain the broadcasting of fare that is expected and appropriate to the situation.

Several incidents from the Black Weekend will illustrate how differences in articulation between news judgment, other-party controls and the broadcasters' concern for situational appropriateness, affect coverage.

The coverage given to Oswald, from the moment of his capture on the Friday until the Sunday when Jack Ruby shot him, came about because the broadcasters judged him to be a crucial news figure; no normative considerations limited coverage; and other-party controls, although expected, did not materialise. Since Oswald was the suspected assassin, any news about him might help answer the central question of how and why the assassination happened. Network correspondents along with other newsmen waited long hours at the Dallas police station, hoping that Oswald might pass by and talk, or that police officers might comment on the case.

A normative consideration that might have limited coverage was that extensive reporting would damage Oswald's right to fair trial. The correspondents in Dallas were mindful of this, one even telephoning the network about it.

I was a little concerned about the civil liberties question here so I called New York. But I got no satisfactory response. They said, "You know we want to cover this big." So I was in there pushing and shoving with everybody else.

News judgment, reinforced by network pressures, prevailed over the normative consideration. In practice, a suspect's right to due process of law has been weak and, in this case, Oswald's right was further weakened by the broadcasters' felt obligation to reassure the audience through keeping it fully informed at a critical moment in national life. A studio correspondent who reminded the public about Oswald's rights, commented:

I wonder what sort of stories or speculation would have circulated if Oswald had been kept out of the news for 24 hours, what rumours about the police using third degree to get a confession, and the unusual protection afforded him. It would plant inarticulate fears in the people about what was done to him. The press had a responsibility to cover the story.

Given their professional interest and responsibility in covering news, the broadcasters feel they cannot limit their own reporting efforts. A network field editor said:

It is the obligation of the news media to seek access to the news that is happening, and as close access as is possible. I don't think

40

it is possible for us to limit ourselves to where we go. This is very possibly the responsibility of others in other fields—lawyers, doctors, policemen. But we must seek access to the news. Philosophically . . . in our system of checks and balances, freedom is never freedom when exercised by one party alone . . . We of the press cannot be the sole arbiter of what is freedom of the press.

The Dallas police did not exercise the anticipated control for they felt obliged, in the public interest, to publicise their investigation of Oswald. They may not have realised that this could be done through pool coverage as well as through individual coverage by many news organisations. Police failure to control the press to any significant degree also arose from an incongruency between expectations governing Dallas press-police relations and expectations governing press-police relations in major cities like New York and Los Angeles.

The Dallas police seem to have little need to control the local press for Dallas newsmen know how far they may go in covering a police story: apparently that is much further than many other police departments allow. The latitude the police give the press in Oswald's case was not unusual. The Dallas police-press arrangement differs sharply from that of some cities where the press persists in news gathering until the police impose clear checks. A Dallas newspaper executive summarised the impasse:

The police in this case were subjected to types of newsmen they have never seen before . . . the very competent and aggressive newsmen who climb over people's backs to get pictures and a story. Here we work hard but we compete on a gentleman's level. There is no rough and tumble scrabbling of the type you get in New York and elsewhere. In New York you have seven or eight papers competing. This was a totally new element as far as the Dallas police were concerned.

While Oswald's coverage came about through lack of articulation between news judgment, other-party controls and normative considerations, the restrained coverage of Mrs Kennedy came about because there was articulation, albeit a vague one. Mrs Kennedy was covered whenever she appeared publicly, and whenever the White House released information about her, for like Oswald she was a central news figure. Unlike news about Oswald, however, news about Mrs Kennedy did not serve the instrumental, affectively neutral function of informing the

41

public, but provided an affective focal point for the news consumer, both because she was the President's widow and because she had established herself as a public figure in her own right. A news executive said:

It's natural that the widow is the central point in any story like this. There is the identification of people with her, especially the young people of the nation. This drew more attention to her than otherwise might be the case.

The restraint the broadcasters imposed on Mrs Kennedy's coverage derives partly from a bereaved person's right to privacy. Excessive coverage would have violated the right and indicated a departure from good taste. A news director said:

An effort was made to show Mrs Kennedy at various steps without leaving the camera on her too long in fear . . . of invasion of her privacy . . . Conscious effort was made . . . not to make any play on this lady's grief.

The restrained coverage was implemented partly through executive directive, partly through other-party control, but primarily through the broadcasters' sensitivity to normative considerations. In keeping with the top news executives' general responsibility for maintaining tasteful newscasting, an executive directed that for the funeral there should be no more intrusion on Mrs Kennedy than necessary. Other-party controls consisted of a request from Mrs Kennedy's aides to the Washington network pool committee that cameramen refrain from taking head-on shots and close-ups of her and her children. Although executive directives and other-party controls would have sufficed to ensure tasteful coverage, it is not clear that they were necessary or that they were even communicated to the broadcasters responsible for televising Mrs Kennedy. In several instances broadcasters subordinated news judgment to considerations of their own. An ABC producer said:

I was struck throughout by the good taste that was spontaneously exhibited. There were no close-ups of Mrs Kennedy . . . [There was] no policy decision but individual cameramen showed restraint.

If the broadcasters had not limited themselves voluntarily it is quite likely that other party controls would have appeared quickly. A Washington news executive said:

[Andrew] Hatcher later said he heard no complaints [from the White House] about the coverage, that it was handled with great

taste ... [The Kennedys] had strong opinions about the coverage ... you never got the feeling they would let you do anything to their disadvantage.

One wonders, then, to what degree the imminent probability of other-party control contributed to self-limitation, and to what degree the broadcasters' awareness that the public might expect Mrs Kennedy's privacy to be respected reinforced their restraint. The questions arise for the broadcasters interviewed the widow of Officer Tippit who was slain by Oswald shortly after the assassination.

The broadcasters felt personally that an interview might invade Mrs Tippit's right to privacy, but professionally they believed her story was news, and the only way it could be obtained was through contacting her for she lacked a public information apparatus. Here normative consideration was subordinated to news judgment. The broadcasters explained that if Mrs Tippit felt her privacy threatened she could have declined to speak with reporters. Thus a problem for normative considerations was defined to be a problem for other party controls. A film editor said of the Tippit interview:

We went after Mrs Tippit in Dallas ... There was a question of trading on her emotions but ... there was a need for a follow-up on [the policeman's death] and I did ask for the [interview]. I ask for things I don't agree with when we are covering a story ... Mrs Tippit was willing but we wouldn't have forced the issue.

A Dallas correspondent explained:

I had to interview Tippit's widow ... I thought ... it was an invasion of her privacy. I am still a little shaky about interviewing somebody right after a death ... the interview went well and she was cooperative ... I suppose it helped the family in the fund drive ... I think the desk in New York was right in making the assignment. It had to be told.

The different coverages given to the widows might be explained by their different abilities to exercise other-party controls, and to reinforce normative considerations, based on their different statuses. Mrs Tippit was an ordinary citizen until her husband's murder cast her into the limelight so she would have had no experience with the press and might not have known how to exercise her technical right to say no had she wanted to do so. There was little likelihood that Mrs Tippit would limit

SUMMARY CHART OF ARTICULATION AND EFFECTS OF THREE FACTORS

news subject	news values	situational appropriateness	other-party controls	outcome
Lee Harvey Oswald, suspected assassin	intensive coverage favoured because it would answer important questions about assassination	recognition of suspect's right to fair trial weak/audience perceived as having to be informed	very few/suspect powerless to exercise controls/police controls expected but police unaccustomed to checking newsmen	intensive coverage that interfered with police work and presented difficulties for fair trial
Mrs Kennedy, the president's widow	coverage favoured because she was affective news figure with whom public identified	right to privacy strong because of high status and public image/public would be offended by coverage that violated privacy	a few requests to limit coverage/high probability of controls if inappropriate material broadcast. Mrs Kennedy accessible only through "gatekeepers"	restrained, tasteful coverage that received compliments from critics
Mrs Tippit, widow of police officer slain by Oswald	coverage favoured because of her connection to events	right to privacy weak because of ordinary status/public unlikely to be concerned about her privacy	none/low probability for any because she had no experience with press	interview conducted and broadcast/some broadcasters object/some complaints from viewers to networks
partisan politics	coverage not favoured because no news at time. Too early to assess political effects of assassination	secular politics in very bad taste during sacred mourning period	political figures refused to make political statements at time.	brief mention of partisan politics after funeral

the press. In contrast, Mrs Kennedy as the First Lady had considerable experience with the press and knew how to protect her privacy. It is unlikely that any newsman would have been permitted to interview her. Mrs Kennedy's high status may also have reinforced the broadcasters' commitment to good taste, if for no other reason than awareness that the public would expect it.

The broadcasters declared a moratorium on party politics, believing that investigation of how Kennedy's death would affect the 1964 presidential election was irrelevant to the main story and a matter that could be handled "even after the funeral" to quote one news executive. The decision not to cover politics involved both news judgments and normative considerations.

Political news at this time would have been in bad taste. Kennedy was assassinated in his capacity as the symbolic and actual leader of his country, not as the leader of the Democratic Party. Johnson was perceived to be the new head of state, not the new Democratic President. Partisan politics, then, were not germane and their examination would contaminate the sacred mourning period with a graceless secular element. Consistent with this nonpartisan view of the assassination, the broadcasters always had Congressional leaders of both parties on television to discuss the country's political institutions.

Even if taste had not eliminated politics the broadcasters would have been hard pressed for news. No partisan political events were happening to provide news nor could any be generated through interviews. Politicians were expected to exercise other-party controls, if for no other reason than the knowledge that political statements at this time might boomerang in the future. One broadcaster said, "You couldn't have gotten anyone to say anything political." Both networks reported incidents where a reporter did address a political question to a political figure and was promptly squelched. A producer said:

I remember throwing out an interview with Goldwater done not by one of our men but by a reporter with an affiliate station who asked how this event affected the 1964 political campaign. Goldwater blew up, and I thought that using [the interview] would [only] compound the bad taste . . . Goldwater was obviously right, the reporter in bad taste.

45

Television and the Kennedy assassination

The coverage of Oswald, Mrs Kennedy, Mrs Tippit and partisan politics only illustrates how news judgment, other-party controls and normative considerations articulate with each other to help determine the coverage news subjects receive. The matter is worth further study, however, for the net result of the articulation of the three factors seems to be a coverage that heightens whatever social solidarity and reaffirmation of values a news event itself evokes in the populace. While this effect may be desirable when collective events like inaugurations are covered, so substantiating McLuhan's idea that television re-tribalises society, it is questionable when other events are covered.

[*13 October 1966*]

... or stay alive;

QUEEN AND PRIME MINISTER—
THE CHILD'S EYE VIEW

Fred I. Greenstein, V. M. Herman,
Robert Stradling, and Elia Zurick

Interviewer: What is a Queen?
Child: Every country has to have a Queen.
Interviewer: Anything else?
Child: And she takes care of the country.

What difference does it make that Britain has a monarch? "Some political scientists," as Edward Shils and Michael Young remarked at the time of Queen Elizabeth II's coronation, "tend to speak as if Britain is now an odd kind of republic which happens to have as its chief functionary a queen instead of a president." Even in the present year, with such notable illustrations of the continuing popular appeal of the monarchy as the widespread, warmly positive reaction to Prince Charles's investiture and the royal family television film, there has been little serious analysis of the monarchy. The evidence is especially weak about the impact of the aspect of the monarchy that Walter Bagehot considered to be its most important function— not the occasional and subtle royal initiatives at Westminster, but rather the Queen's role as a symbolic head and personification of the nation and its institutions.

National surveys confirm the impression that whatever scepticism there may be toward the monarchy on the part of intellectuals, the Queen has extraordinarily widespread support in the general population. But the exact significance of this popularity for Britain is more easily speculated on than demonstrated. Bagehot's own speculations took the form of a variety of elegantly phrased aphorisms—*aperçus* that have a dated Victorian ring and that are not easily put to the test:

"The best reason why monarchy is a strong government is that it is an intelligible government . . . So long as the human heart is strong and the human reason weak, royalty will be strong."

"The Queen is the head of our society. If she did not exist, the Prime Minister would be the first person in the country."

"Constitutional royalty . . . acts as a disguise. It enables our

c

real rulers to change without heedless people knowing it . . . The apparent rulers of the English nation are like the most imposing personages of a splendid procession: it is by them the mob are influenced; it is they whom the spectators cheer. The real rulers are secreted in second-rate carriages; no one cares for them or asks about them, but they are obeyed implicitly and unconsciously by reason of the splendour of those who eclipsed and preceded them."

The purpose of this article is to present in bold outline, with illustrative data from three preliminary studies, a thesis about the nature of childhood conceptions of the Queen and Prime Minister. The thesis is that Bagehot's assertions about the consequences for Britain of having a monarch continue to have a degree of validity and are capable of documentation by studying how British children acquire their political attitudes. Our argument consists of five assertions, the first three of which are straightforwardly factual and the last two of which involve tentative inferences:

1. Very young children in Britain first learn to think of the Queen as the effective ruler of Britain—ie, they assume she rules as well as reigns. To the young child the Prime Minister is merely a helper of the Queen.

2. Children form positive, sympathetic impressions of the Queen. They tend to think of her as a helpful, benevolent figure —one who commands respect and possibly also awe (although not fear). But the Prime Minister, as such, is thought of as simply another individual; his role does not command any special awe. Any particular Prime Minister may or may not receive a favourable assessment, depending upon the child's partisan predilections; but he will not receive the automatic respect accorded to the monarch.

3. The unrealistic view that the Queen rules and the Prime Minister assists her is considerably more common among working class children than among middle class ones. This view of the relationship between the Queen and the Prime Minister erodes with increasing age, but it diminishes much more rapidly among middle class children than among working class children.

4. One legacy for adult politics from these class differences in the acquisition of realistic views of British politics may be the various manifestations of docility and passivity on the part of

some working class Britons that have so often been summed up by Bagehot's term, "deference."

5. A further legacy may be a cool, detached view of the Prime Minister, which is less likely to be found in public response to the national leader in countries that combine the functions of political leader and head of state.

In illustrating these points we first draw briefly on a pair of studies that used more or less standard questionnaire techniques to produce *quantitative* data. Then we draw for illustrative, *qualitative* examples on a depth-interviewing study.

The first questionnaire study was conducted by V. M. Herman and Robert Stradling in the spring of 1969 and involved interviews with 178 junior school children (aged eight to twelve) in three Essex schools, each of which has a roughly 40 per cent middle class and 60 per cent working class student population.

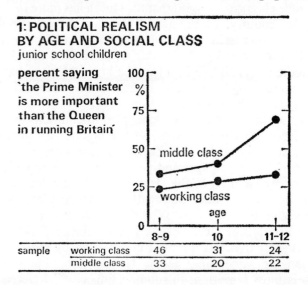

1: POLITICAL REALISM BY AGE AND SOCIAL CLASS
junior school children

percent saying 'the Prime Minister is more important than the Queen in running Britain'

sample		8-9	10	11-12
	working class	46	31	24
	middle class	33	20	22

When asked in an open-ended question to name "the most important person in England," children of all ages and social strata were considerably more likely to refer to the Queen than to anyone else. The Queen was mentioned by about three fifths of the children. The only other figure mentioned with any frequency, the Prime Minister, was referred to by less than half as many children as mentioned the Queen.

Moreover, when asked to name "the most important person *in the world*," the junior school children still referred more often to the Queen than to any other individual. Somewhat less than 50 per cent of them mentioned the Queen in response to this question. The Prime Minister was mentioned less than half as often as the Queen. It is not these pre-adolescent children's unwillingness to assign global supremacy to Harold Wilson, but rather their touching belief in the exalted status of the Queen that is striking.

Figure 1 shows these children's answer to the direct question: "Who is more important in running Britain, the Queen or the Prime Minister?" Only a small minority of the youngest children placed the Prime Minister ahead of the Queen. A handful of the youngest children did not reply, but the great bulk of them—72 per cent of the working class group and 61 per cent of the middle class group—said that the Queen has more to do with ruling the country. By the age of eleven and twelve, political realism had increased, but much more substantially for middle class than for working class children: more than two thirds of the middle class children held that the Prime Minister has more to do with running England, in contrast to only one third of their working class schoolmates.

To see what happens to these political orientations in adolescence, let us now turn to some of the preliminary findings of another study—that by Elia Zurick of secondary school children. Zurick used a paper-and-pencil questionnaire which was filled out by children in the classroom; his research was conducted at various times during the academic year, 1968–69. The question he asked was "Who do you think is more important for Britain, the Queen or the Prime Minister?" The interviews suggest that this question is perceived by most children to mean the same thing as the Herman-Stradling question: "Who is most important in running England?" References to the Prime Minister can in general be treated as reflections of political realism. A very few of the children who say that the Queen is more important seem not to be innocent believers in a fairy-tale conception of British politics, but rather Tory partisans expressing their negative views of Harold Wilson. This, however, merely strengthens Zurick's finding of greater middle class political realism, since the partisan (as opposed to the unrealistic) references to the Queen are largely by middle class children. If these were eliminated, the differences in political realism shown in figure 2 would be sharper.

In figure 2, the percentage of adolescents referring to the Prime Minister is shown by their ages and by the type of their school rather than by their social class. This provides a general indication of social class (given the sociology of educational streaming in Britain) but it also captures a sense of the actual groupings within which adolescent political learning in Britain occurs.

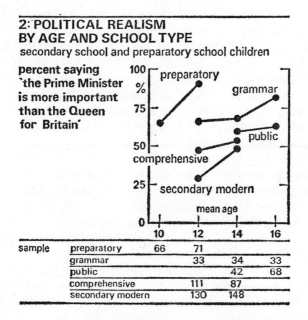

2: POLITICAL REALISM BY AGE AND SCHOOL TYPE
secondary school and preparatory school children

percent saying 'the Prime Minister is more important than the Queen for Britain'

sample		10	12	14	16
	preparatory	66	71		
	grammar		33	34	33
	public			42	68
	comprehensive		111	87	
	secondary modern		130	148	

Figure 2 depicts data on children from two co-educational secondary modern schools in Essex, composed largely of 11-plus failures who range in age up to the school-leaving age: the first three forms of two comprehensive schools, one in Essex and one in London; an Essex boys' grammar school; a boys' public school elsewhere in East Anglia; and finally, for purposes of comparison, a distinguished and well-known boys' preparatory school which sends its pupils on to the most prestigious handful of the public schools. Far more than the actual public school in

53

the sample, the prep school represents in anticipation the stratum of elite public school boys that over the years has held public office in such an astronomical relationship to its actual numbers in the population. The two secondary moderns in figure 2 average about three-to-one working class; the grammar school is slightly more middle class than working class; the two independent schools are middle class or higher and between them include only one child who might be classified as of working class background.

At the age of twelve the great majority of secondary modern children still hold that the Queen is more important, with only 29 per cent mentioning the Prime Minister, whereas about two thirds of the grammar school children and roughly half of the comprehensive children of this age mention the Prime Minister. By 14 the differences between the three groups of children in state education are much narrowed (at least on this exceedingly rudimentary point of political information), but the three types still stand in the same rank order, with the least realism shown by secondary modern children and the most by grammar school children.

Interestingly, the public school sample (which begins at age 14) appears to show somewhat less realism than the more socially heterogeneous grammar school group at age 14; and at age 16 the grammar school children—who, after all, are selected on meritocratic rather than parental-income criteria—exhibit much greater political realism than do children of the same age in the public school. But the most striking finding in figure 2 is that the preparatory school group, although the youngest members of Zurick's sample, are also the best informed. By ten years old, two thirds of these children refer to the Prime Minister; and by twelve years old, nine out of ten of them do.

These statistical skeletons are given flesh by tape-recorded interviews carried out with 52 twelve year old children from about a dozen schools in London and East Anglia. The interviews were carried out in connection with a study by Sidney Tarrow, of Yale, and Fred I. Greenstein of the political imagery of children in Britain, France, and the United States, using a story completion procedure. In the portion of these interviews that concerns us here, the children were asked to tell how they would explain to a foreign child various aspects of their country, including the roles of the Queen and the Prime Minister; they were asked which is more important, the Queen or the Prime Minister, and why they thought the one more important than the other, and they were asked to imagine the conclusions of two stories, one in which the Queen's car was speeding and was stopped by a traffic policeman and one in which a child's parents had made up their minds on whether they approved of a law under public consideration and then found out that the Prime Minister's opinions about the law differed from theirs.

Here, first, is one fairly full presentation of the interview sequence. It provides especially clear illustrations of the main lines of our thesis—that children tend to think of the Queen as the effective ruler, that they idealise her, and that they do not idealise (or defer to) the Prime Minister.

Susan, a student in secondary modern school in a working class section of Greater London, is the daughter of a foreman. She describes herself as a Labour supporter. Susan is asked, first, how she would describe the Queen to a foreign child:

SUSAN: Well it's a member of the royal family that *looks after* the country and her problems [authors' italics].

INTERVIEWER: What sorts of things does she do?

SUSAN: Well she lives in Buckingham Palace which is in the middle of London and she rules over England.

The imagery of benevolence and helpfulness in Susan's description of the Queen has often been found in American children's reports of what the American President does, but rarely appears in British children's accounts of the Prime Minister. Any remaining doubt of how Susan conceives of the relationship between the Queen and the Prime Minister is eliminated by her further remarks:

INTERVIEWER: Suppose the foreign child said: "Tell me what the Prime Minister is."

SUSAN: The Prime Minister is the head of the government which gives out taxes and things like that.

INTERVIEWER: Can you think of anything else that he does?

SUSAN: Well, he's sort of the top of all the ministers that are in the government, and he's sort of the right-hand man to the Queen.

INTERVIEWER: Suppose you were asked: "Who is more important for Britain, the Queen or the Prime Minister?"

55

SUSAN: The Queen.

INTERVIEWER: Now why is that?

SUSAN: Well, she's the monarch sort of thing, she's the head of all of it, but the Prime Minister just looks after the Queen's affairs for her.

In the story about the Queen and the traffic policeman, the interviewer had great difficulty persuading Susan to conceive of the possibility of a royal dereliction:

INTERVIEWER: One day, the Queen was driving her car to a meeting. Because she was late, she was driving very fast. The police stop the car. Finish the story.

SUSAN: Well, really the police wouldn't really stop the Queen driving the car, because somebody would be escorting the Queen to the meeting and that would stop the rest of the cars so she wouldn't really need to be going fast. People have got time to wait for the Queen. She wouldn't really be late.

INTERVIEWER: Let's suppose for the purpose of this question that the Queen was driving by herself in a car and she wanted to go out and away from all the other people and the police stopped her for going fast.

SUSAN: Well, the police might have stopped her, but as soon as they saw it was the Queen they wouldn't take her in for speeding or anything like that.

INTERVIEWER: What do you suppose the policeman would say?

SUSAN: I think he would be astounded, because really the Queen, she doesn't drive the car on her own. And she knows Britain's speed limit, so she wouldn't have gone really fast.

But when the interviewer asked Susan to finish a story in which "Jane's parents are discussing a law that is going to be voted on" and "finally they decide they are against it" only to find "the Prime Minister is for it," Susan exhibits a quite different set of assumptions about the likelihood that a public figure will be fallible or worthy of automatic deference:

SUSAN: Well, if they thought that he was a good Prime Minister they might decide that they want to agree with him but if they didn't like the Prime Minister and they didn't like the law at all, then they would just be against it.

All told, only five of the 52 twelve year olds, one of them a middle class child and four of them working class, have the parents changing their views on learning that they disagree with the Prime Minister; the questionnaire does not make it possible to test the Queen's potency as an agent of opinion change, but the great bulk of the Queen-policeman stories are as respectful as Susan's, even when they do involve police interference with the Queen's driving. Only eight children (five middle class and three working class) suggest that the Queen would be punished "just like anyone else"; the rest exonerate her or mitigate her punishment. A scattering of further assertions about the Queen from various of the interviews helps establish the ubiquity of the themes we have been discussing in the course of this article:

"The police got out of the car and walked over and said, 'What were you doing driving so fast?' Then they noticed that it was the Queen. They said, 'Sorry for troubling you, we thought you was some man in the car.' They walked away. And the Queen went and she was late for her party and couldn't get in. So she complained to the police and they had the two men that were driving the police car sacked for keeping the Queen late."

"Not recognising the Queen a policeman took her to the station, and the sergeant there recognised her as the Queen by her face and her manner and he told the policeman off. He says, 'You silly chump. This is the Queen, not an ordinary person. We're sorry for this delay, Your Majesty, but you usually drive around with a chauffeur and he didn't know it was you'."

"She is the ruler of the country, you know. And anything that she said sort of went, you know. If the Minister of Defence or something like that wanted a castle repaired, he'd have to ask her permission first, if it cost a great deal of money."

"She is a person of royal blood who rules over all of England. And she is the highest person in England. She can do anything with the consent of parliament or the government. [She goes to] visit parts of the empire."

These assumptions about monarchical power are not the result of deliberate inculcation by the schools. They appear much more to result from the absence of any explicit inculcation whatsoever. There is no general consensus in Britain that the schools should be involved in the teaching of civics and contemporary history, at least before the later secondary school years. The vacuum is filled by casual absorption of impressions from family, friends and the mass media and by untutored juvenile reasoning about how things "must work". One Bagehot-cum-Piaget childhood explanation of the Queen's putative supremacy over the Prime Minister is her longevity in office:

"[She is more important than the Prime Minister] because she stays Queen longer than the Prime Minister stays Prime Minister."

Another source of naive inference is based on the impressiveness of royal pomp, as in the following explanation of the Queen's importance by a child who is notably low in political information:

"Well, she's got more things than the Prime Minister and she's got the guards which the Prime Minister hasn't got. And she has all the horses. And that's how I think that she's important. But the Prime Minister has got hardly anything. He has got some things, but not as much as what the Queen has got."

About a third of these 52 twelve year olds exhibited political realism, identifying the Queen as simply a figurehead and the Prime Minister as national leader. As might be expected, more middle class (two fifths) than working class (one fifth) children did so. Alan, for example, who is at secondary modern school and comes from an upper working class family, provides an example of this kind of realism:

"The Queen is the sort of figurehead for the country, and you'll find her head on the coins, stamps and quite a few emblems. It's the British tradition that we should always have a King or Queen. She usually visits a terrible accident and writes sympathy letters to the parents or relations . . . makes speeches on Christmas Day . . . The Prime Minister is a person who rightfully sort of governs the country and he's got men under him . . . I think the Prime Minister is more important. I haven't got anything against the Queen, but the Prime Minister is more important because he governs the country."

Additional information is needed now, based on larger and more varied samples of children—especially at the pre-secondary levels—and on a considerably more comprehensive set of measures of childhood political orientation. Nevertheless, it is clear that at least *some* young British children (we believe *most* of them) begin the development of their political attitudes with the Father Christmas belief in royal rule and Prime Ministerial subordination. At least *some* British children learn quite early in their lives to view the Queen in a distinctly positive light and to see her as a source of benevolent protection, whereas it seems unlikely that many children begin by thinking of the Prime Minister in these terms. Finally, it seems likely that fuller research would support our findings of sharp class differences in childhood political realism.

But this only covers the first three of our five opening points. What about the two final statements, where we argue that childhood political learning patterns help account for the political docility of at least some of Britain's working class citizens and the cool and detached public view of the Prime Minister's role?

Here, admittedly, the connections must be speculative. Early learning in childhood appears to be important for adult attitudes and behaviour in two ways. First of all, early learning occurs at a time of plasticity and openness: the assumptions acquired in childhood frequently appear to be absorbed unquestioned. They become inarticulate major premises, which then exercise a powerful background effect precisely because they are not made conscious enough to be challenged. This may be especially true in areas of discourse—like politics—which, for most individuals, are not matters of very great fascination or concern; areas in which most people act without reflection and on the basis of habit. Secondly, early learning is likely to be important simply because it *is* early. What enters the mind first provides the lenses and categories for later perceptions.

Some later learning, of course, wipes out earlier learning—one's parents come to replace Father Christmas as the source of Christmas benefices. But when this occurs, some of the emotional tone of the early learning may linger, even though its cognitive content is eliminated. This may be what happens in the development of British political attitudes, though it will take subtle longitudinal studies to be sure. The child who begins with the assumption that he is the legal subject of a benevolent but unchecked monarch is not likely, on gradually correcting this impression, to develop the further assumption (common among American children) that the government is there for the citizen to guide and influence. And for many working class children the notion of a royal ruler seems to continue late into adolescence—perhaps even into adult life for a few.

59

Similarly the child who belatedly learns that the Prime Minister is a leader rather than a lackey is not likely at that point to drape the Prime Minister with the idealised, parent-like qualities young British children assign to the Queen and young American children to the President. Thus there develops an adult who can take the Prime Minister or leave him.

[*23 October 1969*]

DO WE WANT OUR CHILDREN TAUGHT ABOUT GOD?

Ronald Goldman

Visitors to Britain frequently register astonishment when they discover that in a country where less than 10 per cent of the population regularly attend a place of worship, there is compulsory religious instruction and worship in all state schools. Americans particularly, coming from a secular society, yet with very high church attendance figures, find religious education in British schools something of a paradox.

They are not the only ones who find it paradoxical. The National Secular Society during the past year has been trying to mount a national campaign, with very limited success, calling for a reconsideration of the religious clauses of the 1944 Education Act. In effect it says that it is intolerable to impose religion upon the young now that we have ceased to be a Christian nation. The British Humanist Association, in evidence to the Plowden committee on primary schools, has also advocated abolition of the 1944 settlement. Some churchmen are equally uneasy about the current situation and feel that the repeal of the compulsory requirements for religious education in schools would do more good than harm. A large and representative group of teachers of religion at a conference held at London University has passed a resolution to this effect.

Religion is the only compulsory school subject in state schools in England and Wales. By law, pupils in these schools must receive some religious teaching and all these schools must have a daily religious service. The 1944 act, which states these requirements, also makes provision for withdrawal of children from religious activities if their parents have objections, and safeguards the rights of teachers who do not wish to teach religion. The act lays down that the daily assembly must not show a bias towards any one religious denomination. The content of religious teaching must be based on a syllabus agreed upon by a conference at which the local education authority, the teachers in the area and the churches are represented. No

61

catechism or feature which is distinctive of any particular religious denomination may be included in an agreed syllabus. Denominational schools, especially Catholic, stand outside these provisions.

In Scotland the requirements are very similar, allowing the same safeguards for parents and teachers as in England and Wales. The denominational aspect, however, is interpreted much more flexibly and the Presbyterian Church of Scotland's influence upon the syllabus and schools is considerable.

The doubts raised by opponents of this religious settlement are many. How representative of public opinion are the views of those who call for a repeal of the religious requirements of the 1944 Education Act? Is religious education under fire? What does the public really think about all this? Has the 1944 Education Act ceased to have public support, as far as religious teaching and worship is concerned?

Since little was known about the state of public opinion on this and related questions NEW SOCIETY commissioned National Opinion Polls to carry out a survey. It was an impartial survey, based upon a systematic probability sample of England, Wales and Scotland. Nine questions were asked of 2,160 individuals above the age of 21 years, representative of regional, sex, age and social class distributions.

The results are overwhelmingly in favour of continuing the present system. In judging their significance it is important to know more about the people who answered the questions. To the question "What is your religion?" the following claims were made by the 2,160 people who answered:

WHAT IS YOUR RELIGION?	%
Church of England	63·4
Nonconformist	10·5
Roman Catholic	10·1
Presbyterian and Church of Scotland	8·9
Jewish	1·3
atheist/agnostic	1·1
other religion	3·0
no religion	1·8

The answers must not be construed as indicating active church membership and attendance. They may indicate a mixture of motives and attitudes, including real belief and affiliation, a wish to believe or to be regarded as believing, an expression of social conformity, or merely a desire to share the social amenities for baptisms, weddings and funerals which the churches provide. There is no doubt that "What is your religion?" is a status-loaded question, and most surveys indicate that people interviewed tend to want to appear to be more religious than their religious activities would merit. There is little difference between men and women in answering this question with the exception that slightly more men (5 per cent) were willing to say that they were atheists, agnostics or of no religion, than were women (2 per cent). The claims made at various ages are of interest:

RELIGION AND AGE						
	21–24	25–34	35–44	45–54	55–64	65 +
base	134	394	435	420	378	399
	%	%	%	%	%	%
Ch. of England	58	63	67	64	61	63
Nonconformist	6	8	7	13	12	16
Roman Catholic	17	15	12	7	9	5
Presbyterian	11	8	9	10	9	7
Jewish	1	1	1	2	2	1
atheist/agnostic	3	1	1	1	2	1
other religion	1	2	2	3	3	6
no religion	3	3	1	1	2	2

The Church of England's loyalties were lowest with the 21–24 age group and highest at 35–44 years. Nonconformist claimants clearly increase with increasing age, but in contrast the Roman Catholics appear to decline with increasing age. The social categories of respondents revealed that those who regarded themselves as Church of England were spread fairly evenly through the upper, middle and lower middle class categories, that the Nonconformists had a marked middle class bias, and that the Roman Catholics revealed a strong working class bias. In Scotland 72 per cent of those interviewed claimed to be Presbyterian. The high figures for the Church of England and the Presbyterian Church are evident in areas where they are the established churches.

Do we want our children taught about God?

Although most people claimed to "belong" to a particular denomination, their estimates of their own attendance are much more modest, and if other surveys are accurate, reveal a fairly truthful and realistic situation. Since the question was asked before Easter and almost exactly three months after Christmas the estimates below will include some people who last went to church at Christmas:

WHEN DID YOU LAST ATTEND CHURCH?

	within 7 days %	within 3 months %
Church of England	6·2	24·1
Nonconformist	2·7	5·3
Roman Catholic	5·4	6·7
Presbyterian	1·6	4·1
Jewish	0·2	0·8
atheist/agnostic	—	0·1
other religions	0·8	1·5
no religion	—	—

These results are, on the whole, consistent with what is known from other sources about church attendance, although they are somewhat on the generous side. Attendance at a place of worship would include not only regular church worship, but "occasional" events such as baptisms, wedding or funerals. Further analysis also reveals that women attend church significantly with greater frequency than do men, that upper and middle class attend significantly with greater frequency than do the lower social classes, that the region with the highest frequency of claimed weekly church attendance is Scotland (26 per cent) and the region with the lowest is the south east (15 per cent). There is a slightly higher rate of church attendance among those who have no children of school age than those who have. Presumably, those with schoolchildren do not have as great a freedom to attend. To support this assumption we can see that the age group who attend least regularly are those aged 25–44 years, who have the greatest proportion of children at school.

All these facts are consistent with what is known from previous surveys. They tend to suggest that the people interviewed were a typical cross-section of our population, the majority not willing to relinquish what is probably a nominal or even sentimental attachment to a particular church.

This is a question important for religious education, for if the vast majority of people reject the idea of a Christian Britain, religious education could justifiably be attacked as an unwelcome imposition upon a secular society. The presence or absence of an established church does not determine whether a society is secular or not: this is largely a reflection of how a society regards itself. From this survey the answers show unmistakably that people view Britain as a Christian society, not as a secular nation:

IS BRITAIN A CHRISTIAN COUNTRY?

	%
Britain is a Christian country	79·7
Britain is not a Christian country	19·0
don't know/no answer	1·3

There are significant variations to be seen when these total figures are broken down:

BREAKDOWN BY RELIGION

	C of E	RC	NC	Presby.
base	521	145	115	88
	%	%	%	%
is	85	78	70	82
is not	15	21	29	15
don't know	1	1	1	3

A statistical test shows that between the churches registering the greatest divergence of opinion, the Church of England and the Nonconformists, the differences are highly significant. This would be consistent with the past history and assumptions of the two traditions. The Anglicans have held to a concept of parish Christianity, in that everyone born and baptised into a parish may be regarded as Christian, whereas the Nonconformists have tended to view society in more secular terms.

Regionally, there is a significant difference between people living in the north and those living in the south east. Northerners (84 per cent) tend to think of Britain as a Christian nation in greater proportion than do south easterners (77 per cent). But the proportion in all areas is still very high.

There is a noticeable increased tendency with age to regard Britain as Christian. The differences between the youngest and oldest age groups are statistically significant. But even 72 per cent of the 21–24 year old group feel that we retain a Christian orientation:

BREAKDOWN BY AGE						
	21–24	25–34	35–44	45–54	55–64	65 +
base	134	394	435	420	378	399
	%	%	%	%	%	%
is	72	78	81	80	80	83
is not	27	20	17	19	19	17
don't know	2	2	2	2	1	1

Before the question "should the present arrangements for religion in schools continue?" was put, the introductory sentence briefly explained the current situation. The overall results, set out in terms of sex and age differences, are shown below:

SHOULD THE PRESENT SCHOOL RELIGIOUS ARRANGEMENTS CONTINUE?						
	21–24	25–34	35–44	45–54	55–64	65 +
base	134	394	435	420	378	399
	%	%	%	%	%	%
yes	86	87	91	93	88	93
no	11	11	8	6	10	6
don't know	3	2	1	1	2	2

Although there are significant differences between men and women there is a slightly greater rate for continuing religion on the present arrangements with increasing age, the overall vote of 90 per cent is overwhelmingly in favour. There are no significant differences between regions, nor between religions on this issue.

SEX	all	male	female
base	2160	1033	1127
	%	%	%
yes	90·0	87	93
no	8·3	11	6
don't know	1·7	2	1

Those who have children at school vote proportionately more favourably (91 per cent) than those who have no children at school (89 per cent) but the differences are not significant. Only 4·9 per cent of parents withdrew their children from religious instruction.

Two further questions were put to see whether people would distinguish between the primary and secondary stages of children where religious teaching is involved. Some writers have suggested recently that "compulsory religion" is happily accepted by children, but is not appropriate for adolescents, who should choose for themselves. The results show only a slight drop in opinion from primary to secondary:

DO YOU WANT RELIGIOUS INSTRUCTION AS IT IS, OR NONE?			
	as it is	none	don't know
	%	%	%
primary school pupils	91·6	4·8	3·6
secondary school pupils	90·7	4·4	4·9

The 1944 act nowhere lays down that Christianity must be taught—it is implied rather than stated. All committees responsible for agreed syllabuses of religious teaching assume that Christianity shall have the major emphasis, although "world religions" are usually suggested for the upper forms in secondary schools. It is difficult enough for a child to grasp the significance of one religion without being faced with confusing comparisons, and it seems educationally sound to delay a systematic comparison of different religions until the years of greater maturity. The idea of a broader approach involving more than Christianity may have a certain broad-minded appeal.

67

Do we want our children taught about God?

Whereas 90 per cent of all people interviewed wish for religious teaching, only 69·4 per cent wish to concentrate upon Christianity. Women wish teaching to be concentrated more

SHOULD INSTRUCTION BE COMPARATIVE OR CHRISTIAN ONLY?			
	all	male	female
base	2160	1033	1127
	%	%	%
compare	22·3	25	20
concentrate	69·4	67	72
don't know	8·2	8	9

than men, and the age differences seen below are strikingly divergent. The older the respondent the greater the tendency to want "concentrated" teaching:

AGE	21–24	25–34	35–44	45–54	55–64	65 +
base	134	394	435	420	378	399
	%	%	%	%	%	%
compare	37	26	25	23	17	15
concentrate	56	67	67	70	73	76
don't know	8	7	8	7	10	9

The age differences may indeed be significant not only statistically, but as straws in the wind. 37 per cent of the 21–24 year age group want a broader curriculum in religious teaching. Reports indicate that students in training for teaching express this desire very strongly. Regionally, this is expressed in our survey between the extremes of Scotland (75 per cent in favour of "concentration") and the south east (63 per cent in favour of "concentration"). These two areas form the extremes of weekly church attendance.

If these replies are typical there is overwhelming support in Britain for the continuance of religious education within the state school system as the educational expression of a society which regards itself, however vaguely, as a Christian country. There is no distinction made in this support by the public between religious education for younger and older pupils, but there is some support (over 20 per cent) for a broader teaching basis than a concentration upon Christianity. It may be that the public suffer from inertia on the question of compulsory religion in schools. It may be that all they want for children is a religion to which they have a sentimental attachment but which they have themselves rejected. It may be that they feel that religion gives to children a good moral start in life. But whatever the motives, muddled or perceptive, the vote is overwhelmingly favourable.

Other surveys indicate similar trends. Despite a drop in weekly church attendance the Church of England National Society points out in a recent report that the number of baptisms per 1,000 live births in 1958 was 579, only 16 less per 1,000 than in 1891. In a survey made in 1964 an investigator at the University of Birmingham issued a questionnaire to parents of sixth formers. Three quarters of the parents replied and three quarters of these were in favour of religious instruction for their children. A group of teachers in Surrey recently reported that in five schools sampled, two primary and three secondary, out of a total enrolment of 2,017 children only 17 children opted out of religious worship and teaching, less than 1 per cent. Similar to this is the conclusion arrived at in a 1954 report by the Institute of Christian Education, that withdrawals were few and were nearly all for denominational rather than agnostic reasons. A survey on the teaching situation in primary schools reported that only 4 per cent of teachers felt unable or unwilling to teach it.

It may be that subtle conformist pressures operate against parents who do not wish to make their children feel peculiar by withdrawing them. They may also be felt by teachers who, despite their legal rights, may feel their chances of promotion would be affected if they were to withdraw from teaching religion. Despite these possibilities, however, the results indicate that repeal of the law is not a live issue.

There is a ferment going on among teachers and within training colleges for teachers concerning the content and aims of religious teaching in schools. These are the live issues today, not the fact of "compulsion." Educators are dissatisfied with syllabuses which appear to stress the historical and factual content of the bible. Research indicates that in primary schools children develop such literal and crude misunderstandings about the bible and its teachings that a more suitable content for religious education, based upon children's experiences and needs, is being sought. In secondary schools, many adolescents feel that religious instruction is rather like a protracted visit to a museum, ossified in a holy time and place, irrelevant to modern life. Much religious education appears to be of 19th century vintage, the bible being regarded as a religious textbook, and knowledge of it is the criterion of "successful" teaching. Yet a report from the University of Sheffield in 1961 indicated that secondary school leavers had a very poor grasp of even elementary bible knowledge after ten years of bible teaching in state schools.

The fundamental issue is basically the effectiveness of religious education. New syllabuses, especially for primary schools, are long overdue. A new look is needed, not for the sake of novelty, but for the sake of our children. Much religious teaching seems only to reinforce crude, magical and immature ideas of God, which have to be rejected as "childish" as pupils grow into adolescence. There is evidence to show that it is the immature religion of childhood which many adults reject today.

Pew fodder for the churches, a detailed knowledge of the old and new testaments, the inculcation of a moral code are narrow and unrealistic aims for religious education in Britain in our present situation. Rather, by personal search, by reflection upon experience, by an exposure to what Christianity has to teach, children in school should be led to a realistic apprehension of the deep questions raised by religion and what it is Christians believe. In this search straight, critical and personal thinking should be encouraged, so that an acceptance or rejection of religious belief shall eventually be made, not on childish or immature grounds, but for adult reasons.

[*27 May 1965*]

... people change,

SOCIAL MOBILITY

David Lockwood

Downward social mobility has always been regarded as a more or less unpleasant experience, but in recent years the costs of "getting on in life" have been attracting as much attention as its more manifest benefits. There is a world, as well as a century, of difference between Samuel Smiles's self-made, self-confident hero, transforming environment to the advantage of society and self, and Richard Hoggart's scholarship boy, anxious and up-rooted in a world not of his own making and hardly of his own choosing.

The problem of social elevation vividly portrayed by Hoggart is also the subject of much fictional, dramatic, and autobiographical treatment. Of course, we know now that Smiles was something of a myth-maker, recording a pattern of opportunity that society accorded to a few and wished to impress upon the consciousness of the many. Is there now a new myth in process of formation; a myth generalised from the testimonies of a few, sensitive and articulate casualties of upward mobility whose experiences teach the cautionary tale that getting on is by no means an unmixed blessing?

The sociologist cannot provide the answer, although he has had the problem on his plate for quite some time. The French sociologist, Emile Durkheim, while sharing the now widely affirmed belief in the value of equality of opportunity and careers open to talent, was also the first thoroughly to explore the psychological effects of the individual's attachment to, and detachment from, social groupings. The disturbance and re-establishment of group affiliations which might be thought to be associated with social mobility is not, it is true, given much prominence in his work on *Suicide*. Nevertheless, the theories of "anomic" and "egotistical" suicide which Durkheim puts forward in that work contain the essence of much that is now being written, spoken, or felt about the psychic costs of individual mobility. His argument in brief was that individuals who are weakly supported by group attachments, or individuals who

73

are precipitated into new social environments to which their previously acquired wants and aspirations are no longer suited, are more exposed to the strains and stresses of everyday existence, and more likely to succumb to them and exhibit pathological behaviour.

Sociologists have been rather slow in taking up this lead. Sharing the view that it is a bad thing for the society and the individual to have square pegs in round holes, they have concentrated on the measurement of occupational mobility and the (in)efficiency of educational selection. As a result, we are less sanguine about existing mechanisms of allocation, more knowledgeable about the stock of talent, and, on a wider comparative basis less prone to generalise, for example, that industrial societies have more mobility than agrarian ones, or that the opportunities for occupational advancement in the United States far exceed those in Britain. Even if the mass of these studies does not directly relate to the social and psychological consequences of mobility, some of their results may help to provide an initial perspective on the problem.

D. V. Glass and his associates found, for example, that the rates of inter-generational occupational mobility have been remarkably stable during the present century as far as men are concerned. This inquiry could not take into account the effects of the Education Act of 1944, but more recently Jean Floud has stated that "it seems unlikely that the postwar movement of educational reform can as yet have brought about any marked increase in the degree of social interchange between the classes established by Professor Glass and his colleagues for the prewar period."

What is happening at the present time is hard to establish. It would seem likely that the number of occupational positions which facilitate upward mobility is on the increase. During the last decade or so, those industries which have been growing most rapidly not only have the highest proportions of white collar workers, but they are also the industries which show the greatest relative increase in their ratios of non-manual employees. Even so, from the facts available, it is questionable whether the increased attention that has been paid to the effects of mobility is simply a product of any sudden increase in mobility itself.

Again, though interest naturally focuses on the experiences of those individuals who have travelled a considerable distance from their origins, the great mass of occupational mobility is of a relatively short-range kind. In the nature of the job structure of the country, most mobility represents either a change within manual employment itself (which may not perhaps be regarded as social mobility at all) or between manual and lower non-manual work.

If there has been no dramatic increase in the amount and range of mobility that is taking place, why then the concern? Perhaps it has something to do with the fact that the mobility which occurs has become more highly institutionalised through formal educational selection. Associated with this, there has obviously occurred some social escalation of a rather sudden and long range character for a very few; and the angry reaction to this process of still an even smaller minority has been accorded a greater publicity than before. It is also necessary to recognise that a heightened concern with the strains of social mobility may be part and parcel of a wider disenchantment with an industrial society.

In such a society, the salient institutions of market and bureaucracy tend to relate segments of human beings to one another in cold, impersonal and calculative relationships, which stand in strong contrast with the warm, intimate sociability of family, friends and neighbourhood in which the full person can relate himself, as an individual, to other individuals. The rationalisation of occupational movement through educational selection is an inherent part of this industrial nexus. People are being selected, elevated or demoted (though to a lesser extent than the official ideology would have it) in terms of specific qualities and achievements, with a consequent subordination of the more primary ties and solidarities. The very existence of such impersonal mechanisms in major areas of the society is bound to cause a certain amount of disturbance, anxiety and tension, not only for those who are mobile, but also for those to whom mobility is a threat—not to mention those who are left at the bottom of the pile.

Under these conditions, any evidence, however slender and atypical, that social mobility produces harmful consequences for the individual, may easily be exaggerated as a result of a diffuse

75

and sub-political hostility to the industrial system itself. In-articulate value judgements in the guise of "committed" social reporting only render more difficult the drawing up of a proper balance sheet of the profits and losses arising from mobility. The unsettling dynamism of an industrial society is inevitably pro-ductive of social dislocation and social conflict. But is this necessarily a bad thing? Is it true, for instance, that deep involve-ment in the "rich full life" of stable working class communities offers the greatest scope for the development of human potential-ities? Or that the sometimes disharmonious encounter between the old-established and the newly arrived is so crippling to the individual and such a dead loss as far as the society is con-cerned? In another context, it was also Durkheim who reminded us that a society designed to eliminate tension and conflict would also be a society that was moribund. Quite apart from needing more facts about the social consequences of mobility, we need a much more explicit analysis of the various standards by which we judge and evaluate the facts.

But the facts we do need. For what evidence is there that social mobility, in the great majority of cases, uproots, isolates, and distresses its otherwise unafflicted victims? One might think that studies of mental health might throw some light on the problem. But in view of the general difficulties of classifying, measuring and accounting for mental illnesses, the results of the very few, mostly American, and by no means consistent, studies which seek an association between social mobility and mental pathol-ogy have to be treated with great caution. Lipset and Bendix, for example, have claimed that "people who are upward mobile, but *not* those who are downward mobile or geographically mobile, have higher rates of mental disorder than those who are station-ary. This suggests that it is not the anomic situation associated with mobility that is responsible for the greater vulnerability, because one would expect downward mobility to be at least as threatening to psychic equilibrium as upward mobility. It is therefore probable that a particular type of ego structure which results from a characteristic family environment is both favourable for upward mobility and vulnerable to mental illness."

According to this theory, then, it is not mobility that causes mental illness; rather both are the product of childhood deprivation. Not only has this theory been vigorously challenged by Srole and his associates, but also the interpretation of the facts on which it is based (a sample of mental patients under treatment). Their own study of *non-hospitalised* population in mid-Manhattan indicated that it was the downwardly mobile group which showed greatest mental distress, while the upwardly mobile group were mentally healthier, healthier even than the non-mobile group. In turn, they put forward the explanation that "upward mobility requires not only appropriate aspirations but also efficient personal mobilisation, such that actually to 'make the grade', sound mental health is a decided preparatory asset and impaired health is not. Downward mobility, on the other hand, is so culturally deviant from group and self-expectations that it can only happen under some initial, predisposing handicap in physical or mental health."

If anything is to be gained from these discrepant claims it is their agreement on one essential point: namely, that even if a connection between mobility and greater liability to mental illness were to be unequivocally established, it would not follow that this increased risk was due to mobility as such (ie, to the alleged disorientation associated with actual social movement). In both cases, there is a clear, albeit contradictory stress upon the important role of the individual's pre-disposition to health or sickness. Only longitudinal studies can eventually clarify the dynamic relationship between such predisposition and the effects of mobility *per se.*

Other factors are also likely to be involved. One of these is the extent of social distance travelled. Another is mobility achievement relative to mobility striving. Other studies have shown that large discrepancies between aspirations and achievements appear to characterise the mentally ill in both the middle and lower classes. This again would tend to suggest that the factor of mobility by itself is by no means the solely, or even saliently, operative factor. Indeed, it may be the lack of mobility, or mobility incommensurate with mobility aspirations, that aggravates the tension and anxiety which in some cases eventuate in mental illness.

Is it also the case that social mobility destroys the individual's pre-existing ties with family, friends, and primary groups? There is again little evidence to draw on, but what there is does not

77

confirm this readily advanced proposition. One study which deliberately sets out to test this assumption is that carried out by Litwak in the United States (*Occupational Mobility and Extended Family Cohesion*). Holding constant the factor of geographical distance, he found that there was no great difference between mobile and non-mobile persons in visiting and maintaining contact with their extended families; and this held true even when extreme upward and downward mobility was considered. He also found that upwardly mobile individuals were not less identified with their extended family than the others.

His explanation is rather interesting. He points out that people achieve status not only by associating with others of equal or greater social position, but also by receiving deference from others. The extended family plays an important status gratifying role for the upwardly mobile. Providing that family visits can be isolated from the visits of friends who are status equals (a condition more likely to be realised in large urban centres than in small rural communities) the upwardly mobile individual can obtain status both by associating with his peers and by gaining deference from his family. Confirmation that upward social mobility does not impair family contacts is also provided in passing by Young and Willmott's research in Bethnal Green.

It is clear, then, that contacts are not necessarily severed by social mobility, although we know practically nothing about the quality of the relationships that may be maintained. But it is not obvious that the greater the social distance moved, the more full of tension the relationship is likely to be. It is in fact possible to argue just the opposite: that the social bond between parents and offspring is likely to be more tense if the upward mobility of the offspring is modest rather than extreme. If it is extreme (the miner's son who goes to Oxford), the manifest differences in education and other achievements may be simply so large that they do not form a basis for potential conflict; especially if the nature of these achievements are a source of family pride, in which case they may confer upon the offspring a generalised "authority" to which the parents are happy to defer. If, on the other hand, the mobility is marginal (the bank clerk's son who goes to a provincial university), it could be that, because they are close enough to be meaningfully competitive, the differences between parents and offspring could lead to tension at many points, not least perhaps in respect of the social and cultural aspirations of the parents themselves.

One final aspect of the problem deserves mention: that is, the ease with which occupational mobility can be translated into status mobility. This has an obvious bearing on the degree of strain which persons moving up occupationally are likely to experience if they seek social assimilation at a new and higher level. A good deal of discussion has arisen over the finding, for example, based on rather crude measurements, that the rates of occupational mobility in the United States are not all that different from those in this country. While interesting in itself, the vital question would seem to be not whether the measures used in this comparison were too imprecise, but whether rates of occupational mobility really tell us anything about social mobility. The United States could have exactly the same amount of job mobility and still be a more "open" society in the very real sense that dollars can be more easily translated into status than pounds sterling. But we should not be too ready in assuming that this is generally the case.

One measure is the degree of intermarriage that takes place between different occupational strata, and the evidence that we have on this point does not again suggest significant differences between the two countries. More particularly, it is possible that the degree of "openness" and "closure" in the two countries varies depending on which level of the class system we are considering. It is possible, for example, that closure is more apparent in this country in the middle of the system, specifically along the manual and white collar dividing line. However, at the elite level, it is by no means obvious that the social assimilation of mobile individuals and groups has been easier in the United States than in Britain.

The more unified nature of the elite in this country, and the more systematic mechanisms for incorporating new blood that it deploys, are well known. On the other hand, many American sociologists have pointed to the tensions between the old-established elites of the East Coast and the new rich in such places as Texas, and have suggested that the relative status deprivation of the latter constitutes a potential for such movements as McCarthyism. Moreover, status differentiation on the

79

basis of ethnicity introduces an element of closure and social exclusion that is almost wholly absent in this country.

It is quite obvious that intelligent discussion of the costs and benefits of social mobility must await more precise research into the various elements that are involved in this process. I have not been trying to dismiss the strains of social mobility. They exist. But we should not exaggerate them, and we should not allow our concern with movement within the class system to distract our attention from the structure itself. If there are human problems and social costs arising from social mobility, there are perhaps more profound and quantitatively more impressive problems arising from immobility.

The mechanisms by which a minority in this country achieve some substantial social advancement are also the mechanisms which affect the life chances and self-esteem of a much greater mass of persons. The fact that mobility has become increasingly institutionalised via the educational system means that while there may be increased chances of intergenerational mobility through education, the chances of intra-generational mobility through work are declining. To enter a factory job with a secondary modern education is to take a job that is more and more a life sentence. It is also to have been allocated in such a way as to give official legitimacy to that life sentence. And it is not simply that there is no alternative channel of upward mobility to the school—for most people, anyway, upward mobility is not a solution. It is rather that human potentialities are systematically cramped at the bottom of our society.

They are cramped, as Basil Bernstein has shown, by the very linguistic apparatus of their social group. They are cramped by selective education whose latent function is to demolish positive aspiration for anything but consumption mobility. Above all, they are cramped by the minimal scope for the exercise of autonomy and responsibility, either in relation to the job itself or the way in which it is organised, that exists at the bottom of highly specialised industrial bureaucracies. We know that for a great many persons in this situation the man is bigger than the job. We know that the manifold reactions by which workers adjust themselves to their work situation are a symptom of this underemployment of their potentialities. We know that it is not necessarily true that people compensate for dull and isolating work by creative leisure and a full social life. We know that people whose work is low in responsibility and initiative are also the people who—once removed from the ritualised sociability of the traditional working class community—find it difficult to form new primary group ties or to involve themselves in the associational life of their society.

Provision for occupational mobility cannot release these potentialities. It is only one part of a wide strategy of mobilisation that society has at its disposal. Historically, the extension of the franchise to the lower classes was a most important form of mobilisation. Political citizenship, by conferring a new status and new rights, was an effective means of incorporating the worker into the new industrial society. But side by side with this process of civic integration there developed an industrial practice whose goal seems to have been increasingly to maximise production by reducing to a minimum the need for any job involvement, other than financial, on the part of the mass of employees. This industrial practice can be, and is being questioned on the lines that altering the job to fit the worker may be more advantageous to all concerned than fitting the worker to the job; and it is hard to believe that a more imaginative mobilisation of human resources at the place of work will not become a major preoccupation in the next few decades. But it would be a pity if the desirability of such measures were reckoned purely in terms of their contribution to productivity. The thought that, at the point of production, we "produce," among other things, human beings, is worth keeping in mind.

[*28 November 1963*]

INTEGRATION INTO WHAT SOCIETY?

Michael Banton

Which is the more important, that the immigrants are coloured, or that the coloureds are immigrant? Early analyses of race relations in Britain saw the newcomers as people who would eventually be assimilated even if it took longer for them than it had for Huguenots, Jews and Irish. The similarities between the new wave of immigration and these earlier ones seemed more important than its distinctive features. However, more recently it has begun to look as if the crude distinction of skin colour will matter most.

If race is to be the dominant feature, then for parallels we must look to the social pluralism of Belgium, Canada and the cities of the north eastern United States. There, members of different minorities enjoy equality in respect of civil rights and obligations, but keep themselves separate in marriage and mutual hospitality, while rivalling one another in other contexts—such as in political organisation. Gerhard Lenski, indeed, sees the controversies surrounding John F. Kennedy's candidature for the presidency as marking, not the end of discrimination against Catholics, but the beginning of a group rivalry that will be taken up by Jews and Negroes.

English society from at least the latter part of the 17th century has shown a remarkable homogeneity. The determinants of class, status, and power in different regions have been very similar and have derived from national institutions. Centralisation was made easier by a fairly dense distribution of population over a small territory, and by common socialising agencies for the higher classes (such as boarding schools and the armed services).

An almost uniform pattern for social mobility was created, while a chain of social groups dictated nationally relevant standards of social acceptance and rejection. Distinctive provincial patterns of speech and behaviour persisted, but a provincial who wished to claim status outside his own region was well advised to study the national norms of civility. The influence of the standard-setting groups gave English society a particular homogeneity in the eyes of outsiders and enabled it to assimilate new groups from within and without its boundaries. The pressure to conform to English conventions was felt by Scots, Welsh, and Irish as well as by people from overseas. In the 18th century at least, coloured people appear not to have been the objects of any special prejudice.

Any host society demands certain standards of newcomers before it accepts them. If the standards are set too high, the newcomers do not try to meet them. If they are set too low, the newcomers do not place much value upon the acceptance accorded them. Yet if the standards are set very high, but still within reach, and the rewards of acceptance kept proportionately attractive, then those who win acceptance will take over the values of the social system and its norms concerning mobility will be perpetuated.

In England, the standards were set very high. The successful immigrant or social climber could not gain acceptance to the upper social reaches in his own lifetime, but by sending his children or grandchildren through the right socialising agencies, he could ensure that his lineage would have a place inside the magic circle. The power of attraction exerted by this mode of signalising and reinforcing worldly success can be seen in the Anglicising of the Irish, Welsh, and Scottish middle classes, as reflected in the social bases of their nationalist movements. It can be seen in the drawing power of titles, honours and social snobbery, in the strength of working class Conservatism, and in the way Jewish citizens have never been a political minority but have acted through existing parties.

A homogeneous society holds a distinctive view of human nature. Americans tend to see the world as man-controlled, and to approach it like engineers who demolish old structures, prepare blueprints and build anew. But the English see the world as something to which man adapts; they approach it like gardeners who plant their seed and cultivate any resulting plants. Even allowing for their general ignorance of human biology, their preference for hereditarian explanations of behavioural variation is striking. Britons rely heavily upon implicit norms of conduct and tacit modes of social training. They more readily become aware of them in breach than in observance: certain things are "not done," but no one likes overtly to teach, or be taught, what *is* "done." Clubs in Pall Mall, like colleges in Oxford and Cambridge, have no name plates outside. Those who are already within the circle do not need name plates, so why put them up? Social patterns like these make it far more difficult for outsiders to gain an entry. They also mean that once people have got in, it is very difficult to throw them out. The old-boy net looks after its own.

Assimilation in past generations could work slowly on small numbers. Its successes have led many well-informed people—Jews and coloured men included—to doubt the value of legislation against group defamation or of any positive programme to foster goodwill towards ethnic minorities. The institutional structure has provided no way in which ethnic variations could be taken into account. Lacking any conceptual scheme for thinking about these matters other than one suggestive of discrimination, the politicians long closed their eyes to the questions posed by the growth of a coloured minority.

Emphasis on the immigration aspect of the present situation has many advantages. It draws attention to the ties with the homeland which are still of paramount importance for Indian and Pakistani communities at least. It takes account of variations in the desire for social acceptance between the different communities and the relevance to British social patterns of linguistic, religious and other differences.

But a salient feature is the readiness of Britons to lump the immigrants together in one category, "coloured." By most criteria, the Jamaicans have more in common with the British than with the Pakistanis, yet people in this country so often assume that colour is the key factor. Those who have lectured on this subject must all know the moment in a discussion of mixed marriages when someone, as if supporting the lecturer, says "and of course, most of the coloured people don't approve of mixed marriages either, do they?" and the lecturer has to go back to the beginning and explain once again how such a statement assumes that "whites" and "coloured people" are, for the purpose in question, homogeneous and mutually exclusive categories. The British create the role, "coloured man." Indians, Pakistanis, Jamaicans, Nigerians and others are classed together not on account of shared objective characteristics but because

British culture operates with this kind of classificatory scheme. Organisations that have tried to represent all the coloured communities have always found the task difficult because the only thing they have in common is the experience of discrimination.

In recent years other developments have made this shared experience more important and an emphasis on the racial perspective better justified. The growth in the number of children born in Britain who have a coloured parent or parents shifts the emphasis from immigration. It looks as if urban trends characteristic of the United States may be recapitulated here. The immigrants have gone to the areas where the jobs were, and this meant going to the areas of housing shortage. They found accommodation most easily in the twilight zones of urban decline, and residential concentrations have started to appear. This intensifies the problem in the schools, and parents in some localities have complained vehemently that their children's educational progress is being retarded because many immigrant children in the classrooms do not speak English properly and require extra attention.

It now looks, moreover, as if British society has become much less homogeneous since the second world war. The old social and political elite has been identified and pilloried as the Establishment. As new individuals have risen to positions of power and influence, they have seemed less inclined to seek a place in the traditional social elite. National distinctiveness is being reduced by the uniform technological requirement of industrial production and the ease of travel. American ideas of competitiveness and diversity evoke stronger echoes. It seems no longer helpful to think of integration as a single process operating across the whole society, and preferable to assume that there are different processes of integration in separate spheres (politics, work, leisure) of a partially independent character.

When someone ignorant of economics discusses our balance of trade problem, he does not get a serious audience. Yet much discussion of racial questions has been allowed to neglect the facts uncovered and analysed in sociology and biology. At the extremes people have been able to represent the difficulties as if they stemmed simply from the immigrants' presence (solution: send 'em back) or from British illwill (solution: love your neighbour). In between, the attempts to attribute complex phenomena

85

to simple causes have been equally depressing. Teachers have been inclined to see racial questions as suited to discussion in scripture classes or in school debates—as if the task was to exercise opinion rather than to teach facts and their interpretation. Moralising prevails. Yet noble motives are rarely sufficient and the consequences of a person's action may conflict with his intention.

For example, girl students sometimes deprecate racial discrimination and wish to demonstrate to coloured students that not all white people are prejudiced. So at a university dance a girl might show that she was not unwilling to dance with a coloured student. Other coloured students would notice this and conclude that here was one girl who was not prejudiced. Some of them who had asked English girls to dance would have been turned down and might well have found the experience a little humiliating. They would therefore be more inclined to seek dances from a girl whom they defined as unprejudiced. So the girl who initially wished to show only goodwill might find she was receiving a whole series of invitations to dance from coloured students. She might well find it more difficult to say no to them than to white boys. If the white students saw her dancing with one coloured student after another they might infer that she did so from choice, and refrain from asking her to dance with them.

Nor might that be the full extent of her troubles, for, since many of the coloured students come from countries where women are allowed less freedom, they might interpret her behaviour as a desire for greater intimacy than she actually wished. A whole series of predictable consequences, which were no part of the girl's original intention, might flow from her initial willingness to dance with a coloured man.

Analysis of interracial avoidance suggests that British behaviour is influenced by two particular pressures:

1. A desire not to be *exposed* to dealings with a coloured man who does not know the norms of the relevant relationship and may involve other parties in fuss and embarrassment. (More common in some work situations.)

2. A desire not to be *identified* with a coloured man in those relationships in which a person is supposed to be free to choose his associates. (More common in leisure.)

Some immigrants in the 1950s quickly learned the cues by which the natives judged whether a stranger knew the social code. Many became skilled in exploiting the ambiguities and the cues themselves. For example, E. B. Ndem reported that former seamen in Manchester who wished to be taken for students might sport university scarves, and that even illiterates could sometimes be seen with folded copies of *The Times* or *The Guardian* under their arms.

At their workplaces, many men associate with persons of inferior status while on the job; they do not have to worry about being identified with them, for their role in the organisation legitimises the association. But with a man's choice of companion at the lunch table in the canteen, or of his partners in leisure time activities, the pressure of what others may think becomes more potent.

This is particularly relevant to the feeling that no ordinary person would want to live next door to a coloured family if he had any choice. The growing identification of coloured people with neighbourhoods of urban decay, and with the various problems of schooling and health that centre upon them, is affecting the image of the coloured man. Earlier, the things English people associated with him were negative; he was rejected because of beliefs about what he was not, rather than because of beliefs about what he was. The coloured man did not belong at any particular point on the social scale, for (relative to the total coloured population) there were quite a lot of coloured doctors, students and persons of standing. Nor was the coloured man identified with the local scene, because the coloured students were returning to their homelands and the domestic situation was not in the forefront of people's minds. Attitudes seem to have been hardening. There is now more of a tendency to associate positive features with the coloured man, to see him as a permanent resident with dependants, and as someone at the bottom of the social hierarchy whose presence is linked with trouble of one kind or another.

The kind of integration that can be achieved depends on the kind of society Britain is becoming. Considerable fluidity remains. Whether events will approximate more closely to an interpretation in terms of immigration and assimilation, or to one which envisages movement towards a pluralistic pattern of racial communities preserving their distinctiveness in respect of marriage and leisure-time associations, will be decided by the reception accorded to the present second generation of immigrant children when they leave school. There is not a long time to wait for an answer, for it has been estimated that by 1978 one in six of the school-leavers in Birmingham will be a young coloured person. Can any changes in social patterns be predicted?

Someone who is accepted in one situation may be rejected in another. On the early 1960s it seemed as if this resulted in a three-step pattern of social acceptability (see diagram, which is based on the results of a national survey directed by Professor Melvin M. Tumin; the full data are to appear in his forthcoming comparative study of ethnocentrism in Britain, France and West Germany).

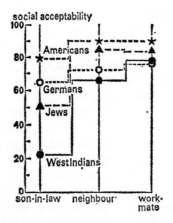

On the first step, two Britons out of ten were inclined to reject West Indians as *fellow-workers*, by comparison with two out of ten who would reject Germans, three out of 20 Jews, and one out of ten Americans. Such rejections seem to stem from ideas about coloured people as strangers, and the rejection of the second generation might be expected to fall to a level comparable to that displayed towards Jews.

On the second step, between three and four Britons out of every ten were inclined to reject West Indians as *neighbours* or friends, compared with under three for Germans and rather more than one out of ten for Jews and Americans. These rejections were presumably attributable primarily to fears of identification, and, since the second generation of immigrants would be almost as visibly different as their parents, the rate might remain near to that shown towards Germans.

The last step in social distance is that represented by *marriage*. Almost eight out of ten Britons reject the idea of being related to West Indians by marriage, compared with less than five for Jews and Germans, and two out of ten for Americans. In this matter fears about exposure and identification are combined. In no relationship can differences of habit and custom have more immediate implications than in marriage. Mutual involvement is at its peak for if either party loses patience with the other, the imposition of sanctions hurts the would-be punisher as well as the punished. By no normal relationship are the members of two family groups more closely identified than by marriage. It seems unlikely that these factors will operate with very much less force for the second generation of immigrants.

For many years now, some people have said they placed their faith in the younger generation, believing that when white and coloured grew up together there would be little hostility. Opposed to such optimism has been the observation that young people very often take over the attitudes of their elders when they succeed to their roles. Industrialisation increases social competition and certain forms of group tension, but its influence is not uniform. Just as there are discontinuities between situations, so there is a step-like pattern in the individual's life cycle. Adolescence is a step between the ascription-oriented world of the family (where your role as, say, "son" is "given") and the achievement-oriented world of adulthood. The youth culture facilitates transition from the one to the other.

In this phase the teenager is oriented to his peers and is under pressure to form sets or cliques based on the more easily recognised principles of distinction. Racial difference can therefore suddenly acquire much greater significance in adolescence, particularly since young people at this time start thinking about marriage and exploring its preliminaries. Adolescent dating is usually selective and often highly competitive; so mixed groups in which there is familiarity between boys and girls tend to be exclusive.

Whatever efforts are made in the schools, the new generation of coloured school-leavers will start their adult lives under a very great handicap. Their dilemma may be whether to accept an inferior status or to mould a new identity. For children of Indian and Pakistani parents the major conflict may well be the domestic one as parents try to draw their children into the culture of their homeland. But the parental generation of West Indian immigrants often displays a deep ambivalence towards English social patterns: on the one hand is a powerful desire for acceptance: on the other, a reaction against discrimination and dissatisfaction with the restrained outlook of the English. The West Indian community in Britain does not readily form associations to advance its interests. Some do not wish to see their group organise itself politically for fear of antagonising the English. West Indians therefore cannot support one another in adversity as much as Asian groups can. Were there a sharp increase in racial tension, morale in the West Indian community might become precarious. These same factors will probably increase the stress upon children who grow up in West Indian homes.

What is certain is that the interracial patterns of the 1970s will be the creation of the British rather than of the immigrants.

[9 November 1967]

THE DANCE INVASION

Orlando Patterson

The revolution in British pop music and dance is generally seen as having its roots in United States popular culture. People are not generally aware of the particular influence, in this revolution, of a music and dance form (called the *ska*) which is prevalent among the Jamaican lower classes. To examine this influence is a useful corrective to the usual studies of minority groups. These studies nearly always assume that cultural contact is a one-way process. They conceive of a dominant culture (the host community) and a minority culture (the immigrant or minority group); and, from then on, only the problems of the minority group in adjusting to the host society's culture are seen as worth analysing. But cultural contact and social assimilation are never one-way.

Ska is what the music and dance are called in Jamaica; in Britain, in its undiluted form, it is the "blue-beat." The *ska* is a unified form—ie, it consists of a unique, easily recognisable rhythm which is identified with a special kind of dance. This kind of form has a long tradition in both African and European culture. In Europe, as early as 1300, unified forms like the *ductia* and the *estampies*. More modern examples are the waltz, the tango, the foxtrot. The early period of rock-and-roll lacked unified music and dance forms, until Chubby Checker introduced the twist.

The *ska* was created around 1961 by the lumpenproletariat and urban lower classes of Jamaica. The music which accompanies the dance consists almost entirely of a monotonous, pulsating and compulsive rhythm. In Jamaica this is usually emphasised by the guttural grunts and groans of the dancers, who act like an exhausted person gasping for breath. The melody and lyrics are always secondary, serving mainly as a framework for the rhythm. The dance, accordingly, is of more interest.

It is usually performed in couples but there is little coordination or sexual specialisation in any of the movements. These

91

tend to be very flexible. The dancer stands with his feet slightly apart and his body bent from the waist, as in a bow. The body is then straightened and bowed to the rhythm of the tune, the neck plunging in and out like a turkey. There are several hand movements, the most characteristic being a muscular jerk convulsing the whole body. It is carried out with the arms held out in front of the dancer, slightly bent at the elbows. The movements of the legs tend to vary with each performer.

The *ska* began to make its impact on British popular culture less than three years after it had emerged from the shantytowns of western Kingston. At first it was heard and danced mainly in the discotheques and nightclubs of Soho and Brixton, most of which had formerly specialised in rhythm-and-blues, jazz, and other aspects of the predominantly Negro elements of American popular art. In 1964, however, Millie, a Jamaican teenager, produced a *ska* version of an old American pop song called *Lollipop*. It was an immediate success and, retitled as the blue-beat, the *ska* soon became popular among the young people in Britain.

After its heyday in 1964 the blue-beat seemed to go the way of so many other fads in modern popular arts. But though the more obvious elements of the rhythm have declined, the accompanying movements have become the basis of British popular dance, and the modified *ska* is now referred to by various other names such as the "shake" and the "jerk."

The diffusion of the *ska* among the British has brought about several changes. The first is the greater muscular play given to various parts of the body, and to the body as a whole, while dancing. This is a conception of dancing wholly alien to the west European, and particularly to the Anglo-Saxon, dance tradition. The traditional posture has been to keep the torso fairly straight, at times even rigid, with movements restricted to the legs and the shoulders. Second, spontaneity has become increasingly important in dancing: improvised muscular contortions, especially from the waist upwards, are carried out within a loosely defined pattern. Third, there is the disappearance of stereotyped conceptions of masculinity and feminity. In dances like the veleta, the military two-step and almost any other of the old-time forms, there was always a strong emphasis on the masculinity and aggressiveness of the male partner who was expected to lead the woman, and the coyness and delicacy of the female who followed. Now the female dances in exactly the same fashion as her male partner and in many instances appears to be even more aggressive.

Finally, the communal framework of British popular dance has shifted rapidly from "organic solidarity" to that of "mechanical solidarity." The traditional west European popular dance forms required some specialisation among the dancers. This type of organic solidarity—each dancer performing a specialised role, harmonising with the rest towards a given aesthetic goal—received its classic exposition in the ballet. New dance forms are

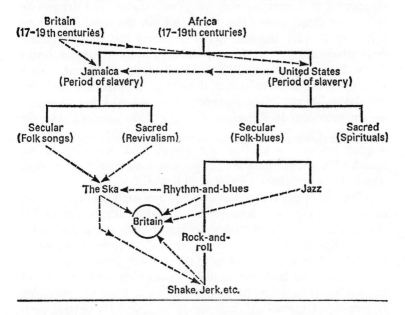

"mechanical" in that they consist of each individual performing all the possible moves or roles required by the dance. Any solidarity among the dancers derives from the sameness of every movement.

I believe these developments stem from New World Negro culture and culminate a cultural diffusion that spans three continents (Africa, North America and Europe) and several centuries. How did this diffusion come about and what factors led British youth to accept these elements of Negro culture?

The diagram shows the spread, in time and space, of elements which finally converged on Britain. Now unexpectedly, they go back to West Africa from which, during the 17th, 18th and 19th centuries, the vast majority of the New World slaves came.

Slavery in the New World disintegrated the culture of the African slaves. But those parts of the slaves' former culture which were least offensive—or least relevant—to the functioning of the plantocratic slave regime, had the best chance of survival. As in the United States, so in Jamaica (though with some differences), this included the music and dances of Africa.

They did not survive in their pure forms. As soon as the masters discovered that many of their rebellious slaves used drumming to communicate across the island, all but the most innocuous forms of it were banned. Second, placed out of its original cultural context, what formal dance structure existed broke down, becoming extremely individualistic and informal. Third, what persisted of the culture of the whites in Jamaica, influenced the slaves. By the 1760s European-type sexual affectation had grown prevalent in Jamaican dancing. One account says the male dancer has "all [the] action, fire and gesture . . . as serve to display before his partner the vigour and elasticity of his muscles," while the female ". . . puts on a modest, demure look which she counterfeits with great difficulty."

After Abolition, the ex-slave population went through a series of religious revivals. These meant a rapid decline in the secular dances which had developed under slavery. But music and dance —especially if it still showed marked African influence— survived within the ceremonies of the new religious cults. During slavery, all that had survived of African religion was a cult known in the island as Myalism. This came from the surviving fragments of former African secret societies. Its central ceremony was a death-and-resurrection dance. Towards the end of slavery this cult fused with the fundamentalist Baptist Christianity of Negro American slave missionaries, brought over to the island by their loyalist masters after the American Revolution. The fusion produced a new religion in Jamaica—what is now known as Poccomania.

The *ska* or blue-beat largely derives from the dancing and music inside the Poccomania cult. There was a slight revival of secular music and dance at the beginning of this century.

Revived slave dances and songs soon merged with musical influences from Latin America and other parts of the New World to produce the *mento*—a kind of Jamaican version of the Trinidadian calypso. By the mid-1940s, however, Jamaica was swamped by popular American music. But it is significant that the acceptance of this new American influence was highly selective. The most popular songs in the island were almost always rhythm-and-blues, especially among the predominantly negroid lower classes.

The lack of a genuinely Jamaican music and dance form was strongly felt by the working class and lumpenproletariat. Towards the end of the 1950s, they turned to the native Poccomania cult and borrowed its music and dance. When combined with the Negro American rhythm-and-blues, this became the *ska*.

I have already explained how the *ska* arrived in Britain. Rhythm-and-blues was always popular among a small group of the British public, almost from the moment it became widespread in the United States. Over the past four years or so, it has got much more popular. Much of the supposed originality of the Beatles and the Rolling Stones and the mass of their imitators is a direct borrowing from the pure rhythm-and-blues. Such cross-pollination is not uncommon. In its transmogrification into the shake, the jerk and other similar forms, the *ska* reveals its impact not only on Britain, but also on the United States where it was vigorously promoted by the Jamaican government and tourist board. These dance forms came to Britain via America.

So much for the *ska*'s background and process of diffusion; but the crucial question still unanswered is: why have these alien patterns of recreation established themselves in Britain?

Till recently, British society has been one of the most remarkable experiments in living. It had a culture that was unusual among western societies both for its homogeneity and stability, and for the complexity and sophistication of its internal mechanisms of change, adaptation and social control. As long as the underlying pattern of conflict within the society remained the same, these highly complex mechanisms remained efficient in their resolution of whatever new forms of conflict emerged. But when the underlying pattern of conflict in a society changes, as it has in Britain, two things follow: (a) new mechanisms of adaptation must be developed; and (b) the very complexity and

95

sophistication of the traditional techniques come in the way of resolving the new types of conflict.

One of the basic factors in the rock-and-roll revolution was the shift by the entertainment industry toward the youth sector of the population. Youth-orientation emphasises virility, action, sensationalism, speed and violence. The violence factor, more than any other, makes the youth-oriented, hedonistic ethic unacceptable to the traditional system in Britain. This system is conspicuous for its compromise, conciliation and the avoidance, at whatever cost, of any overt form of violence. When overt violence does occur, it is either considered as deviant and treated as such, or canalised into socially acceptable forms of behaviour.

Today a large part of the population thinks that a certain type of violence and aggression is both necessary and desirable. But the only response of British society has been to treat this behaviour as merely another form of the traditional pattern of deviance. So a self-fulfilling process occurs. The alienated youth population identifies its incipient hedonism with the traditional forms of deviance. It has no other way to express its violence, and almost all other aspects of its hedonistic ethic are frustrated by the still largely Protestant-oriented older group. The young people realise that whatever they do will be interpreted, in any event, as simply another form of deviance. Only this can explain the sheer anarchy and meaningless iconoclasm of the smashing up of seaside resorts, destroying public telephones, wrecking trains or desecrating cathedrals.

Similar patterns of youth violence are observable in the United States—for example, the Newport and Fort Lauderdale riots. But with its more flexible and heterogenous culture, and its fuller recognition (if not acceptance) of the nature of such forms of non-deviant violence, the United States has, to some extent, developed the necessary adaptive cultural techniques for dealing with it. There are the beat movement; certain aspects of the civil rights and other political movements; the emergence of new recreational forms and literary and cinema productions specially oriented to youth; and the significant reorientation of the attitudes and values of the older group to meet the demands of the younger sector.

With one exception, British culture has failed to provide the institutional techniques to meet the new situation. The exception is music and dance. This is one of the most significant means of expressing not only the violence, but all other aspects of the hedonistic ethic. As in all other spheres of traditional culture, the music and dance of Britain could not satisfy the demands of its new, alienated youth group. Popular Negro music and dance like the *ska* is essentially the recreational pattern of an alienated people, developed to express the rage, the anger, the violence and the vitalism of a sub-culture which, for various historical reasons, is basically hedonistic in orientation.

It was what the youth of Britain lacked.

[*15 September 1966*]

ATTITUDES TO ILLEGITIMACY

Raymond Illsley and Derek Gill

Sociologists and social anthropologists have noted many societies which view pre-marital sexual relations with tolerance, but none in which illegitimate birth gets as much approval as legitimate birth. With one or two exceptions, sanctions against illegitimate birth are severe.

The evidence overwhelmingly suggests that condemnation applies, not primarily to pre-marital sexual relations, but to the birth of a child without an identifiable and responsible father—a child who cannot easily be fitted into any lineage system or inheritance laws, who may lack material support and the presence of a full family to introduce him into the culture of the society. The condemnation of illegitimacy, on this interpretation, goes with an ordered arrangement of procreation which will ensure clear responsibility for the creation of new members, their maintenance, and their introduction into society.

The point was made very forthrightly 30 years ago by Crane Brinton in his book on laws passed after the French Revolution about illegitimacy: "Bastardy and marriage in this world are quite supplementary—you cannot have one without the other. In another world, you may indeed separate the two institutions and eliminate one of them, either by having marriage so perfect—in various senses—that no one will ever commit fornication or adultery, or by having fornication so perfect that no one will ever commit marriage. But these are definitely other worlds."

It is true that we could virtually abolish illegitimacy and the stigma attached to it by permitting easier divorce, giving effective sex education, making contraceptives freely available, permitting abortion on demand, and by introducing new legal and administrative support for the mother and her child. In the past, at any rate, society has preferred to retain these sanctions (which are supports for marriage) and to condemn the act of illegitimacy. Some sociologists maintain that illegitimate status and its stigma are necessary to reinforce acceptable sexual and marital

98

behaviour. Every unhappy unmarried mother is thus an advertisement for marriage.

If condemnation of illegitimacy is the defence of marriage, what does this imply for the state of marriage when illegitimacy ratios increase sharply? This question is relevant today because of what one American investigator called "the amazing rise of illegitimacy in Great Britain" (see diagram).

In 1945 the British illegitimacy ratio (illegitimate births per

ILLEGITIMACY RATIOS 1911–64

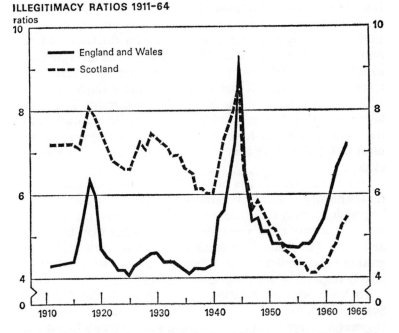

100 births) reached very briefly its highest point during this century. This did *not* mean there had been a wartime decline in sexual morality. The proportion of British girls conceiving outside marriage remained remarkably stable before, during and after the war. But pregnant girls who, before or after the war, might have married, were prevented from doing so by the death of their partner, or by his absence in the forces or by their own absence from home. A similar rise, probably for similar reasons had occurred during the first world war.

Apart from these two wartime peaks, the illegitimacy ratio in

99

England and Wales had, till recently, been fairly stable since the beginning of the century at what we would now consider the extremely low level of about 4 per 100 births. After the second world war, it looked for some years as though the ratio would fall back again to its accustomed level. From over 9 per cent in 1945, the ratio had almost halved by 1953–54.

Scottish experience was rather different. In the late 19th century, the ratio in England was already less than 5 per cent; but it was still as high as 12 to 13 per cent in Scotland. From the 1880s the English ratio remained stable; by contrast, the Scottish ratio fell slowly and spasmodically, but quite markedly, until in 1939 it was only 6 per cent, compared with England's 4.5 per cent. Just after the second world war, the Scottish rate continued to fall; and in 1952, for the first time since these rates were recorded, it crossed over and was lower than the English ratio.

Does this mean that the immoral 18th century Scots have become converted to the good life in the mid-20th century, while the virtuous English have become suddenly degenerate? We must seek the truth in a more prosaic and patient sifting of the evidence.

Unfortunately, this has not yet been thoroughly carried out for the history of the late 19th century and the early 20th century. The high Scottish ratios derived mainly from the rural areas— ratios in county areas were consistently higher than the towns and cities. The gradual depopulation of rural Scotland, by emigration or assimilation into urban areas and urban culture, is largely responsible for the decline in illegitimacy.

To learn why rural ratios were high in Scotland (and in Scandinavia), we rely on more dubious, if colourful, evidence. It is sometimes said that farmers wanted wives who could not only bear children, but also bear sons. The surest test of this ability was to try it out first and marry later. We have yet to see proof of this hypothesis. Alternatively, it is said (and for this there exists some evidence in Scandinavia), that pre-marital relations were permissible in these small, stable, tightly-knit communities, because it took place according to traditional procedures which permitted ready identification of the father. Furthermore, since both parties remained in the same community and were available for marriage at an appropriate time, marriage could be postponed until after the birth of a first or even a second child if a farm or farmhouse were not available. These are interesting hunches which need to be checked and compared, for example, with rural Ireland where, despite the oldest age at marriage in western Europe, the illegitimacy ratio was (and is) very low.

We have better evidence on the distribution and causes of illegitimacy in urban Scotland in 1949–52 which was the mid-point between the wartime peak and the postwar trough. Barbara Thompson, studying all illegitimate births to Aberdeen women, found that rather less than half of these births were first births to single women. The remainder consisted of:

1. A small group (5 per cent of illegitimate births) of married, widowed or divorced women having their first child. Most of these women were cohabiting steadily with their partner. Illegitimacy occurred because one or both partners could not marry—casualties of the divorce laws.

2. A larger group (12 per cent), again mostly married, widowed or divorced, who were also cohabiting steadily but with a man by whom they had previous children.

3. A group of similar size (12 per cent) who had had previous legitimate babies and were now having their first illegitimate baby. In Dr Thompson's judgment, the usual sequence was marriage breakdown, followed by a subsequent liaison, rather than breakdown stemming from the illegitimate pregnancy.

4. A large group (22 per cent), again mostly married, widowed or divorced women, who had illegitimate pregnancies by two or more men.

These findings contain a number of surprises, particularly the high proportion of illegitimate births among women who had been married, among cohabiting couples, and among women having their second or later baby. The results indicate that, just as important as the unmarried mother and her child, is the *married* mother and her illegitimate children.

One further finding deserves mention. In Dr Thompson's study, an illegitimate first birth is overwhelmingly a feature of the lower socio-economic classes. It rises from 2 per cent in the professional classes to 18 per cent among catering workers and cleaners. Illegitimacy, says Dr Thompson, "tends to be associated with unskilled, unattractive or menial occupation." Insecure conditions during upbringing, broken homes and general family disorganisation were frequent in the history of many mothers.

What has happened since that early postwar period? The ratio fell until 1954–55 in England and Wales, began to rise again, and by 1966 had risen to 7.7 per cent (see graph again). The increase was sharp and unexpected. Looking back with hindsight the trend was already obvious earlier because the ratio first started to rise in London and the south in 1953. The Scottish ratio fell until 1959 when it too began a sharp upward rise.

One can trace the spread between these two geographical extremes. After London, the increase appeared next in the conurbations and large cities further north, and then in the smaller cities, and finally in the rural areas. In each case the increase began in the south and appeared later in the midlands, the north and finally in rural Scotland, the area which had had the highest ratios earlier in the century.

This pattern of spread is at least consistent with the introduction of new social and sexual behaviour spreading from urban cultural centres through the media of communication to the remoter areas.

Other evidence leads in the same direction. The number of illegitimate births to *married* women, based on Aberdeen experience, has not changed much in these years. But since the *total* number of illegitimate births has increased, they form a diminishing proportion of the total. The new component is the increase in births to single teenagers. These births comprised 13 per cent of all illegitimate births in 1951 in England and Wales, compared with 27 per cent in 1964. The increase is not, however, entirely due to teenage pregnancy—the legitimacy/illegitimacy ratios are rising at all ages.

There has been a corresponding rise in pre-nuptial conception (where the partners marry before the child is born). Added to the increased illegitimacy ratios, this amounts to a big increase in pregnancies begun outside marriage. The preponderance of the lower social classes in conception before marriage has decreased. The steepest rise here is among the upper and more educated groups.

Thus the trends point towards: (a) urban areas, (b) younger unmarried girls, and (c) the upper social groups. Their origin apparently lies in the sophisticated urban culture. It is not merely a question of illegitimacy, but an increase also in extra-marital conception. We cannot conceive of any interpretation based on genetics/racial origin/original sin which would explain the trends we have witnessed. And these trends are widespread over western industrial society.

When, in the 20th century, people's attitudes to illegitimacy softened slightly, a psychiatric model of explanation became fashionable. By saying that the unmarried mother was mentally ill-balanced, society could give some personal sympathy and understanding without condoning a deviation from moral norms. The explanation undoubtedly held good for a minority whose disturbances led them to a sexual rebellion against society or family: it perhaps held good for even more whose treatment by society, once they became pregnant, produced unbearable strains. But major reversals of the kind we have been looking at cannot easily be explained psychiatrically. One cannot accept the image of an Oedipal problem spreading from London to the north and to the rural areas.

Many other historical periods, cultures and social groups have had high illegitimacy ratios. It is more profitable to examine these for parallels.

The most common causal factors put forward in our own society so far have been lack of education income or "security" —ie, a general sense of deprivation and uncertainty which leads a woman to accept transient affection and to lack any motive to plan. But these explanations, like the psychiatric one, do not fit current trends. Indeed they seem to be in direct opposition.

The most cogent explanations are those which postulate a breakdown of cultural norms. The most obvious example is drawn from African slaves transported from their separate cultures to an agglomerate slave society in the New World. Similar situations have arisen in developing societies, when people from peasant societies, with stable systems of arranged polygamous marriage, are drawn into an expanding and industrialising urban life. The cultural norms regulating their sexual and marital behaviour are no longer applicable or cannot be enforced. But a new set of norms, more appropriate to urban industrial society, has either not yet evolved or not reached the stage at which all groups of society are committed fully to them.

In Britain we have not undergone such dramatic migratory upheavals, but social changes over these last decades have been rapid and far-reaching. Have we reached the stage at which our major institutions are undergoing fundamental change, or at which sections of our population no longer feel committed to upholding or conforming to them?

The question really has three parts. Has there been an increase in extra-marital intercourse and a weakening of the sanctions against it? Secondly, has there been a weakening in the sanctions against extra-marital conception? And finally, once a woman or girl is pregnant, is the pressure to legitimacy by marriage weaker than formerly? Let us take these questions in turn.

First, then, extra-marital intercourse. Adolescents do reach sexual maturity earlier now. This may mean that the sexual drives among the young have also grown stronger.

But much more important is the earlier marriage age of the last decade. This greatly alters the social position of unmarried teenagers. Many of their friends are married and have had sexual intercourse: some of them also have children and family responsibilities.

Can you be an "adolescent" when your contemporaries are adults with sexual experience and such responsibilities? This confusion of adolescent and adult roles in our teenage population reaches into many other spheres. Their earnings are high, compared with the past and with their responsibilities. They are important targets of a competitive retail market. They will attain the vote shortly.

This occurs within the context of a newly emerged teenage culture. This simultaneously rejects both adolescent status and adult authority/establishment values. To be a "teenager" gives one a label which legitimates one in behaving in ways disapproved of by adults. This behaviour is transitional in two senses: (a) transition from adolescence to adulthood, and (b) transition from the norms of one generation to those of another.

We have concentrated on teenage change because the biggest increase in illegitimacy relates to the under-twenties. But more general factors may also have led to more pre-marital and extra-marital intercourse. There is the increasingly overt value placed upon sexuality in postwar society, not merely in the news media, but in the marriage manuals, medical writings and marriage

104

guidance councils. Sex is good, sex is fun, it is equally enjoyable by men and women. Its mutual enjoyment is an essential feature of modern marriage, which emphasises partnership and mutual satisfaction rather than unilateral benefits. When you pretend that the grapes are sour (and they were indeed sour for many women), an injunction against their consumption outside marriage may be effective. But when you extol their taste, the injunction is more difficult to enforce.

What of the second stage in this question? Even if there is more extra-marital *intercourse*, need there be more extra-marital *conception*? Several forms of contraception are freely available and their existence better known now. Ultimately, this may be a deciding factor. The sharpest rise in illegitimacy occurred before the introduction of the safest form of contraception—the pill. Mere availability, however, is not enough because pills need consistent use. The public arguments which have taken place about providing the pill for unmarried girls, show how undecided our society is. In general, society wishes to prevent unintended conception by the most efficient means, but it fears the emergence of a generation which does not cherish chastity.

This is the climate, the crisis of values, to which the younger half of our population is exposed. For most mature adults—who make laws, policies and pronouncements—it is a theoretical ethical question. For the younger, and particularly the unmarried part of our population, it is a practical, everyday question. Until society settles for itself the moral behaviour which it regards as acceptable, there is no clear guidance for the individual.

Finally, when unintended pregnancy occurs, what are the current pressures which decide whether it shall end in marriage, illegitimacy or abortion? Again, present-day British society does not speak with the unanimity of earlier decades. Abortion is now permissible under a political compromise formula which can hardly be regarded as stable. It leaves the decision to the medical profession because they are technically fitted to carry out the operation. Doctors' values, however, are as ambivalent as society's at large.

A couple's decision to marry or not, if marriage is technically possible, must be influenced by the importance attached to

105

marital status *as such*, compared with expectations about the stage of marriage and the stigma attached to illegitimacy. The value that modern marriage puts on personal relationships, mutual satisfaction and equality, acts as a deterrent to automatic marriage. And this is especially so among the upper social groups. They emphasise this type of marriage and try to subordinate specific decisions to a long-term rational goal.

This is not perhaps the same "breakdown of cultural norms" that has occurred in more disrupted societies with high illegitimacy ratios. But the ambiguities reduce people's commitment to conventional institutions and weaken the sanctions against illegitimacy. We are in transition between an older sexual/marital pattern and a new code. The new code will be based perhaps on pre-marital sexual experimentation, safeguarded by more perfect contraception and the backstop of abortion. But during the transition, many individuals are caught in the penalties and stigma that survive from a more clearcut moral order. In this conflict a strong teenage culture provides the young with temporary protection.

[*14 November 1968*]

THE FOUR-GENERATION FAMILY

Peter Townsend

My purpose here is to call attention to a little-known fact about old people in industrial societies, and to dwell upon its implications.

In 1962 a cross-national study of persons aged 65 and over was carried out in Denmark, Britain and the United States. Probability samples of around 2,500 persons in each country were interviewed during the same period of the year. Questionnaires and methods of sampling, interviewing and analysis had been standardised. One result surprised the investigators. A substantial proportion of the elderly populations were found to have great-grand-children—as many as 40 per cent in the United States, 23 per cent in Denmark and 22 per cent in Britain.

The existence on a substantial scale of families of four generations is a new phenomenon in the history of human societies. The emergence of a different structure brings new patterns of relationships but also different experiences of ageing. How has it happened?

This development is not attributable just to improvements in longevity. Average ages at first marriage have diminished and for women in the United States, for example, have been relatively low throughout this century. The age of parenthood has also been diminishing. In the United States the median age of women at the birth of their first children was 23 for those born between 1880 and 1890 but is down to between 20 and 21 for the latest generations to marry. Because of the decreasing number of large families the median age at the birth of the last child has fallen more sharply. Earlier marriage, earlier childbirth and fewer large families inevitably contribute towards a narrowing of the average span in years between successive generations. The larger number of great-grandparents in the United States than in the European countries is attributable in the early decades of this century to the higher rates of marriage, the younger age at marriage and the birth to a larger proportion of women in the early years of marriage of several children.

It would of course be profitable to study the family life cycle in more detail. Among the British sample, for example, it seems that the women had become grandmothers on average at 54 years of age and great-grandmothers at about 72. The men had become grandfathers at 57 and great-grandfathers at 75. One immediate thought of relevance to our understanding of human personality is the scope that exists for structural variation in family building habits. Some women become grandmothers in their late thirties, others not until their seventies.

These structural variations have been given little attention by sociologists and psychologists. If there are shifts of emphasis in family-building practices then there are likely to be big changes in the patterns of family relations and in the types of relationship and of problems experienced by the elderly. With increasing age old people tend to find themselves nearer one of two extremes—experiencing the seclusion of the spinster or widow who lacks children and other near relatives, or pushed towards the pinnacle of the pyramidal family structure of four generations which may include several children and their spouses and 20 or 30 grandchildren and great-grandchildren.

Previous theories about the changes that have taken place in family relations and in the care of the aged during the process of industrialisation need to be qualified heavily. When we compare what the family does now with what it did a hundred or two hundred years ago we are not comparing like with like. Instead of 1 or 2 per cent of the population being aged 65 and over, there are 10 or 15 per cent. There is the same contrast between developing and advanced industrial societies. In the "older" type of society old age may have a kind of pedestal prestige. Like the population age-pyramids of pre-industrial societies that the demographers produce for us, the extended family may have only one surviving grandparent at the apex of a structure consisting of a large number of children and other relatives. Nowadays there may be two, three or all four grandparents alive and often a great-grandparent too. The structure of the kinship network has changed and this has had important effects on the ways in which this network is broken into geographically proximate groupings of households and types of households.

108

The structure of the extended family—understood as a group drawn from the network of kin whose members meet every day or nearly every day and exchange a variety of services—has changed because of the pressures induced by changing mortality, birth and marriage rates. The relations between ascendant and descendant kin and affinal kin have been strengthened as compared with those with collateral kin: parents and children and in-laws count more, cousins, aunts and uncles less. There is greater stability at the centre. More people marry. More marry young. More survive in married couples until an advanced age. Consequently the number of middle-aged and elderly spinsters acting as universal aunts has diminished; there are fewer "denuded" immediate families (ie, families of parents and unmarried sibling groups in which at least one member is missing) and fewer extended families of certain types—such as widowed women linking in households with their brothers or sisters for the purposes of rearing children and overcoming hardship. The broken marriage and the broken "home" are no longer dominant constituents of the extended family in a group of proximate households. A model type of extended family is beginning to replace a wide variety of types of families and households, ranging from lone individuals at one extreme to "kinship" tribes at the other. This family does not necessarily consist of *all* children and grandchildren of an old person, say, but only some of them.

What are the implications for old people in their relations with their families? They are dividing into two broad categories —those belonging to the third and those belonging to the fourth generation. Those belonging to the third generation more often have a surviving husband or wife than did persons of their age at the turn of the century. Fewer have single children remaining at home and grandchildren who are in their infancy. Since they represent the "younger" section of the elderly, fewer of their children will have to look after them in infirmity, or illness, and they will have more energy to spare for their grandchildren. In various ways it is likely that the rapid relative increase in importance of the third generation, with its younger age-span, will result in much greater emphasis being placed in the future than formerly on reciprocal relations between the second and third generations. This will alter, and complicate, the whole

109

pattern of kinship activity. Moreover, a fourth generation of relatively frail people is also being established—for the first time.

The nature of the problems of old age is therefore changing. A common instance in the past has been the middle-aged woman faced with the problem of caring for an infirm mother as well as her young children. A common instance of the future will be the women of 60 faced with the problem of caring for an infirm mother in her eighties. Her children will be adult but it is her grandchildren who will compete with the mother for her attentions. The four generations of surviving relatives may tend to separate into two semi-independent groupings—each of two generations. Similarly, there may be a shift of emphasis from the problem of which of the children looks after a widowed parent to the problem of how a middle-aged man and wife can reconcile dependent relationships with *both* sets of parents.

Changes in population structure have far wider and deeper effects than I have been able to indicate here. Insufficient attention has been paid to them in discussing relationships between parents and their children, between husbands and wives, between generations and generally among households and families. The data about the emergence of the four-generation family suggest that the structure of the kinship network has been changing more rapidly than has been supposed. It is therefore likely that changes in family organisation and relationships may have been affected less by changes in industrial and economic organisation and more by changes in population structure. This may constitute an argument for reviewing and revising not only theories of change in the process of ageing but also theories of urbanisation and the social effects of industrialisation.

[*7 July 1966*]

THE DECLINE AND FALL OF THE INTELLECTUAL

J. P. Nettl

The framework within which intellectuals operate is necessarily universal, while that of bureaucrats is organisational. They live in a different cosmos, as it were. There is for intellectuals an almost Lutheran conception of immediacy between the individual and the universe, without any intervening obstructions. The bureaucrat gives primacy to the intermediate level of the organisation—which mediates between the individual and the universe (and downgrades the primacy of both).

I need hardly stress how the notion of bureaucracy, and particularly of bureaucratic power, is anchored in the idea of modern society. However modernity is defined, it has in it strong if not dominant notions of industrialisation, which in turn has increasingly come to mean scientifically directed technology. This is not the place to discuss the justification of the scientific label. The point is that most people do regard modern society as more scientific and more technological than anything in the past. If they condemn it, they condemn the organisation of its science and technology too.

The edges of the original over-neat marxist distinction between capitalist science and technology as totally irrational and inhuman, and the socialist version as totally rational and humane, have become very blurred in the last 20 years. Theories of convergence increasingly place the fundamental frontier not between capitalist and socialist but between highly industrial and underdeveloped societies. Bureaucracy in this context is what Max Weber called it long ago: "the application of rationality to administration and government."

It may not be a perfect transposition from nature to society, from the laboratory to the human organisation, but it is intended to be the best we can do in this direction at the moment, given that human beings are not chemical particles or thermodynamic units. Bureaucratic power is the application of the most rational and scientific social power we have, modelled on the power

111

generated for the control of complex physical structures or technological systems. Bureaucratic power is an essential component of modernity.

The intellectual is always something of a voluntarist. He may describe the future he wants or sees in the most objective terms. In lurid contrast to a sickly, despised present, he may show it to be inevitable or merely desirable: but in either case he knows it has to be struggled for. That is why intellectuals are so frequently identified with revolution. This identification with revolution (or counter-revolution) is not based so much on the ideological or utopian element in intellectual thought as on its needing an action component to achieve it.

As modernity advances, the intellectual retreats. For one thing universality is no longer regarded as a validation of intellectual status but as an arrogant and unjustifiable claim, at best the stigma of the dilettante. Respect and competence come not from universal Aristotelean wisdom but rather from detailed knowledge and technical qualifications. The right to speak with authority is no longer inherent but has become an external attribute which is attached to a person like abbreviated titles of degrees after a name. The last man who was said to know everything, Francis Bacon, died nearly 350 years ago.

Since one cannot know everything, intellectuals who do wish to speak with authority on the wide range of social phenomena have increasingly to go in for a severe form of reductionism. Hence we find that today's intellectuals increasingly concentrate on what they hold to be the one dominant aspect of life, whether it be the psychoanalytic unconscious, the evils of industrial capitalism, the ugliness of our cities (Lewis Mumford) or the imbalance between the two generic parts of our brain (Koestler). I don't think that this plethora of reductions to single basic causes has ever been as great as it is today. The bureaucratic response is rather to concentrate on diversity of interests and knowledge, and to accept it as normal; no total explanations are either possible or desirable.

Reductionism is only one rather feeble response to modern complexity. Politics—the arena *par excellence* of dashing ideas —is itself becoming a specialised business with its own professional qualifications. Persuasion has little part in it, except as a means of teasing or screwing resources out of the invisible men in government. And this type of persuasion, the political scientists keep telling us, is no amateur business of "mere" convictions nowadays but a highly skilled technical affair of lobbying and fixing. Problems of right and wrong in politics are much less relevant—at least in the actual political process. On the subject of protest against the Vietnam war and related matters the late Johnson administration repeatedly went on record to the effect that everyone has the right to protest and dissent but that this must not disrupt or interfere with politics or administration.

Finally there is the area of culture. Intellectuals have always validated their efforts at persuasion on the fundamental grounds that their ideas and actions would improve the quality of human life. Such a claim implies a unity of cultural perceptions among those they address. This area of postulated relevance has, of course, varied enormously. Greek intellectuals spoke only to citizens, not foreigners, or slaves, and usually not to artisans. Marxists traditionally spoke to workers and other intellectuals, though Chinese and Cuban marxists have broadened their area of persuasion substantially. Christ spoke to all, as did at least some of his disciples.

But today, as high culture and mass culture become differentiated, and as specific efforts are made to rescue minority cultures from the lethal encroachments of the mass media (by providing them with mass media of their own), the cultural arena of intellectual concerns has shrunk to a narrow island of inbred reverberation lapped by a sea of indifference and commercialisation.

Edward Shils has described the position as one of "high professional proficiency in many fields, each talking to itself, a highbrow, more or less literary-political culture tinctured by marxism, isolated from the rest of the culture and fearful of contamination by it, and also speaking only to itself—and under all this a layer of unserious philistinism." Instead of legitimating themselves for society as a whole, intellectuals merely legitimate each other. They have become each others' reciprocal articulators and audience, no more.

The intellectual is forced into precisely the position which Raymond Aron has characterised with such scorn: "Radical criticism has abandoned the attempt to reshape the world or to change it, it is simply content to condemn." Condemn, that is, not the order of society but its rationality—condemn science.

Now intellectuals have had to flee from hostile environments before. Ironically, there was a time when they "fled" from the chaos of Europe to the good order of China in the 18th century, from the jungle of competitive capitalism to the ordered society of the Soviet Union in the 20th. As modernity advances they now come to recognise increasingly that, from their point of view, the United States and the Soviet Union are not much different, and if they reject one they must reject the other.

Where can the intellectual go? One possible refuge is provided by the developing areas, many of them seething with revolutionary movements. The most powerful among them, China, is most emphatically determined to reject the "modernity" of Europe and America. But in China's case, the errant European intellectuals were given short shrift, for the Chinese reckon to solve their problem by specifically Chinese means without benefit of emigrés in flight from the west.

Both the Algerian and the Cuban revolutions have had their share of European emigrés. We need only think of Sartre glorifying the "new men" in Algiers and Havana. But if the most recent tendencies are anything to go by, the intellectual vision of revolution in underdeveloped areas is much more concerned with processes than with utopias, with means rather than ends—for the ends have so often proved disappointing.

Régis Debray's *Revolution in the Revolution* is an intellectuals' handbook on how to make a revolution, not a marxist or any other analysis of why revolution is necessary and what it should achieve. This preoccupation with process, with technique and strategy, is thus the intellectual's concession to bureaucratic modernity even though it may be an inverted mirror image of it. Once the argument shifts on to the ground of power, intellectuals inevitably accept the organisational framework dictated by their opponents and to that extent become denatured as intellectuals.

Another refuge for intellectual concern has been the field often described as "international relations." Here, modernity itself lags sadly. Instead of an abstract international society, we are still in a conflict-ridden world made up primarily of individual communities and states. Apart from a tentative beginning in

114

regional groupings here and there, it is still very much Hobbes's state of nature. Since there is no international organisation—at least no effective one—this is still a fruitful Eden for intellectuals. There has accordingly been a glowing concentration of effort in this field, such as the work of Toynbee, Spengler and Sorokin, to mention only three. The universal concerns of "modernity-rejecting" intellectuals like Marcuse have a strong international overtone.

All seek to overcome the inhibiting organisational domination of individual societies in the modern world and regard their problems on a global scale. And yet science is catching up rapidly, it is already breathing down the necks of the intellectuals in international relations. Kenneth Boulding states that in stable systems science is not necessary for human behaviour; precisely in *unstable* systems it is. This simply means that we can take our science for granted in modern societies and regard it as common sense. In the international field, where nothing can be taken for granted and conflicts are at best always just around the next corner, science is essential. Looming behind the Kahns and Kissingers and their "scientific" analyses of conflict is a rationality that carries bureaucratic power in its hip pocket. Hence it may not be too long before bureaucratic rationality takes over the international field as well.

Already in the mid-1920s a deviant marxist called Bruno Rizzi wrote a book called *La Bureaucratisation du Monde* in which he predicted precisely this. When it does happen, we may obtain the benefits of the same rational-scientific order which exist in advanced industrial societies (if they are benefits).

So much for the intellectual's escape routes. He may of course stay at home and become a social scientist. Modern societies make an important distinction between gatherers and processors of knowledge. The latter have higher status than the former. The United States, as the preeminently modern society—and its challenger, the Soviet Union—both invest more heavily in the collection of information than in its processing. France—perhaps lagging in the modernity competition by having a disproportionate number of intellectuals—is more concerned with information processing. At the moment, in America as well as the Soviet Union, the processing of information—which necessarily implies a higher degree of selection and judgment—is in the hands of politicians and administrators. But social scientists with growing self-confidence are increasingly claiming a share in it.

If it is true, as a commentator from the World Resources Inventory at Southern Illinois has stated, "that our capacity to determine and evaluate future goals lags far behind our ability to fulfil goals we set ourselves," this would seem to suggest a fruitful field for intellectual activity.

But does it? It seems to me that the social scientist, far from being a new form of intellectual, may really be his mortal enemy as well as his replacement in society. Although the areas of concern may be the same, the social scientist approaches them with very different premises and intentions.

He is primarily concerned with the collection of facts and their interpretation, as a potential scientist. He shudders at the claim to possess values of his own; at the very least he goes through the ritual motions of laying them aside when engaged in his work. His claim to participate in the shaping and enunciation of social goals is based on his scientific capability, his "possession" of certain skills and in particular his access to facts, not on any preeminent concern with the quality of life. At best his alternatives, when he offers any, are derivations from options arising out of different means to unquestioned ends, ends that are themselves "givens," not transformations of reality, not visions of fundamentals.

When one of the culture-heroes of the social science profession like Raymond Aaron claims that problems of race relations, inequality, the retention of a bit of natural greed amid the forests of urban concrete, are not the business of the ideologist but are best left to the engineer, social or physical, then it is clear that the scope of the problem is being defined in a radically unintellectual or anti-intellectual manner.

The social scientist is not asked to accept, reject or even analyse modernity in its fundamental aspects but to explain it in some particular, not necessarily related, sectors. The problem for anyone who would combine the role of intellectual and social scientist, who wishes to bring intellectual activity up to date in a social science context, is therefore not as simple as Edward Shils makes out: "The critical and solicitous care for the whole in the proximate future must be the charge which American intellectuals take on themselves, if American society is not to become

116

the victim of the parochial preoccupations of specialised techno-logical experts. If academic social scientists and freelance publi-cists or amateur social scientists are not critics . . . no one else will be."

An admirable prescription. Yet the future with which they must concern themselves is "a relatively short-run future . . . less prophetic than it was in the great age of revolution . . . less global . . . more piecemeal and contextual—more concerned with par-ticular problems . . . though with the ramifications and pre-conditions over a wide area, with the alternative solutions to *particular problems.*" Whether we like it or not, the basis of social science criticism differs radically from that inherent in the intellectual role. We might say that social scientists escalate their criticism only when necessary, and remain within the par-ticularity of limited problems whenever possible, while intellec-tuals generalise by definition and deduce to small problems only in terms of particular application. The "social science solution" for intellectuals may mean no more than to prettify preferences, clothe economic desires or demands in a moral garb and give to interests the attractive patina of values.

Finally the intellectual may presumably abandon analysis of, and argument against, a hostile environment altogether, and turn instead to action—the dissolution of *logos* in *praxis* which Marx adumbrated, and which a few marxist intellectuals like George Lukacs tried to formulate in detail—and which Lenin, Mao and Castro (to name only some relatively recent and suc-cessful ones) put into practice.

There is no shortage of activist causes throughout the world at the moment, but interestingly most of those at home do not lend themselves readily to intellectual participation. The student protest movement in the United States and Europe and the activism of American Negroes share a distrust of intellectual articulation, matched only by a rueful failure on the part of intel-lectuals on the other side of the fence to "understand" what is happening. Youth has withdrawn from society before; think only of Jahn's German gymnasticists at the beginning of the 19th century, of the rucksack-humped hikers of the early 20th, escaping from society into nature—at the time they all gave their elders as incomprehensible and healthy a fright as hippies do today.

But I do not believe that the gap in advanced societies between the activism of the young and the underprivileged on the one hand, and the attempts of intellectuals to understand and analyse it sympathetically on the other, has ever been as great as it is now. The voice of Byron and Shelley, of the romantics, has no equivalent today.

Analysis is a poor substitute for lyricising at the best of times. There are isolated and individual attempts by intellectuals to put themselves at the head of movements of fundamental dissent and rejection. The work of Georges Bataille and Jean Genet in France, which make crime into a counter-system of virtue against the profanity of the material world; the existential approach to psychiatry by R. D. Laing in England, which inverts the notions of sanity and madness—these are indications of determined attempts to dig a solid intellectual foundation for anti-system rejection. But in general the plaint of the Polish novelist Witold Gombrovich holds only too true: "Born as we are out of chaos, why can we never establish contact with it? No sooner do we look at it, than order, pattern, shape is born under our eyes." Chaos versus order, absurdity versus reason, intellectualism versus science—the very manner of posing such alternatives predetermines our choice.

The future looks gloomy for what we have come to regard as intellectuals. Will criticism in future be increasingly particularistic and limited to little bits? Will cataclysms go unrecognised and unexplained, because science can only explain mishaps? Or will science itself produce a new type of intellectual whose radical criticisms, ideologies and utopias will come from within science and not outside or against it? Will social scientists perhaps provide a means of returning to more fundamental criticism by refusing the supportive task that modern society and their own self-definition have assigned to them?

Or will the intellectual continue for a time as an attenuated relic of an individual personality type, kept and polished in quaint survival in the hothouses of highly specialised cultural media, of little or no relevance to society as a whole? At this time we can only ask such questions, not answer them.

[*17 April 1969*]

118

... or stay the same;

YOUNG MARRIAGE

Paul Barker

You will see them in your High Street this Saturday. She carries the shopping bag: he manoeuvres the Silver Cross. While the wife goes into the dry cleaners, her husband joggles the pram handle up and down. The baby is a few weeks old. Its parents also are young, perhaps only 19. They seem to be enjoying themselves. The sight is the sign of a new social phenomenon, but not quite the one that most observers seize on. Young marriage in 1964 is mainly the story of the teenage (or thereabouts) husband.

Forget about teenage brides. There are more of them than there used to be—two and a half times as many as in 1938. But they aren't a novelty. Already before the war more than one bride in ten was a teenager. Young husbands, by contrast, are a genuine innovation. The change in ratio is fantastic. Five prewar brides married under 21 for every underage groom. In the 1950s, the ratio was down at four to one; now it is three to one, if not lower. The corollary is that there are more very young *couples*. At least 10 per cent of marriages are between minors. Even if a girl before the war married young, her husband married old.

All the advanced industrial countries are experiencing this shift towards earlier marriage. Economics is an important cause. Jobs for almost everybody and good wages for the young mean that a big barrier is gone; and irregular work with poor pay deterred men more than women: they had to support the family. Full employment has helped the blue collar workers rather than the traditional white collar men. (It has only made insurance clerks dissatisfied as having security as their job's apparent chief reward.) And young weddings are more characteristically proletarian than bourgeois. So the best place to check on how they work out is a district like South London around Camberwell: where ordinary people live but the pattern of life isn't complicated by the Jewishness of Whitechapel or the colouredness of Brixton.

What is the combined impact of a young husband and easier money? How does a young couple's life differ from their un-

121

married friends'? Do they still see the old gang, or does marriage immerse them? What effects does a child have? And what is the young marrieds' relation to Mum? (Why also have mother-in-law jokes died out?) I had long talks with young couples in and around Camberwell to find out.

None was older than 23, none married longer than 18 months. The husbands' jobs spread from skilled work like printing to warehousemen or packer. All the couples except one wife had left school at 15. That wife, who had taken GCE, worked in a bank. She would stop work when she got pregnant. The other wives observed this same divide: they were either mothers/pregnant or else they went out to a job. The job was partly for the money, partly for the interests of it. Some husbands felt it wasn't right for a wife to work but their view didn't win: their age makes them more a companion who advises than a father substitute who commands. Only one pregnant wife, however, was reluctant to cross the divide when the time came. She wanted to be back at work in two or three years; other girls thought they would wait at least till the children had left shool.

For social workers, young marrieds are a curious gap in their knowledge. The couples see as little of them as they often see of their friends. They vanish from the youth clubs and even from the discotheques. The Peckham Disque has only had one married couple back in a year. The people themselves will have to speak. Like Peter Docherty.

Peter is 18, his wife is 21. Their chubby daughter is 9 months' old. Peter earns about £16 a week as a plumber's mate. Before she was pregnant, Maureen made tea in a works canteen. Housing plays the biggest part in their plans.

"Jobs are all right now, but not housing. Round here it's diabolical: a right take on. When we got married we lived in furnished rooms. The bloke there, he's Greek. We paid £4 10s just for two rooms. He was willing to sell for £350, but where could we get that? I worked it out he must be making a fortune: they paid £5 10s downstairs, another on the same landing as us paid £2 10s, and upstairs was £4 10s again. He never gave no receipt or rent book. I reckon he was fiddling the tax people."

They live now with Maureen's parents, having the front room, furnished, for their own. The baby sleeps in the grandparents' room "because it's warmer." The Dochertys still pay £4 10s but it includes board. Peter is trying to get a two room unfurnished flat in a tenement block. A relative set him onto it. The block is probably due to come down, and he hopes that will mean a council flat. The printers were the only husbands I met who were thinking of a house of their own. Everyone else's ideal was a council tenancy: they moved into condemned property or became lodgers in Mum's council house for the chance of being re-housed.

"We wondered once about going to a New Town," Peter Docherty said. "But we found there was more to it than there seemed. The husband has to be passed by a board, then find lodgings and get a job, before you get a house. I don't think that a reasonable proposition. It put me off. And my wife wasn't keen. I wasn't that keen myself: they want skilled men there, and what use is a £5 10s apprenticeship to me?"

Like Jack Clark, a printer, whose wife offered coffee instead of tea, these husbands' determination was "to earn as much money as I can." Work ambition was fairly limited. A bus conductor wanted to become a driver. A 19 year old soccer professional simply intended to stay in the game as long as they'd let him. Peter Docherty would stay in plumbing, though he hoped for his own business eventually. Even the warehouseman was content with his job: he worked long hours and could sometimes get £30 a week, not all of it passing through the taxman. Most incomes, most weeks, were between £11 and £16.

The money was for the home or for saving. Only couples without children (actual or imminent) spent much outside.

"We don't want a child for about two years," Brenda Collier said. She is 22 and gets £8 to £9 a week at the gummed-paper works where her 23 year old husband, John, earns £11 as a packer. They were engaged at 17, "but we felt we were too young to marry; besides, we wanted a nice wedding and didn't want to marry into debt." After two years of saving they had their five bridesmaid, 80 guest church wedding last spring. (They followed the new etiquette: if you want a big wedding, you help pay for it —usually everything except the caterer.)

We sat drinking tea among the bright flowery wallpaper, the gilt framed mirror, the splay legged furniture. The television, which they had bought outright, was on. In the corner stood a large radiogram. It had been handed on by Brenda's mother, who lived round the corner in a prefab, when she bought a new one. Mum was drinking tea with us. Couples are anxious to start up away from home and be independent: living with in-laws is only a last resort. But they still see a lot of their families. To go there for a cup of tea and a chat is the most frequent outing. Brenda Collier is at her mother's every day.

They had had the flat for a year before they moved in. They took off the encrusted layers of wallpaper, filled the cracks in the plaster, got a carpenter friend to build cupboards over the sink on the landing. They got the whole place furnished in advance. Almost everything was paid for cash down. Only £1 a week goes out in hire purchase, for the bedroom suite and gas cooker.

The Colliers were exceptionally prudent. A local clergyman was probably thinking of them when he said: "The amount that young couples start marriage with amazes me." But others were just as serious minded about home; as averse to hire purchase (£2 10s week was the highest debt); and as determined to have as well equipped a place as they could afford—whether they could find decent premises or not. Living with in-laws generally followed a wedding hastened by pregnancy (sometimes a wedding planned anyway; sometimes, as with the Dochertys, "we couldn't really say if we would have got married without the baby"). But it was a dismal business to find an alternative; and the alternatives themselves could be pretty dismal.

The Langhams live in the tenements that the Dochertys are hoping to move into. It was a block like Islington's Beaconsfield Buildings (where Philip, the husband, was born). A boarded off cellar by the door sent out a repellent stink of drains and tom cats. "We had the sanitary in to have a look at it," Margie Langham said. "But they just put their head in the house and said: 'You've got a lovely home here. There's lots worse off than you.' And went away. It used to be a debtor's prison here in the old days, I've heard. Shakespeare had something to do with it."

In a way the Langhams class as reckless. But not given the economy of the Britain they have always worked in. They spent in the context of money coming in. The house was littered with knickknacks that Philip had bought for it (some of them got cheap at work). Margie had a 59 guinea washer, alone among

124

the wives I met. "But it's a dreadful machine. I've seen a nice one at 109 guineas. We shall have to get a new suite, too." There was nothing wrong with the red moquette, but it was only a two piece. Margie felt it wasn't a real suite without a settee.

The Langham marriage came nearest to a probation officer's opinion that "marriage here is traditionally a battleground." When Margie met me at the door in her curlers, she looked ten years older than her actual 20. I could hardly talk through the semi-bickering backchat of husband and wife. "Don't want them," Philip said when he came home to the apple pies Margie had baked. "I knew you'd say that," she replied, accepting that men were difficult. Margie spent most of the day out, seeing relatives or old girl friends, but Philip didn't raise a finger to do ordinary chores and wasn't expected to. Nonetheless, home and an old car were his two real interests. He only went to the caff to see his mates if Margie and he had a row.

Most husbands moved cheerfully into helping with the house. Their age has something to do with it. Before marriage their pattern of life is like their wives'; often out, plenty of clothes, lots of entertainment. Then the sudden plunge into either marriage (with a baby) or into saving. After the marriage it is natural that they should want to, or feel they ought to, continue to share the pattern. They enter marriage trailing all kinds of traditional attitudes derived from their parents' homes. ("Conscious rejection doesn't prevent the influence coming through," a psychologist remarked to me.) Some husbands draw the line at washing up. Some must have one night a week out with the boys. One said, "I'm in favour of hitting women; especially if the wife degrades herself" (not that he did). But the Clarks' habit of spending every other Saturday "looking in the shops and dreaming what we shall have when we get a house" points the way forward. Mother-in-law is no longer a joke because son-in-law shares her interest in homemaking.

The first child has a more shattering effect on the premarriage pattern than the wedding itself has. The Colliers live rather how they did before they married: ladies' darts on Tuesdays; men's darts on Thursdays; a drink, a dance or a party on Saturday night. John also goes off to watch Spurs on Saturday. That is his only solo excursion. (Sport, or a trip to the betting shop, is the one all male pastime that survives engagement and

125

marriage.) On the seventh day the Colliers stay in. With a child the routine becomes one night *out* a week, when a grandparent or an unmarried friend of the wife's can babysit. "That's the way the cookie crumbles," one 22 year old husband said, after a week of marriage. But his wife was six months gone and had another child (not his) already. Peter Docherty's dedication to fatherhood was more typical.

He dandled young Carol on his knees and told me all about her teething troubles. He helps to bath her and likes to take her for walks on a Sunday: "it's only a shilling to Regent's Park." He explains: "When you're married and got a little baby, it's something to work for. You've got your responsibilities. Before, I never knew what home was. It was always the all night caffs for me. I'm not all that interested now. The boys are getting married anyway and that." Like Philip Langham he used to be a Rocker. Philip now justifies his car as a way to take the expected baby out. Peter hasn't any transport at the moment: he wants a second hand motor bike; but only, he says, for going to work.

Marriage counsellors emphasised to me that it wasn't the age in years that counted if a marriage was to work. It was emotional maturity. Young couples could have that as well as older people. The difficulty with some young marriages is that the marriage can be merely a sortie in the war against parents. Which leads to trouble.

In theory, Peter Docherty's marriage might look like that. When the Dochertys are in (ie, most of the time), they watch television or play the records that they still buy. Sometimes they have friends in. Peter's aunts come round regularly. All this resembles the other couples. But Peter's mother never comes.

"There's lots of hatred in my family. I never got on with my mother. I couldn't miss her. She ran off with my uncle after my father died. I always got on golden with my dad. When he died, I tell you, doctors do cry. It isn't just something you see on the television." Peter was never out of trouble with the police. The baby was born before they married because he was doing time in a detention centre for robbery with violence. But he isn't stupid. In the centre he made sure he earned full remission. "It's meant to be a short sharp shock and it is and all. They have you just like a lot of bleeding sheep: you're not people." He intends to stay clear: next time it would be three years.

Marriage, whatever its other virtues, can be at least a short-term cure for delinquency. It can even help a 40 year old go straight, a local probation officer said to me; it has a still stronger effect on the adaptable young.

Peter was a father to please any marriage counsellor. Maureen was happy enough to shop, housekeep and look after Carol. She didn't mind that she had to wash by hand. Young wives, like young husbands, are resilient. But just as Peter helped with Carol, so it was certain he would make sure Maureen got the vacuum cleaner, fridge and washer she wanted when they found a house of their own—where he would do as much home decorating as other young husbands.

It always comes back to accommodation. The National Marriage Guidance Council have found that in marriages of less than three years, living conditions are one of the chief troubles (ie, symptoms if not diseases) that people come to counsellors with. Infidelity stays near the bottom of the list: this is an older person's reaction to marriage difficulties; it appears near the head of the council's list for marriages more than 18 years old. On both lists income comes last.

The economic circumstances which have produced young husbands have also reduced the prime worry: bread. With that out of the way, young couples are doing their worrying about the roof and the veneer of the sideboard. I was surprised how seldom education—either their own or their children's—was mentioned. But I shouldn't have been. Education is third priority. When the housing problem has gone the way of unemployment, there will be the clamour for education that today, at this level, is lacking. And 18 year olds may have the vote then.

[*17 September 1964*]

ARE HUSBANDS GOOD HOUSEWIVES?

Ann Oakley

With the emancipation of women has come the virtual equality of the sexes—or so many people believe. They also believe that one sign of equality is the increasing employment of married women, while another is the greater readiness of husbands to help in the home.

The conventional argument has logic in its favour; it seems that one consequence of equality *should* be men's increasing domesticity. But we know very little about the degree to which men's participation in housework and childcare has increased, or otherwise, in the last 50 years. Several studies report that the husbands of employed women help more in the house than men whose wives are not employed. In manuals of advice for working wives, the husband often has a prominent place. In *How Working Mothers Manage*, published in 1970, the first three chapters are "Husband," "Guilt" and "Children," in that order. The author says, "The first and most vital necessity for a working wife is the right husband." But the comment made by one child of a participant father ("you ought to buy mummy a Christmas present because she does help you with the housework") reflects a parental division of labour which is the exception, rather than the rule.

To connect men's greater participation in domestic and childcare tasks with the increasing employment of women suggests that the change has occurred on a practical, rather than an ideological, level. In a dual-job marriage, the husband may indeed help put the children to bed and then prepare the evening meal. But in his thinking about the proper roles of the sexes, does he actually believe in the domestication of the male? And does his wife? Is their behaviour merely a personal adjustment to a situation in which housework bores educated women and the cost of living is constantly rising? Or is it really symptomatic of basic changes in the acceptance of the old dogma that a woman's place is in the home, and a man's is outside it?

128

Taking a random sample of women who lived in west London, I examined the division of labour between husbands and wife. The women were selected from the practice lists of two doctors in the area—one with a predominantly working class list, the other with mostly middle class patients. All the names chosen were of married women aged between 20 and 30, with at least one child under five. They were selected on an alphabetical basis. Many of these women turned out to have moved away from the area, or to be otherwise unavailable for interview. The final 40 were divided equally by class; 20 middle class and 20 working class.

The main aim of the research was to study women's attitudes to housework—consequently only the wives in these families were interviewed. Of these, 34 were full-time housewives; one of the remaining six was employed full-time, four had part-time jobs occupying an average of two hours a day; and one worked every Saturday. Because of the low incidence of employment in this group—reflecting the national pattern for women with young children—the division of labour between husband and wife cannot be entirely considered a response to external factors. Furthermore, if ideological change is occurring in the role defined for the husband/father, one might expect it to be most clearly revealed at the stage of the family cycle when the wife is more or less a full-time housewife.

During a long, detailed, depth interview, women were asked which household and childcare tasks their husbands regularly helped with—ranging from shopping, general housework and washing up, to putting children to bed, buying children's clothes and supervising their play. They were also asked about what they believed should be the respective roles of husband and wife in the home. The results were of two kinds: firstly, information about the extent to which husband and wife share housework and childcare tasks: and, secondly, information about the ideology which underlies the roles of each.

One of the first facts that emerged is that husbands (and wives) commonly make a distinction between housework and child-care: the degree of sharing in one area may be quite different from the degree of sharing in the other. Traditionally, research has assumed a convergence between the two, but this seems to be untrue of marriages in this sample.

One marriage illustrated this discrepancy. Mr B works as an inspector in the cleansing department of a local authority, and his wife was a nurse before her marriage. There are two children, aged six and two. Mr B helps a great amount with the children: he regularly gets the two year old up in the morning, dresses him, and puts both children to bed. During the part of the interview which asks about childcare activities, he came into the room and at one point asked the two year old whether he would like to go to the lavatory. The child acquiesced and the father bore him off, but came back and reported no success. "It's a great problem, that," he said, and then proceeded to launch into a monologue on the problems of toilet training this child, punctuated only by brief comments on the part of his wife. He did not appear pathologically obsessed by this topic (as some parents can be) but seemed to be emotionally involved in it in a way more typical of mothers, than fathers, in our society. Within the sample, he was one of the most participatory fathers.

Compared with this, his participation in household tasks is low. His wife said that he does "just little things": he clears the table after the main meal and makes a pot of tea at lunchtime and in the evening. He does no washing up, shopping or cleaning. Husbands were rated as high, medium or low on their participation in childcare and household tasks, and Mr B came out as high on childcare and low on housework. In fact, 15 out of the 40 husbands did more in one area than another.

The most usual pattern was for husbands to share more in childcare than housework. A plasterer's wife with five children, who does two hours' paid domestic work every evening, said: "If he comes home from work before I come home, he'll even have the twins done for me. I don't ask him, he just does it." But as far as housework goes, she said: "On Sundays he'll probably do the potatoes and greens, but that's it. I suppose he might wash up once a week if you're lucky."

Another wife explained: "He helps a lot with the children. He plays with them in the evening while I'm washing up and keeps them quiet, and sometimes he'll help me to bath them and put them to bed. Very often he says, 'You undress one, and I'll undress the other'." But does he help with the housework? "No. He works a long day. I wouldn't expect him to." Her husband's

130

job is that of carpenter, and the three children concerned are aged four, two and a half, and eight months.

Both these women were working class, and this particular pattern—more help with children than housework—appears to be more typical of the working class marriage. Three of the middle class housewives got more help with housework than childcare, whereas none of the working class husbands was simply not, according to his wife, "baby-minded." Childcare is "a mother's job: my husband plays with the baby, but he's frightened of things like bathing him." (This child was a year old.) Fear of the unknown may motivate a dislike of childcare tasks: "My husband holds the baby, but he would refuse if I asked him to do anything else. He thinks it's my job. I think he doesn't really know what to do."

Overall, class differences appeared rather more in the area of help with housework than with childcare, as the table shows:

HUSBAND'S HELP WITH HOUSEWORK AND CHILDCARE, BY SOCIAL CLASS

	No. of respondents	housework			childcare		
		high	medium	low	high	medium	low
working class	20	2	1	17	2	8	10
middle class	20	4	9	7	8	4	8

To explain this difference, it is necessary to look at the beliefs people hold about the roles that men and women should play in the family—at the ideology which shapes role-behaviour. Not one of these housewives questioned their primary duty as being that of looking after the home and the physical needs of the family. Housework was spoken of as "my work" ("I can't sit down till I've finished *my* work"); the interior decor of the home was referred to as belonging to the housewife alone ("I clean *my* bedroom on a Monday"; "I tidy up *my* sitting room in the morning"; "I wash *my* basin every day").

The role of the housewife was thought of as an occupational one equal to the man's role outside the home. ("I've got my job, he's got his.") Even where husbands help with childcare, the housewife described this as an activity done "for" her: "Some-times he'll *help* me to bath them." Fathers are, therefore, at best, only aids to the mother who retains full responsibility for, and control over, what is done in the home.

Four questions proved invaluable as a means of finding out beliefs held about roles in marriage. The first of these, perhaps somewhat surprisingly, is: "Does your husband ever change a dirty nappy?" (or where there were no children still in nappies, "*Did* your husband . . ."). This question was deliberately aimed at the boundaries defining the father's role in childcare, and the responses it received suggest that it does indeed do just this.

Here are some of the replies:

"No, never! He won't. He just hates the idea. I don't know why. He's funny like that." (Working class: two children aged three and a half and nine months.)

"You're joking! He says, 'I'm not doing that—it's a woman's job'." (Working class: two children aged two and three.)

"He's changed a nappy once or twice but he does not make a very good job of it. He wouldn't change a dirty nappy—I wouldn't expect him to." (Working class: three children aged four, two and a half and eight months.)

"No! He absolutely refuses. He says, 'No thank-you, goodbye, I'm going out.' If I'm changing a nappy, he runs out of the room. It makes him sick. He thinks that it's my duty." (Middle class: one child aged four months.)

"He might do it under protest. But I think he tends to think that's not what he *should* do." (Middle class: one child aged four months.)

Clearly, the duties of even the most participant father rarely extend as far as this task. To the working class man, changing nappies which are dirty rather than merely wet is simply "a woman's job." Although the middle class father might not make exactly the same claim, he also appears to feel that this particular task cannot rightfully be expected of him.

These and other comments show just how much agreement exists in these marriages about what the husband/father's role should be. While a few of the women remarked that they would like their husbands to be prepared to change the occasional dirty nappy, even these women accepted, like the rest, that the physical side of childcare is basically the mother's responsibility.

"He's a very good father—he plays with the children" was a comment often voiced by both working class and middle class housewives. To play with the children in the evenings and at weekends; to take them off the mother's hands on a Sunday morning; to be interested in their welfare; and to act as mother substitute in times of illness or childbirth—this defines the father's role for these husbands and wives.

Care of small babies is not expected, and pram pushing is still regarded by some as emasculating—for example: "He wouldn't push a pram, neither would his brother." "I wouldn't let him take the baby out—I don't mind when they turn two or three. I wouldn't like to ask him to push a pram, oh God no!"

Some wives with male babies give the impression that their husbands are withholding an active role in childcare until the child is recognisably masculine: "He wouldn't buy anything for a baby, but he would for a boy, I think." "He won't take him out on his own—only with me. He reckons he's going to play football with him, though."

Husbands who won't push prams, and who withdraw from contact with tiny children, tend to be working class. Among such men, the belief that these activities are inherently feminine seems strongest: perhaps one could say that middle class husbands appear to be more enlightened about just what is at stake in the negotiation of sharing tasks with their wives.

Three other questions provoked statements of belief about the "proper" roles of the sexes in marriage: "Do you agree with men doing housework and looking after children?"; "What would you think of a marriage in which the wife went out to work and the husband stayed at home to look after the children?"; and "Have you heard of the women's liberation movement?" (If the answer is yes: "What do you think about it?")

The impression these housewives gave was one of conservatism, even of a reactionary backlash against the democratic ideology of sex-equality. "I don't agree with men doing housework. I don't think it's a man's job . . . I certainly wouldn't like to see my husband cleaning a room up." "I don't think it's mannish for a man to stay at home. I like a man to be a man."

"Unmanly," "unnatural," "unmasculine" and "henpecked" were words which constantly appeared in these replies:

133

"I've seen a lot of husbands who are that way, and it really makes me rather sick. I just don't think it's right—it just doesn't seem manly . . ."

"I don't mind if they do their share, but not too much. They should *help*—but not all the time, like there's a chappie here who goes out on a Sunday with a pinafore on him. I don't like that, I don't think they should broadcast it, it's not genuine."

"I don't like a real molly of a man with an apron on all the time . . ."

One working class wife makes the distinction between help with the housework and help with the children quite clear: "I agree with them looking after children and bringing them up with the wife, but I don't really agree with them doing housework. I don't think it's their job. I don't think it's their job to come home and do their wives' work in the evening."

Sometimes comments about the women's liberation movement show a real fondness for the man's point of view: "I think it's ridiculous. Well, I always think it's a man's place to be head of any family and what they're trying to do is put the woman up above the man—and it'll never work. It's degrading the man, isn't it?"

Only six women agreed with the reversed-roles marriage as an arrangement which might suit some couples, and of which they wouldn't disapprove for its castrating tendencies. Two women out of the 40—one working class, one middle class—approved of some points made by liberation movements. The middle class woman said she would never join such a group, since she felt the movement was opposed to the idea that women—any women—should stay at home and care for their children. The working class woman was vehement in her support: "I think I would have been a bit of a Pankhurst. You walk down the street and the men look at you and it's degrading . . ." and so on.

In describing what they think about women's liberation, these women make statements about what they believe the roles of the sexes should be. These beliefs, in turn, help build up the division of labour between husband and wife. It is, of course, impossible to know whether they report their husband's views correctly (but on the other hand, what reason would they have to lie?). It is also impossible to generalise with conviction on the basis of a

134

sample of this size. Yet these interviews provided some interesting lines of thought.

In practical terms, the help these husbands give their wives is somewhat limited: 15 of the 40 were assessed as low on participation in both housework and childcare. The average husband in this category did the washing up, and made tea, occasionally, and minded the children some of the weekend to release the wife for household chores. Not only did some husbands contribute very little, but the level of participation throughout the sample could hardly be described as high. This limited help is paralleled by an ideology which views the male as domestically inept and alien to the wife's world of housework and children.

Husbands are not regarded as domesticated creatures, nor is domestication set up as an ideal. In the light of this, it seems more probable that the help the employed wife gets from her husband (according to other research), is a response that is purely due to the fact she is employed. It signals no necessary or direct change in the concept of the male's role.

While it appears true from this sample that men think of themselves as, in a sense, "active" fathers, it seems that they limit their activities mainly to playing with or supervising children. Based on what the father does during his restricted hours at home, these assessments of fathers' participation could not be expected to show an absolutely equal division of labour between the sexes; but what they show is a lot less than this. To put it simply, these men seem to avoid all but the sheerly pleasurable aspects of childcare. The physical side, like the bulk of the housework, is in most cases avoided.

From a male-oriented standpoint, it is easy to see how playing with the children has been brought into the concept of the paternal role. It is a pleasant activity: changing dirty nappies is not. In fact, one could say that this enlargement of the father's role is an unfortunate development for women, who stand to gain nothing from it but temporary peace to do the household chores ("he plays with them in the evening while I'm washing up"), while they themselves stand to lose some of the very rewards childrearing has to offer.

The housework equivalent of "playing with the children" is "washing up." Washing all the family clothes, cleaning the floors, making the beds, cooking the meals, remain feminine

135

activities. It is perhaps less easy to see how washing up has come to be sanctioned as a male activity. Maybe it is because this task calls for limited time and energy and has to be done during the time husbands are at home. At any rate, the presence of British husbands at the kitchen sink does not appear to mean that they are fast becoming "househusbands" in the sense in which women are "housewives." However great the dual-role problems of modern woman, modern man does not seem willing to solve them by creating the same dilemma for himself.

[*17 February 1972*]

BETTING-SHOP DREAM WORLD

John Barr

Affluence has penetrated into Hackney. The surest signs of it are the busy betting shops which have appeared in nearly every street—more than 50 in the borough as a whole—displacing laundries, cheap clothiers, ragmen.

This, of course, has happened in 15,000 places throughout Britain and is the unsurprising result of the Betting and Gaming Act of 1960. But the impact of betting shops is undoubtedly greatest in urban areas and especially urban working class districts. For not only are there more shops in proportion to the population in such areas, but betting shops by their very nature are particularly designed to appeal to the working class. Conclusions based on a study of betting shops in Hackney would in all likelihood apply to similar districts: Stepney, Bethnal Green, Shoreditch, where relatively few residents have credit accounts with bookmakers and where before 1960 street betting particularly flourished. The conclusions would apply less to Mayfair, Hampstead, Chelsea, where credit betting by telephone is still the rule and where gaming clubs are more enticing than betting shops.

Looking then at Hackney, how does one measure the impact of betting shops, examine their role, fix their place in the community? The answers are best sought from the interested parties: the bet shop proprietors; the people who live in streets where bet shops have appeared; those involved in the legal, social or economic consequences of bet shops (the police, magistrates, churchmen, welfare workers); and, most of all, the punters themselves.

Albert Shaw owns a large, independent betting shop near the Salvation Army Congress Hall. Like most bookmakers even in Hackney he announces himself on his shop sign as TURF AC-COUNTANT—the 1960 Betting Act has given bookies a new respectability. Also like practically every betting shop proprietor in Hackney, he was in the pre-Act days an illegal street bookie with a staff of runners, setting up streetcorner pitches, dodging

137

down alleyways and vanishing through obscure entranceways at
the arrival of the police. He no longer has runners: "The good
places where runners go are already taken up." Today he em-
ploys a manager, assistant manager, chalk man, settler, and two
counter girls.

The girls "adore" their jobs, say the hours are "lovely" (11–5)
and are coolly amused by the punters: "Suckers, all of them, but
it gets into their blood, they can't give it up . . . wouldn't know
what to do with themselves if they did." On a Saturday, his best
day, Shaw's turnover is about £1,000, on other days "maybe 15,
20 per cent less." About 90 per cent of the turnover goes on
horses, most of the rest on dogs; "12s 6d is a typical bet."

In general the police don't bother him: "Once in a blue moon
a constable comes in and pokes around." He says his shop,
unlike some, attracts few layabouts; the same faces there for
long periods each day are, he suggests, shift workers at the markets. He says he is strict about minors: "Always ask the questionable ones their age . . . still if they say they're 18 you got to
accept it. Sometimes I catch them out, ask 'You 17?' 'Sure,' he
says. 'Okay, then get out!'" Fights are very rare. What does
worry him are the doping coups at dog tracks: "Course I've got
a grapevine with other bookmakers . . . just the same, you got to
be on your toes." He claims no protection rackets operate in
Hackney bet shops today, though with a droll half grin adds:
"There *was* some incidents in this area a year or so ago."

Max Steadman is manager of a chain shop near the Public
Baths. He has a string of grievances. He thinks there are too
many bet shops in the area. He would like to stay open after
6.30. He wishes the law allowed TV in the shop: "These days the
punters come in, lay one bet, then run round the corner to home
or a pub and watch the race on telly. They'd more likely stay if
we had a set, and if they stayed, well . . ." He's unhappy about
the petrol bombs thrown in some of the chain shops recently
(not his), guesses they were done by other bookies because the
victims were offering punters better terms.

Steadman admits his is a pretty rough shop: threats from dis-
gruntled punters, fairly frequent fights among customers, a lot
of layabouts—"regulars that make a living by betting . . .
the worst ones I sometimes sling out." Not surprisingly "the
coppers are always coming in . . . it's a bad thing, bad for the

business, customers fear the police." He often takes more than £1,000 a day: "small punters, big punters, all kinds, housewives that play the dogs like it was bingo, betting on the trap numbers. The average bet is 10s, but £100 is not so uncommon."

To the police, betting shops are a relative blessing, freeing men who before 1961 were tied down dealing with illegal street bookies. In 1955, the Metropolitan Police made 5,000 arrests for street betting, in 1964 only four. Constables from Hackney police station, with 33 bet shops in their area, now visit them all at intervals of every one or two months. The most common offences are doors left open, so that passers-by can see the posted odds, and minors placing bets. Children loitering outside the shops are sometimes a nuisance. Police do not look on the shops as "dens of vice," though they agree "shady characters" are sometimes attracted to them. They do not think the shops are used for drug passing. If they know that a wanted criminal is a keen punter, they search the shops, otherwise not.

To the local magistrates, betting shops and their consequences are mainly uninspiring routine. Punters chased by their creditors; applications for new or renewed bookmakers' and betting shop licences. Both objections and defences are much the same in all cases. Applicants for new licences proudly cite long strings of pre-1961 street betting convictions as proof of their professional qualifications. A session at the local magistrates' bench last week was typical and gives an insight into the subculture of the betting shop world.

Two of London's most affluent bookmakers were on hand to defend themselves against aggrieved punters and fellow bookies. Both men were expensively dressed, cool, professional, proper representatives of turf accountancy (now Britain's sixth largest industry). Both fit the description by the principal of the London School of Turf Accountancy writing in *The Sporting Life*: "The status of turf accountancy has risen immensely . . . more intelligent and progressive types [are] leaving commerce and taking up turf accountancy as a career."

One of the men was applying for renewal of his bookmaker's permit. His objectors were a burly man in paint spattered trousers and shredded cuffs and a housewife in kerchief and shredded cloth coat; both claimed immense sums were due to them (£9,800 and £987) for winning tickets on a Dagenham dog

139

race last year. The bookmaker explained patiently: the race was an alleged coup, the case was *sub judice*, payouts had been held up pending a court decision in November. Besides, he had a rule never to pay more than £1,000 per ticket. "But it says no limits in your rule book," the man protested. "The gentleman must have a book years old." Another objector suddenly appeared, a young man with horn rimmed glasses and a bright blue shantung suit. The bookmaker had given him only £15 on a winning treble. "I was shocked, there was £300 due." It appeared the young man had filled out his bet slip wrongly; he was lucky to have got anything. "And he refused to give me a rule book . . . and an underage girl took my bet!" No one took these objections seriously. The bookmaker's permit was renewed.

The second bookmaker wanted a licence to open his 131st shop. He would buy a rundown place, his new shop "would bring up the standards of the neighbourhood." Was there a need for another shop in the district? "Certainly . . . you can walk 600 yards from the place and there's only one small betting shop." His objector was the bookmaker with the one small shop —8 by 8 feet. The big man said not more than twelve punters could squeeze into that place, the small man said 30 could and if they didn't believe him just look in on any Saturday. The big man said he would impose no limits on winnings in his shops; the little man admitted he had to have limits, "but the punters don't mind." The new shop would ruin him; the only other trade he knew was coal merchant. The decision was delayed. But it was clear from the day's proceedings that the small bookie and the even smaller punter are no match for the big boys.

Some churchmen and welfare workers feel betting shops certainly create problems in the community, but not to the extent one might imagine. The Rev H. A. S. Pink, rector of St John-at-Hackney, says: "Betting has not loomed large" among the problems brought to him. There may be a reluctance to admit excessive betting to a church official: "I sometimes have a shrewd suspicion they are not telling the whole story." But he cited one recent case: a man who had gambled his pay packet away in bet shops, pawned everything, had large rent arrears. The rector assisted him with £4. He never saw the man again.

A Hackney psychiatrist frequently sees distressed wives of obsessed punters. He tells them to say to their husbands: "Go ahead, gamble it all away, I'll manage somehow myself." This approach, he says, often works.

When betting becomes not so much a leisure pastime, more a way of life, the punter becomes a candidate for Gamblers Anonymous. At last week's GA meeting three compulsive punters from Hackney who have now stopped gambling confessed in the "group therapy" session: Mr A, taxi driver: "In 30 years' gambling I had a bloody good time mind you. At first it was a thrill, then an elation, finally it got so I couldn't stand it . . . I lost the love of my wife and family, when I was gambling I couldn't care a damn about them . . . that is one debt I will never be able to repay." Mr B, factory employee: "I owe £2,624, been in and out of prison seven times. I used to go round the works borrowing from x in order to pay y, from z to pay x." Mr C, salesman: "I started gambling at 14, first bet was 6d each way, won on a 20 to 1 shot. One marriage broken up through compulsive gambling. When I took out a mortgage, when the next child came along I couldn't accept the responsibility . . . at three minutes to two I found myself back at the bet shop for the first race. It reached the point where you feel your guts aren't yours."

But most punters stop short of these ruinous extremes. Over at Stan Farrow's Hackney shop one sees the more characteristic punter. On Wednesday of last week, day of the 2,000 Guineas, life at Stan's went like this:

9.55 am: Outside, leaning against frosted windowpane decorated with rampant horses, is Little Sammy, most regular of regulars, sometime electrician's mate, now on dole "for the moment." Moments for Sammy are measured in months. Beside him is Molly the charwoman, happier than usual, clutching a winning ticket on last night's dogs. She puts 1s a day on one race, always trap No. 3.

10 am: Stan opens door. Door isn't frosted but has bright plastic ribbons. You could look through them if you wanted to. He smiles a bit grimly at Sammy, more genially at Molly, Sammy strides straight to counter ("He holds up the counter, he does," says Stan). Molly collects 5s 6d winnings, sets to sweeping up the crumpled bet slips, bashed newspapers, fag ends. The room she works in is 12 by 18 feet, no seats, austere like almost all bet shops. (One large Hackney shop does have chairs, appropriately enough rows of old cinema seats; some West End shops

141

have a posh room upstairs, plush chairs, carpets, minimum bet £2.) On the walls are signs: ABSOLUTELY NO LIMIT (large letters) subject to new rules (small letters). There are crude frescoes: greyhounds dashing over green fields, huntsmen and hounds. The atmosphere not unlike a night club the morning after, but with all the velvet stripped off, furniture packed away. Stan tears down yesterday's papers, pins up today's sporting pages. He lays out bet slips in neat piles on the narrow counter that runs round the room.

11 am: Sally the cashier arrives, is soon engrossed in painting her nails. Little Sammy, after hours scrutinising papers, makes his first selection, shoves 2s across. Shapely young woman comes in, puts down £1: "It's me mum, not me." Comes every day, says Stan. Two building labourers appear to collect winnings on last night's dogs. "Testing! Testing!" The Blower warms up for its daily commentary on the odds and races. A young mother slips in, places 1s each way on Spanish Express. Her baby is in the pram outside.

12 noon: Stan's settler arrives, so does the chalk man, who wipes off blackboard, begins meticulously printing two o'clock Newmarket runners. Seven men in shop now, all engrossed in sporting pages. Despite fellow punters, betting is a lonely pastime, faces often suspicious.

1 pm: Pace quickens, 17 present, 11 of them West Indians. They work shifts in the Underground. Except for Blower testing, almost silent up to now, but West Indians chatter, laugh, argue good naturedly over virtues of Pepperpot. Men string in and out, most don't stay long. Already have selections on scraps of paper, just transfer them to bet slips, pay money and leave. But West Indians linger. Little Sammy places another bet, then slips out for sandwich at pub.

2 pm: 22 men, 17 of them West Indians, more laughter, last minute scurry to counter as day's first race begins. A few groans when it's over, no particular elation even from winning punters.

3 pm: Place packed, 2,000 Guineas about to start. Still, little excitement. Confirmed punters blasé, even if they win it is only drop in ocean. Infrequent, more excited punters are in pub next door watching it on TV.

Shop almost silent as Blower relates race. One West Indian mutters "Go, go!"; another, "Come on Silly Season, come on!"

142

Lots of men twisting newspapers fiercely, sucking deeply on roll your own fags. Suddenly it's over. Only two men tabbed Niksar to win. They don't look specially happy.

4 pm: Down to six men, including Little Sammy. His luck bad today, puts another 2s on 4.15. Four kerchiefed factory women arrive. Each put 1s on dogs at Park Royal.

5 pm: Little Sammy and two others. He's quit for day, doesn't chase his losses. Sally leaves for day. Stan playing darts with settler in back room.

6.30 pm: Postman hurries in, leaves wager on night dogs. Only Sammy left: "That's it, Sammy." Stan taps his shoulder, Sammy shuffles out reluctantly. Stan locks door behind him. Sammy hesitates at first corner, looks up at Congregational Church. Huge sign asks "How long is it since you went to Church?"

These men and, less frequently, women who spend varying time and money in Hackney bet shops do it for different reasons, offer different explanations. Albert Walker, 23, West Indian dishwasher, spends 10–11 am each day in shop before starting work, earns £10 a week, wages 5s a day, has trouble reading form. It took him 35 minutes to write out slip for races at "Empson" (Epsom). "I always go for a treble, I never win . . . but one day I might, there's always that hope isn't there?"

George Plummer, 71, pensioner, loses £1 a week, spends every afternoon in same shop. "'at's off to the Queen today," he says. He always wages on the Queen's horses. Why does he bet? "It's my life."

Pete Underwood, 33, plumber's mate, earns £17 a week, wages "maybe two quid a day." Used to be addict of dog tracks, gave them up when bet shops came in. Like most, reckons he spends more now than before. "It's entertainment, that's all."

William Clarke, 59, part time presser, spends all free time, all money except for essentials on the dogs. "Lose? Yes, I lose, but I get tired of myself . . . I can read the papers, read a book maybe, but I get tired of myself . . . you know what I mean?"

Terry Crowson, 18 inside the shop, 17 outside it, market worker, earns £9, spends £3 on horses. "Just look for me at five minutes to two, I'm always around. Why? It's there, isn't it?"

Harry Mull, 51, unemployed labourer, has lived on betting for three months, "doubles only, horses only . . . dogs are a racket,

143

all fiddled." Always goes to same shop, likes the service: "They've got limits in some shops, some shops are no good at all." He chases losses, puts a big wager on the last race if he's lost all day.

Mary Newton, 37, housewife, takes a 2s flutter each day. "Comes out of the housekeeping . . . I would never have bet on street corners, it didn't seem right."

Tom Tyler, 24, unmarried postman, bets £1–£2 a day, has no system, "Nobody does, nobody knows a thing about betting." Follows advice of newspaper "experts." "It's rubbish that blokes spend too much in betting shops . . . you've got to do something with your life, haven't you?"

Hackney punters may live in one of the local authority slum clearance flats; more likely they live in streets like Churchill Walk or Lesbia Road, in two storey grey or dun brick terraces, quasi-Corinthian columns at the doors, bow windows with optimistic bright green or magenta paint round them.

A door-to-door survey in Lesbia Road, which is within two minutes' walk of four bet shops, revealed a lot of opposition: "The shops are a bad thing . . . all comes out of the housekeeping money don't it? . . . Shouldn't allow them . . . People should spend their money on their homes if you ask me . . . They ought to kick all married men out of the shops . . . I'm not a punter, I'm not mad that way . . . It's undesirable, those shops . . . you know what I mean . . . attract scruffy types . . . foreigners. Too many shops . . . a bad influence on children." And so on.

The door knocking also brought some defensive opinions: "How else will I make anything? You tell me. I mean real money . . . how else? I get eleven quid a week . . . Sure you pay for the bookie's holiday, so what? It's something to do . . . It's a thrill . . . Don't bet myself, but the shops don't bother me . . . It's all right for those that like it."

What conclusions can be drawn? In those confirmed punters one recognises in embryo the personality factors which Gamblers Anonymous detects in the compulsive gambler: an inability or unwillingness to accept reality ("Sure, it's a kind of dream world . . . but better than the real one outside," a Hackney punter admitted); immaturity ("It made me feel big to go into a cheap bet shop and lay down £50," confessed a GA member); emotional insecurity ("I just like it here," one Hackney regular said, "it's

144

familiar, I know where I am"); and dishonesty (the wife of one obsessed punter said: "He bet heavily for years . . . he told the most fantastic lies and yet I believed him").

In the less confirmed, more typical punters, one detects boredom as a principal drive. It is something to do. Austere as they are, bet shops are a kind of social centre. They offer entertainment, thrills. There is always the chance of the big one. The very existence and easy availability of shops increase the temptation. More women bet than before. More men bet more. There is the chance to bet all day, the quick payoff. In the street pitch days it was usually one bet a day, with payoff the next day—if the bookie hadn't vanished. Now it's sure.

Most punters admit they lose, many agree it's a "mug's game." But they're philosophical about it, it's a pastime and you pay for it. Bet shops have made that pastime more respectable. If you still have puritanical hesitations, well those high frosted windows make it so that no one sees you in there. The shops are an attraction for young people, make them feel adult. For the aged they are even more appealing: dry, warm, free, a place to waste days and to meet friends. You can spend the last of a lifetime pouring over form charts.

But most of all, in working class areas, betting shops are an attraction for the poor and underprivileged: the immigrant, the casual labourer, the man on NA, the pensioner. The 1951 report of the royal commission on gambling recommended licensed bet shops in order, among other reasons, to afford poorer people, unable to establish a credit rating, an opportunity to bet legally. In an area like Hackney, this egalitarian aim has if anything been over-realised.

[*6 May 1965*]

CRIMINAL FAMILIES

Mary McCullough

In my experience there are likely to be, in an urban borough, two or three families—certainly not more than six—who have produced three generations of delinquents. These families all have a good deal in common. In describing them I cannot, for reasons of confidence, give actual case histories and so the account of my imaginary family, the Norths, does not apply to any real family, although the material used is true to life.

Tom and Mary North each have one or two convictions for minor offences, and Mr North has a business—"dealing" with a horse and cart. They are in their sixties and are already great-grandparents, having had 14 children, eight boys and six girls. Two of the boys died violently, one killed in a car crash while being chased by police after the commission of a crime and another murdered in a foreign port during a brief spell in the merchant navy. One of their girl children died from natural causes. There are 35 grandchildren so far and the oldest grandson (who has three convictions) already has two children.

All the North sons became criminals, graduating via probation and approved school to borstal. The youngest boy is still there but the other five have also served prison sentences of varying lengths. They are known to be very violent—one served eight years for seriously injuring a man in the course of a robbery and another who has two convictions for violent crime is also suspected (although without sufficient evidence to justify a charge) of murder in similar circumstances.

One of the North daughters has three convictions for minor offences and two have one each. One of the latter and another daughter have also been before the juvenile court as being exposed to moral danger. These four have all been on probation or under supervision and two of them have been in approved schools. But none of the girls has been in prison or borstal; and all except the youngest who is still in an approved school have married, some into the criminal fraternity. Only one of these marriages seems to be going to last. Another daughter has had

146

seven illegitimate children by five different men and the remaining three daughters have left their husbands and are cohabiting. North girls, however, never become prostitutes.

Less is known about the third generation because some of the family have moved out of the borough, but five grandsons and one granddaughter living locally have been convicted of larceny. Currently one grandson has just left borstal, one is still there and a grandson and granddaughter are in approved school.

There are some relatives of Mr and Mrs North living in the district, and their families present a very similar general pattern although the criminal activity is not quite so concentrated.

The Norths are experienced (if not very successful) criminals, habitually and continuously dishonest. A typical record for man in his late twenties would read:

Age 11, larceny (probation): age 14, larceny (probation); age 15, robbery with violence (approved school); age 17, possessing offensive weapon (detention centre); age 18, factory-breaking (borstal); age 20, insulting words and behaviour (fined), grievous bodily harm (15 months); age 21, taking and driving away (9 months); age 23, housebreaking (3 years); age 26, assault, factory-breaking, taking and driving away (4 years).

At any one time there will be two or three of the North brothers, and a nephew or two, at liberty in the district, all well known in the local criminal network, able to drive a lorry and climb a wall, physically strong and not averse to violence but stupid and only too likely to be suspected by police and to make unfortunate admissions under skilful questioning. These are not master criminals, not even skilled craftsmen. They are the rank and file, the unskilled if experienced labourers in the field.

Judging by the way they live, they do not make much money, but when they get a few pounds—or a few hundreds—they can have terrific spending sprees for a night or two. Indeed one is driven to the conclusion that money is not so important to them as it is to most law-abiding citizens.

The Norths' relationship with the police is a strange one. Of course, the family are hostile to the police and full of accusations about brutality, the fabrication of evidence and so on; but they will not hesitate to go to the police for help. For example, it was Mrs North's practice not to make any arrangements for her frequent confinements but instead to send one of the children to the nearby police station when labour commenced. She considered that she then got the best possible service in the prompt provision of an ambulance and an emergency hospital bed, with no effort on her part. Members of the family have been on good terms with particular CID officers with the reasonable supposition that the relationship is maintained by the police because they find them useful as informers.

Over the years the Norths have been subjected to various forms of residential training. They follow older brothers and uncles through the remand home and they have been to various approved schools, borstals and prisons. Their response is invariably negative; and judging from progress reports this would seem to be obvious to the most optimistic member of the staff. They are persistent absconders wherever absconding is possible. They can always be sure of shelter and help from relatives so that they can stay on the run for months.

Their response to probation is equally lifeless. They will carry out the letter of the order—report fairly regularly and so on, and be civil and in a way friendly enough. But they are successfully slippery and evasive when it comes to finding and keeping a job, occasionally truculent if pressed. The hopelessness of their case is as obvious to probation officers as it is to the staff of residential institutions, and this cannot just be put down to giving a dog a bad name. There are competent and sincere workers in both settings to whom a bad name is a stimulating challenge, whose optimism has been blunted and social awareness sharpened on the Norths.

These families are maladjusted to society and isolated, or perhaps islanded would be a better word, *as a family* rather than as individuals. They are separated from respectable neighbours in the streets where they live and they do not work with them. They are not, emphatically not, upwardly mobile. They are not reached by the rewards of the welfare state and the affluent society, neither are they deterred by its punishments. The greatest real punishment to the average citizen for social failure or crime—that of loss of self-esteem and reputation—does not affect them. They expect to spend long periods of their lives in prison; and although they resent it, they regard it as an unavoidable misfortune like illness. Jack North remarked once that he

148

was about to spend his first Christmas at home for eight years—and was in prison again by the end of January.

The Norths mix with problem families, with people from the criminal and drug subcultures, with occasional isolates and from time to time with the poorer kind of new immigrant who may not belong to any of these categories but who presumably cannot yet identify or be identified with normal society. Apart from these, their main contacts with the outside world are with police, the staff of correctional institutions, probation officers, other social workers and teachers.

Yet criminal families are viable as families and indeed have great survival potential. They are not to be confused with problem families. They live in houses, not rooms, and never seem to move. Whatever else happens, the rent is paid. There is plenty of food, warmth and sufficient if shabby clothing and furniture. They hang together. As families they demand help in cash and kind from social, charitable and religious agencies, but they look after their own sick, mentally defective and aged.

Cruelty to children in the sense of deliberate neglect, excessive punishment or sadism is unknown, but family life is violent. Although details are never available, there is reason to suppose that occasionally the children may be hurt—perhaps in the course of drunken brawling among their elders. I have never known them seek, or willingly agree to, the removal of one of their children from home, and removal to approved school is hotly contested. Illegitimate children of each generation are absorbed, often into the grandparents' family. Grandmother is apparently the dominant figure, the kingpin of the group domestically but not criminally.

Family life is confused, full of shifting feuds and often violent: but it has strength and warmth and this may be one of the reasons why residential training is so uniformly unsuccessful. Deprived children and young people from coldly rejecting homes may have their first experience of warm and positive relationships with staff and fellow residents in institutions, and so may begin to absorb ideas and patterns of behaviour from the loved persons. But the best institution cannot offer the Norths what the family offers. What is more, they have to suffer living there stripped of the family's protection—they are *alone* there in their isolation from society.

149

The family will even occasionally offer a sort of mock-up of Victorian authority. Parents and elders are loud and emphatic, if not always effective, in their disciplining of children and young people. But it is not always clear what standards are being upheld. "When I got out of borstal my Uncle Joe gave me a telling off and knocked me down [Uncle Joe has a terrible criminal record]. Then he told me to keep out of trouble!" This was related with pride and approval but it was not clear whether not getting into trouble meant just not getting caught or not engaging in crime—possibly the latter because the speaker was a frail youth of a nervous temperament apparently unsuitable to a criminal career.

Criminal families are riddled with secrets in a truly Dickensian fashion. Is your mother really your mother or your adopted mother, and if the latter is she actually your grandmother? If so, which of your aunts is really your mother or could it be that one of your uncles is your father? Would it really be incest to go with and possibly marry your half-sister because really her father is not (as is generally supposed) the same as yours but is a chap her mum met while your dad was on remand that time? These hints of incest recur, but family vagueness makes them hard to pin down. They upset everyone very much and cause bitter quarrels.

Members of the family would appear to be of uniformly low average intelligence but one or two of the children are actually subnormal. Not one single child ever does well in school, and a five year old North faces and expects ten years of boredom, humiliation and failure as he follows his uncles and aunts and his older brothers and sisters to the local school. Small wonder that they long to leave, although few celebrate this event as dramatically as Barry North. He listened in silence to his headmaster's parting homily but turned back at the gate to break window after window with the aid of a crate of milk bottles, until the police arrived.

There are no obvious signs of serious mental ill health among these families. As far as I know, no member has been in a mental hospital or received psychiatric treatment as an out-patient. Members of the family, and particularly the children, often look sullen and depressed, and a number of adult members complain of frequent headaches and dizziness, usually blaming these on having received severe blows on the head. In the case of the men these are said to have been inflicted by police officers, whereas the women blame departed husbands or lovers.

These families do not seem to be part of our world at all—of the expanding, scientific world. Indeed they live lives little affected by the industrial revolution. They do not take the well-paid employment in factories or on building sites available to unskilled labourers. Apart from crime they engage on their own account in such occupations as breaking up old cars, dealing in scrap metal or "rags and bones," or carting and selling coal. One has a paper stand. They do odd jobs in house decorating and repairing, spray cars and so on, sometimes using skills acquired in prison.

All these occupations slot conveniently into the edges of crime and none of them involves working indoors. In a thickly populated industrial area, ten miles as the crow flies from open country, they keep horses and work with them, and magnificent racing greyhounds coil by their fires. Younger boys keep pigeons and chickens. They have been known to catch and sell wild birds. Apart from their criminality, their distinguishing feature is this way they are cut off in space *and* time from the mainsteam of society. With very little change in occupation and way of life they could have survived in the dark ages.

It is tempting to speculate as to the earlier history of these families. There are settled gipsies in the district, and also settled barge-dwellers from the canal which runs through it, and I do know of one instance of a gipsy ancestor. Whatever the explanation such families seem to survive, little affected by social pressures and social change.

[*24 August 1967*]

NON-SWINGING YOUTH

Bernard Davies

Watching *Top of the Pops* in one of Lancashire's dockland youth clubs. On the screen, swaying bodies, gay and fashionable clothes, space-age decor, music to match. The weekly ritual confirmation of youth's popular image. Freedom, wealth, confidence, unconventionality—all unmistakably symbolised.

Around me, a different scene. Fashion caricatured. Skirts short and revealing, but not truly mini—only turned up at the hem. Hair, both boys' and girls', long but simply straggling, without style, sheen or grooming. No bell-bottoms or frills, snappy waistcoats or high-necked shirts. Just tired and shapeless sweaters (not even Marks & Spencer) and stained blue-denim jeans. Faces pale, drawn, probably undernourished. Movement lethargic, without spark, without conviction. A microcosm of Lancashire's imprisoned youth.

Of course, the comparison may not be altogether fair. For the studio visitors to *Top of the Pops*, this was at least a big night out; but for the youngsters by my side it was clearly just any night, and in a club, moreover, whose unpainted walls, stone floors, poor heating and rickety furniture were hardly a temptation to dress up.

Yet these young Lancastrians in the youth club cannot in my experience be regarded as exceptional. Theirs is an anti-image in which the supposedly essential traits of present-day youth don't feature. What seems to characterise so many of their lives is not wealth but privation and even outright poverty. These young people are mostly not angry and active, but apathetic and unassertive, especially in the face of "them." Even where few minorities threaten them directly, a deep-seated bigotry often bitterly obtrudes, as they seek to defend the little they do possess. Far from challenging the world around them with an insistent individuality, they seem personally and socially incarcerated; their talents are consistently underrated, their vision constricted, their most personal modes of expression stifled. Each self-image they

152

have created for themselves has been repeatedly deflated, all futures prematurely and permanently foreclosed.

The point of stirring all this to the surface is not to paint one more of those black, outsider's portraits of the north. It is rather to question *in general* how accurately the widespread image of contemporary youth fits with the realities. Lancashire may have triggered off such thoughts, but evidence can be accumulated from much farther afield that everything that is young does not swing.

Take, for example, the tag of affluence. Mark Abrams attached it to young people very firmly, with revelations about the hugeness of teenage consumer spending. This he fixed in 1960 at £950 million, and ever since the bulging teenage wage-packet has simply been taken for granted.

Yet, when one begins to look closely, some contradictions emerge. In the first place, Abrams was concerned with unmarried 15 to 25 year olds. This upper age limit was bound to raise the total spending figure sharply, but it disguises important age differences. Abrams discussed only *total* expenditure and average earnings. He said nothing of how many high-earners were hiding how many low ones. He offered no regional or local differences and so threw no light on how young people in London compare with those from the north or Scotland.

Such discrepancies do exist. It is not just that I feel them when I see youngsters huddling and cuddling in the bus shelters or against the railings of Atherton, Tyldesley, Ince-in-Makerfield and elsewhere. Nor is it just that I hear of them even more personally when I talk with shopgirls, waitresses, factory hands and other young workers. Much more convincing is the research evidence which is now available, drawn from larger groups in other areas.

Cyril Smith, in his Bury study, *Young People at Leisure*, concluded that "the popular picture of affluent teenagers grossly over-simplifies the very real differences in income among them." The amount of money available to the young people he studied in 1963 varied greatly with age and sex. In general over 90 per cent of his 17 and 18 year olds spent £2 a week or less, and nearly 40 per cent of the 18 year olds spent under 15s.

In Scotland, according to Pearl Jephcott in *Time of One's Own*, the picture is not very different. Despite overtime, bonuses and

153

increases for age, she found that between 1964 and 1966 41 per cent of young people aged 17½ *and over* were earning only £5 to £7, with a further 15 per cent falling below this amount. The wages of girls during the first two years at work rose from £3 or £4 to £5 maximum, while a mere 7 per cent of the whole under-21 group she interviewed had more than £9 a week. Spending money was of course much less: 59 per cent of the 15 to 17½ year olds had less than £1; 81 per cent of the 17½ to 19 year olds had less than £3. Pearl Jephcott's conclusion, inevitably, is that "the popular image of today's adolescent as having money to burn was certainly not true of the great majority of these Scottish boys and girls."

Once one examines the teenage image in this detailed way, one discerns all sorts of other cracks. Take youth's reputation for unconventionality and unorthodoxy. Research findings on teenage values and attitudes do very little to confirm it. In *Youth and the Social Order*, Frank Musgrove's general thesis is that "the broad picture of contemporary youth is not of a population either actually or potentially deviant—or even particularly adventurous." Such chapter sub-headings as "The realism of youth" and "The conservatism of the young" reveal where Musgrove stands. They are supported by his own and other evidence. Thus, he reports that statements like "Boys (or girls) of my age should be allowed more freedom," get very little teenage support. But statements concerned with young people "acting their age" or being "responsible" are approved by a majority.

Inquiries into the specific views and standards held by teenagers tend to reinforce this conservative picture. True, on sexual morals, an NOP survey, published in the *Daily Mail* in November 1967, suggested that, in their *attitude* to pre-marital sex, girls are equally divided, while two thirds of the boys are in favour. This, however, says nothing of actual *behaviour*. According to Michael Schofield's authoritative and widely quoted 1965 survey of nearly 1,900 young people (*The Sexual Behaviour of Young People*), this seems to be much more conventional. Only 11 per cent of the 15 to 17 year old boys interviewed, and 6 per cent of the 15 to 17 year old girls, had had sexual intercourse. The corresponding figures for the 17 to 19 year old age-group were 30 per cent and 16 per cent. Thus, by the age of

154

20, only a third of the boys and one sixth of the girls, were sexually experienced; most of the experience was gained after the age of 16 (the law, of course, may have an effect), and the vast majority of these sexual encounters were with a single partner.

Peter Willmott's conclusion in *Adolescent Boys of East London* (1966) is very similar: "Those we talked to suggested that by 18 something like a third or half of the local boys would have had intercourse"—though many of these, it is clear, had done so either with a small number of highly promiscuous girls, or only with the one girl with whom they were going steady." A more recent study in the midlands, whose comparability with Schofield's or Willmott's work is not clear, suggests some noticeable shift towards permissiveness in the last few years. Yet from the solid evidence available, long after the so-called teenage revolution got under way, it is clear that, far from being one of gay and irresponsible abandon, the path of sexual experience along which young people travel has until now been most striking for its conformism, or at least for the way it would appear to mirror adult morals and behaviour.

Perhaps it is not surprising, therefore, that in what they want and expect from their own future family lives and careers, young people again reveal much that is most noticeable for its resemblance to adult responses. Adolescent aspirations in these areas are only minimally tinged with the fantasy and idealism one might expect. They apparently stay firmly within boundaries which any "sensible" adult might lay down for them.

Professor C. A. Mace noted in 1962, in his introduction to Thelma Veness's study, *School-Leavers: their aspirations and expectations*, that "few young people have the ambition to become millionaires, peers, film-stars, even Lord Mayors of London. They are on the whole realistic, setting their sights to the reasonably attainable." The average boy's "peak ambition lies somewhere in the middle management in industry or similar status in other occupations or professions . . . At 23 he gets married, and his wife bears him two or three children who thereafter are apt to become the centre of his ambitions. The ultimate objective is retirement on an adequate pension." The picture of the "average" girl is, according to Professor Mace, very similar.

155

Thelma Veness herself found that over a third of her sample, when asked what they might especially want to be in the future, responded by pointing to an ordinary sort of job. She concludes that "a large number of these boys and girls have tailored their ambitions to fit what they are in fact likely to do." (Some of her results, however, revealed that such realism did not exclude a good deal of day-dreaming or resort to fantasy.)

This absence not only of idealism but even of burning personal ambition—this striking emphasis on pragmatic, traditional values and aspirations so little different from those of their elders—is equally discernible in other spheres of young people's lives. It can be seen, when their views on political, religious and social issues are sought. The NOP survey I quoted earlier also revealed that 68 per cent of the young people interviewed wanted the death penalty restored, so that this emerged as top of a list of "reforms" desired by the young—hardly a rallying cry for social upheaval! As many as 30 per cent would have sent all coloured immigrants back home (even before Enoch Powell's Birmingham and Eastbourne speeches), and almost as many were against abortion law reform as were for it. Sixty per cent of the boys and 76 per cent of the girls said they believed in God.

It follows logically that the anti-authority feelings, said to be so prevalent among the young, were little in evidence in the NOP survey. In the list of "most popular personalities" Mother was No. 1 and Father No. 5, the Queen No. 2, Harold Wilson No. 4. President Johnson No. 6 and Prince Philip joint No. 10. The footballer Bobby Charlton was the only sportsman to get a mention. The only pop idol, Elvis Presley, cast an unmistakably dated shadow even two years ago.

This only confirmed what E. M. and M. Eppel had found in 1966 in *Adolescents and Morality*. Among the young people they talked with, nearly two thirds were prepared to accept orders either without qualification or provided the person giving the orders had thought about them in advance, was sure they were right, or gave them in a reasonable and humane way. Only a quarter of the sample appeared uncompromisingly hostile to authority.

Whether one is relieved or appalled by this widespread adolescent conservatism depends on one's starting point. To those who read only press reports, or watch only television newscasts, such

156

a portrait of youth may bring relief. The more radical will see it as evidence of repression of the young, their premature moulding according to adult models, their direction into restricting channels.

Both would be right, in a way. But for the purposes of policy towards youth, quite apart from the question of understanding, the adolescent anti-image must be accepted, once and for all, as a fact. Even among university students, few are active radicals; and students are a tiny minority of youth. A great deal of education, not least in the youth service, still seems to be carried out on the assumption that it is only to greater affluence, independence and alienation among the young that adults must respond. Yet the first need is to help youth out of its strait-jacket.

In traditional youth organisations, in youth clubs, in more recent youth work bodies such as the Duke of Edinburgh's Award Scheme and the Young Volunteer Force Foundation, and in the schools themselves, the motives of exploiting what is socially "beneficial" and damming up what is socially "destructive" still predominate. Control remains the first, though rarely the explicit, priority. Genuine teenage self-expression—which, I repeat, at present *we have not got*—is still an undervalued and even feared objective.

The real lesson of the research on young people's condition and philosophy is that we don't need some coordinated movement to keep most young people in check, but we do need an enormous programme to release many more of them from the mould (curriculum reform in the secondary schools may be at any rate a first step). For every individual young person who frightens or undermines the established order, many more are going to have only a tiny opportunity to discover what is most individual in their personalities. Penned into a pattern of badly-off homes, run-down schools and poor jobs, they are going to remain poor (emotionally as well as, sometimes, financially), to adopt blind prejudice against any group threatening their uncertain stability, to be convinced of the inevitability of their own limitations and even failures—and to reproduce this pattern of humble acquiescence in restricted lives in the generations that succeed them.

Behind the headline-snatching students and hippies and

157

swinging kids, the truth of these youngsters' condition may seem difficult to discern and even more difficult to act on. Yet whatever *Top of the Pops* may communicate, those Lancashire teenagers in that youth club exist; and they are far more common than most of us care to admit.

[*3 July 1969*]

WORKPLACE INEQUALITY

Dorothy Wedderburn

The thesis that the British working class is getting more bourgeois in its way of life has come under fire from John Goldthorpe, David Lockwood and their colleagues. Their main evidence covers work, family and community life and is drawn from a case study in one particular place, the car town of Luton. Further relevant data are now available from a national survey. They cast light on general differences in conditions of employment.

An inquiry by the Department of Employment and Productivity, published in 1969, revealed that a marked gap remains between the earnings of manual and non-manual workers. But differences in fringe benefits, in security of employment and in opportunities for promotion are all, it is now recognised, important aspects of the total "market" situation in which workers find themselves. It is particularly significant when one finds this kind of inequality in the basis for treating workers even within the same area of interest—as where an occupational pension scheme exists for both manual and non-manual workers but where entitlement is calculated differently. But no systematic data have been gathered on these variations in the employment relationship as a whole.

This was why, with financial assistance from the Social Science Research Council, I conducted an inquiry into how the employment situation of male workers in manufacturing industry varies. Christine Craig, of the Cambridge Department of Applied Economics, collaborated, and with the help of the Department of Employment and Productivity we selected a stratified random sample of manufacturing firms and sent a postal questionnaire to them in mid-1968.

How to collect the information presented a problem. We needed data about a wide range of conditions of employment in a form which would not only reveal any significant differences between what are commonly called manual and non-manual workers, but also whether, within the non-manual group, there

159

was any further stratification. Firms were therefore asked to supply information about a "typical male worker," aged 35 to 40 with five years' continuous service in each of six occupations which we had chosen as representative of broader occupational groupings where terms and conditions of employment might be similar. These six occupations were: operative or semi-skilled manual worker; foreman in a plant or works; general routine clerical worker; draughtsman or technician of similar standing; professionally qualified employee who is a member of middle management; and member of senior management.

A response of 55 per cent from the sample of 815 establishments was encouraging, particularly as those who replied were very like the original sample in their geographical, industrial and size distribution. I give the results as percentages of all the establishments that responded.

Taking all employment conditions together—from fringe benefits to discipline—our survey shows a big gulf between manual workers on the one hand and non-manual workers on the other (see table). In every respect, manual workers are worse off than their non-manual counterparts; and in many cases the differences are very large indeed. The data suggest that there may be another division with the non-manual employees— foremen, draughtsmen and clerical workers as one group, and management as another. But even where these two non-manual groups diverge, they are still more like each other than they are like manual workers.

Differences are perhaps smallest for private occupational pension schemes, where the Government Actuary's surveys show a considerable extension of coverage in the last ten to 15 years. Even so, one quarter of the establishments in this sample had no scheme for their manual operatives, whereas each of the non-manual grades was almost completely covered. As important for lifetime income expectations is our finding that nearly half the manual workers' schemes provided a pension calculated as a fixed sum per year of membership, whereas three quarters or more of the non-manual schemes provided pensions based on final salary or on salary in the last years of service. Here is a gross example of inequality of treatment within the same area of interest.

SELECTED DIFFERENCES IN TERMS AND CONDITIONS OF
EMPLOYMENT

	per cent of establishment in which the condition applies					
	opera- tives	fore- men	clerical workers	tech- nicians	middle managers	senior managers
holiday: 15 days +	38	72	74	77	84	88
choice of holiday time	35	54	76	76	84	88
normal working 40 + hours per week	97	94	9	23	27	22
sick pay—employers' scheme	57	94	98	97	98	98
pension—employers' scheme	67	94	90	94	96	96
time off with pay for personal reasons	29	84	83	86	91	93
pay deductions for any lateness	90	20	8	11	1	0
warning followed by dismissal for persistent lateness	84	66	78	71	48	41
no clocking on or booking in	2	46	48	45	81	94

Sick pay illustrates how important an employer's discretion
can be for non-manual workers. Of these establishments, 43 per
cent made no provision for supplementing the national insurance benefit of their manual workers when they could not work
because of sickness. Only a tiny proportion of the non-manual
grades, however, were without some extra provision. But in
almost a third of the establishments, payment, even for the non-
manual grades, was discretionary. Where there was a scheme,

161

non-manual workers were more likely to have any national insurance sick benefit deducted than manual grades were, presumably because manual operatives, when sick, would be receiving only their basic pay, which in many cases would be well below their normal earnings. The specified length of time for which the different grades were officially entitled to sick pay did not vary much. But additional time, over and above that formally specified, was allowed for operatives in only half of these establishments. Between 85 and 90 per cent of them allowed it for non-manual grades—frequently, again, at the discretion of the employer.

Our inquiry did not attempt to collect data about levels of earnings, but in exploring some aspects of methods of payment it cast additional light on the results that the Department of Employment and Productivity published last summer. The department's survey showed, for instance, that the average earnings of a worker rise with age up to a peak and then decline before retirement whether he be manual or non-manual. The percentage increase in the case of manual workers, however, was much less than for non-manual workers and the decline was much more rapid and marked. Manual workers aged from 60 to 64 were thus, on the average, earning less than their younger workmates. Non-manual workers of the same age were still earning considerably more than their juniors. In other words, if we were to take account of these differences in the expectation of earnings over the life cycle, inequalities between manual and non-manual workers would be even greater than an examination of levels of earnings at a point of time would suggest.

Two forces compound to produce this result, we found. Opportunities for promotion from one grade to another are greater for non-manual workers than for operatives. Moreover, in 80 to 90 per cent of the firms, all the non-manual grades had the possibility of an annual pay increase, but this applied to only a fifth of the operatives.

Another important side to earnings is their predictability and regularity. Nearly all the establishments in our sample paid their management grades a fixed annual salary by monthly cheque or credit transfer. Between two thirds and three quarters paid their foremen, clerical workers and draughtsmen or technicians salaries that were also fixed on an annual basis. Some

162

30 to 40 per cent of these middle grades were paid by cheque or credit transfer, and about half received their payment weekly. But operatives were paid—98 per cent of them in cash—a weekly wage which could fluctuate considerably with overtime, bonus and piece-rate earnings.

A slight variation in the dominant pattern of differentials emerged over hours of work. Both operatives and foremen, because of their intimate concern with the production process, worked the longest hours and were also more likely to work shifts. In only 50 to 60 per cent of the establishments were no operatives or foremen working shifts. In, at the most, 7 per cent of establishments did any of the other non-manual grades work shifts. Holidays were longer for all the non-manual grades who were also more likely to be able to choose when they took their holidays.

Hours of work, pensions, sick pay, earnings, are all, as I have said, aspects of the market situation. Our inquiry was limited by being carried out by post, but it also attempted some preliminary investigation of what might be called social relationships at work. The physical arrangements of production tend to minimise contact between manual workers and non-manual grades, except for foremen. But some segregation was also the rule in nearly half of those establishments where there was a canteen, and in 40 per cent of those where there was sports and recreational facilities by the different groups. Nor could our inquiry look into the often sharp contrast in the physical working conditions of the different groups of workers, and the differences in their exposure to risk of injury. Both these are important for any general assessment of workplace inequality.

Our inquiry did, however, explore several areas of disciplinary practice. Clocking-on was general for manual workers in the responding establishments. We found that 98 per cent made their operatives clock on and 90 per cent made automatic pay deductions for lateness. One third made their foremen clock on and another fifth had them book in, but only 30 per cent imposed any regular penalties for lateness. Only 6 per cent of senior management booked in or clocked on, and only 4 per cent had regular penalties. In cases of persistent lateness, 84 per cent of the establishments said operatives would be given a warning and then dismissed. Only just over 40 per cent would do this for

163

management. For the management grade promotion prospects were likely to be affected.

It seems clear that far more discretion is exercised in disciplining non-manual workers than manual workers. Discretion of another kind is also evident in another socially indicative area. Most establishments said that they would give time off to all grades for domestic reasons, such as death or serious illness in the family. But only 29 per cent of the manual workers, compared with 80 to 90 per cent of the non-manual workers, would be paid for such time off.

These data suggest that the kind of treatment which the non-manual worker gets at work reflects an assumption by the employer that values are shared—that the non-manual worker will "behave responsibly," will "have the interests of the firm at heart" and "not abuse privileges." The manual worker is more often subject to formal rules and prescriptions. On the other hand, he is far more likely to work for an employer who recognises a trade union to negotiate on his behalf. Of the responding establishments in our sample 84 per cent recognised a trade union or association for operatives, a third for foremen, 20 per cent for clerical workers, 43 per cent for draughtsmen or technicians, and hardly any for management grades. The figure for non-manual workers appears high compared with those for union membership given in the research report prepared for the Donovan commission on trade unions and employers' associations. The explanation may lie in our inclusion among "associations" of bodies which would not generally be regarded as "trade unions," as well as the fact that the percentages I give here relate to the establishments, not to their membership.

The wide inequalities revealed by this survey have important implications for the understanding of employees' behaviour *outside* work, and this would repay further investigation. Differences in the length of the working week, in the flexibility of timekeeping, in the constraints of shift work, are important for the way a man can organise his social life. Manual workers may remain marked off by such differences. Differences in the regularity of earnings and in the pattern of life-cycle income suggest that assumptions about a convergence in the consumption patterns of manual and non-manual workers may indeed, as Goldthorpe and Lockwood have argued, be misplaced.

Differences in workers' experience of authority, of discipline in the workplace, and of how improvements at work are won, have implications for attitudes towards collective, as opposed to individual, activity.

But perhaps more immediately relevant is whether such inequalities are a major factor in the present industrial relations situation. Some employers are busy negotiating a reduction in these differentials as part of a productivity deal (ICI, for instance). Some of these employers are interested because they believe it will affect "the attitudes to work" that motivate their manual workers: others, because they genuinely believe that certain differences are unjustified: yet others, simply to attract particular kinds of labour that are in short supply. "Staff status" for manual workers has become a fashionable discussion point, although it can mean vastly different things. Both the Donovan report and Barbara Castle in her white paper, *In Place of Strife*, thought it a good thing to eliminate "outdated social distinctions between hourly-paid employees and those on staff conditions."

We carried out attitude studies among manual workers and two grades of non-manual workers at two very different firms, as part of this research, in order to explore some of the implications of reducing differentials. Would equality of treatment cause unrest among non-manual workers who would see their status as being eroded? The limited evidence from our case studies suggests that this may not, in general, be an important factor. The non-manual workers had some misgivings, particularly those who were closest to manual workers, like the foremen, about their possible loss of privileges. But there was a good deal of support for eliminating what were seen as unjustified differences of treatment over (say) sick pay and pensions.

But, for the manual workers, it did not seem that the elimination of "outdated social distinctions" was very important in bargaining. They expressed a strong desire for absolute improvement in pay, physical working conditions, security and regularity of earnings; but they did not use the superior position of non-manual employees in their own company as a reference point.

The situation, we found, closely resembled the prewar position summarised by W. G. Runciman: relative deprivation (a

165

feeling of inequality, compared to the group usually used as a yardstick) "was, as far as can be inferred, less in magnitude and frequency than the objective inequalities might lead one to expect." If "equality," therefore, is offered in any way at the expense of, or as a substitute for, absolute improvement it may be an unacceptable bargain for manual workers.

[*9 April 1970*]

SIR, WRITING BY CANDLELIGHT

E. P. Thompson

Let the power workers dim the street lamps, or even plunge whole districts into utter darkness, the lights of righteousness and duty burn all the brighter from 10,000 darkened drawing-rooms in Chelsea or the Surrey hills. "Sir, May I, writing by candlelight, express my total support for the government in their attempt to halt the unbelievably inflated wage claims now being made?" inquires one correspondent to *The Times* (12 December 1970). Undoubtedly he may and will.

Historians have often paid tribute to this peculiar character of the British. It is in grave adversity, in states of emergency, that they have noted this flaring-up of the British spirit. Only then do those proper guardians of the conscience of the community—the retiring middle classes—shed their usual reticence and openly articulate their values and commitments.

One infallible signal of such a time of bourgeois renaissance is the epistolary *levée en masse* of the readers of *The Times*. Such *levées* are infrequent; when they occur, one senses the presence of History. One such took place in February 1886 after the "Trafalgar Square Riots," when unorganised unemployed demonstrators—after listening to some exciting rhetoric from John E. Williams, John Burns and H. M. Hyndman of the Social Democratic Federation—broke into a brief rampage through the West End, smashing shop windows, looting and even throwing bricks at select London clubs. Worse riots occurred, in most years, in some parts of the country: but not on such sanctified ground as Pall Mall.

"Sir," wrote one unfortunate gentleman, whose carriage windows were smashed in the rioting: "I am a subscriber to various charities and hospitals, which I shall discontinue. I have always advocated the cause of the people. I shall do so no more."

But wounded and long-suffering righteousness, on these occasions, takes second place to the firm disciplinary mode. "Sir," demanded one correspondent in 1886, "What is the use of having

167

a highly-paid Commissioner of Police, with proportionately highly-paid deputies, if they are afraid of the responsibility attaching to their posts? . . . When there is a kennel riot in any kennel of hounds, the huntsman and whips do not wait to get the special orders of the master, but proceed to restore order at once."

Another correspondent (11 February 1886) produced an example of the genre so rich that it has to be quoted at length:

"Sir . . . On returning from the Prince's Levée I was walking through Pall Mall, in uniform. It was gradually filling with very suspicious-looking 'unemployed' at that time, two of whom, turning towards me, one said, rather significantly, 'Why, who the —— is this chap?'

"As I passed the War Office entrance, formerly the Duke of Buckingham's, a blind fiddler, led by a little girl, came by . . . playing some odd tune or other, when a young guardsman on sentry stepped out and said, in a commanding tone, 'You stop that noise' . . . I thought, 'Now there is a man of common sense and of action.' It was a little thing to stop at the time, but when the snowball which a child or a blind fiddler could set rolling on the top of the hill reaches the bottom it has become in this country an immovable monster, in other countries a destroying avalanche.

"On the 10 April 1848, I was sworn in a special constable between Buckingham Palace and the House of Commons. At the former we had a battery of Horse Artillery hidden in the stable yard. I asked the officer commanding what he was going to do? His answer was, 'We have our scouts, and if we hear of any gatherings we could run out and sweep the Mall or the Birdcage-Walk in two minutes, or command St James Street and Pall Mall in three.' He would not wait till mischief was done. Are those days quite gone?

"Your obedient servant, Wilbraham Taylor."

Such high heroics can rarely be repeated, just as the true physical *levées* of the bourgeoisie against the plebs (the Volunteers against the Jacobins in 1800, the Yeomanry against the poor of Peterloo, the Specials against the Chartist 10 April, the debs and Oxbridge undergraduates against the General Strike) are too few to satiate the desire dramatically to beat the bounds of class. So the epistolary cry goes out for someone—

the government—to discipline *them*, and put them back in kennels.

John E. Williams had been reported, in 1886, as having deplored that the unemployed were not well enough organised— not to riot and destroy property—but to occupy the banks, Stock Exchange and government offices. "Sir," wrote one *Timesian*, "if correctly reported Williams must be an atrocious miscreant, compared with whom Gashford in *Barnaby Rudge* is a virtuous person."

December 1970 produced little in this genre of comparable quality, perhaps because Electrical Workers' leaders are scarcely typecast as communist or trotskyist fiends. (Perhaps the nearest was the letter—14 December—from Nicolas Bentley, suggesting that Robert Morley, who had dared to declare his solidarity with trade unionism, must be a "callous reprobate.") But the old theme of "there ought to be a law against . . ." has been fully orchestrated. This was very evident in another vintage epistolary year, 1926.

One mine-owner addressed himself (5 June 1926) to the subject of the mineworkers' officials: "Their one object is to squeeze as much money out of the industry as it will stand, to the detriment of the proprietors who have taken all the risk incidental to coalmining." (A rigorous statistical examination of the number of coal-owners killed in mining disasters might not bear this out.) The Bishop of Durham came baying up behind (22 June): "Trade unions now include in their ranks a great number of young men whose boyhood was spent during the war, when every kind of discipline was weakened . . . These lawless youths are well-fitted to become the janissaries of Communist Revolution."

Trade unions were "the mocking caricature of anything . . . democratic," and their rank-and-file were "the hopeless tools of the ruling clique." They could only be held down by stronger law. The compulsory secret ballot, then as now, was one grand recipe for the extirpation of strikes, from correspondents pathetically anxious to believe that if only the workers expressed their minds *in secret* they would turn out to be chaps just like themselves—or, rather, chaps *convenient to* themselves, compounded of all bourgeois virtues of prudence, self-help, and deference to

169

property, but emasculated of the bourgeois reproductive system
—the drive for *money*.

Such themes, announced in 1926, have, if anything, become
more pronounced with the epistolary *posse commitatus* of 1970.
Should strikes be forbidden by law? asks Sir H. T. Smith, from
Wallingford (11 December). On the same day the "long-suffering public" found a spokesman in H. P. Rae: deeply perturbed
about invalids dependent upon "continuously functioning
kidney machines" (which they aren't), he demanded: "why the
hesitation in putting in troops *now*?" "The vast majority of the
public," he assured *Times* readers from his Chelsea address,
"are sick to death of the squalid attempts by the unions to
tyrannise" etcetera. Mr Tennet of Shottermill Ponds, Hasle-
mere, also found (12 December) that the workers were "(mis)-
using their monopoly position," and Richard Hughes, from the
United University Club, suggested "a national one-day token
lock-out (by employers) in support of the . . . Industrial Relations
Bill."

Mr Flamank of Solihull (also 12 December) wanted to see the
formation of "an emergency service corps," which could, at the
Home Secretary's whistle, "move in and run the services."
Those encouraging industrial unrest, "be they communists, shop
stewards or militant students, are just as much our enemies as
were the Nazis." (Perhaps one can hear an echo of Wilbraham
Taylor and the Horse Artillery over Birdcage Walk?)

Such situations tend to make the bourgeois feel, with a sudden
flash of insight, their own value in the world: they bear its weight
and (*vide* the coal-owner) its risks upon their shoulders. "Think
what the feeling would be," exclaimed Lord Midleton (28 June
1926), "if any pit were closed for the day and all wages lost to
the men because the managing and controlling staff required a
day off!" A similar thought occurred to Mr Reade (14 December 1970): "Sir, If manual workers can work to rule, why not
wage clerks too?" Aha! The argument is final: what if we, who
have the money, stopped letting you rotters have it ! ! !

It is not to be thought that in such national emergencies, the
bourgeoisie is solely concerned with such paltry matters as
money or comfort or class power. Not at all: the full moral
idealism blazes out. Thomas Hughes, the Christian Socialist
author of *Tom Brown's Schooldays*, came unhesitatingly to his

post in the correspondence column in 1886: these modern socialists he found to be "notorious ruffians," and "If Mr Chamberlain will consider whether he cannot be getting Messrs Hyndman & Co a year or two's oakum picking instead of 'receiving their views in writing' he would be doing all honest folk more service, in my judgment."

At such moments *Timesian* correspondents always know unhesitatingly what are the thoughts and needs of "all honest folk" or of (see *The Times*, 14 December 1970) "the welfare of the entire community" (Rose Cottage, Westhumble, Surrey). But it was left to the honest folksman, Sir Alan Lascelles (The Old Stables, Kensington Palace), to come forward as shop steward of "an immensely larger union—namely, the union of British citizens" (17 December).

In 1926, however, the immediate requirements of the "entire community" were pointed out to the striking miners in more dulcet tones, since they had made the tragic error of being manoeuvred into a bitter, wasting, strike during the summer months, and the readers of *The Times* were suffering, not from empty grates, but from an over-full sense of moral outrage. At such a time the clergy select themselves as the proper admonishers. The Dean of Worcester advised the miners (8 June 1926) that if they capitulated to the coal-owners' terms they "will have won a great victory—a victory of their nobler over the lower self." The Archdeacon of Chester addressed the same homily with greater fervour: capitulation by the miners "would be good Christianity . . . an act of personal self-denial . . . of personal self-renunciation for the sake of others, following the supreme example of the Greatest Figure in history."

One has yet to notice, in 1970, correspondents congratulating the power workers, who called off their work to rule, on their good Christianity, or likening Frank Chapple to the "Greatest Figure" in history. (Nor did *The Times* publish such congratulations from rural deans in 1926, when the miners returned to their pits defeated; after all, such letters, if read at the pithead, might have induced moral complacency, and, as events were to show, the nation was to expect a good deal more Christianity from the miners in the coming years.)

But—let us be fair—there has been one change in the genre in recent years: the clergy, generally, do not push themselves forward so obtrusively, nor do they presume so readily to express the conscience of the nation on socially-divisive issues. Their role, as national conscience and admonishers of delinquents, has been passed over, in good part, to David Frost and Malcolm Muggeridge. Some small part, perhaps, has been taken over by that new conscience-bearer, the middle class housewife, who, being out of the hurly-burly and puerility of industrial warfare, can watch all things with a wholly objective eye and instantly detect from her kitchen the national interest. Thus, on 11 December, a correspondent from Prescot, Lancs:

". . . the radio is dead. The television is dead. The electric heaters are dead. The kettle is dead. The fridge is dead. My washing machine is dead. My iron is dead . . . Goodness knows how many *tragic* deaths may result . . ."

It is (she concludes) "an exhibition of power surely grotesque in its selfishness."

All dark and comfortless: we stalk the drear world of the psalmist or space-fiction writer: all that inanimate world of consumer goods, animated each quarter by the insertion of money, lies inert, disobedient. All flesh is grass, we know; but what (O ultimate of horrors!) if all gadgets turned out to be grass also? It is the Rebellion of the Robots, recorded by the author of Ecclesiastes.

Grotesque and selfish the power workers' action may have been. How can one know? Facts have been scarcer than homilies. Reading the press one learns that one has been living through little less than cosmic disaster. One had thought that one's neighbours had suffered little more than power cuts for several hours on three or four days, but the mistake is evident. Outside there, in the darkness, the nation had been utterly paralysed for week upon week; invalids dependent upon "continuously operating" kidney machines lived two or three to every street; armed robbers prowled the darkness with impunity; not a hospital in the country that was not lit solely by candles, with surgeons operating upon month-old babies by the light of a failing torch.

A comparatively few individuals, wrote a correspondent from Richmond (12 December), were inflicting upon the public "catastrophic injury." Why not "issue an order *withdrawing all legal protection* from the persons and property of the workers concerned," and the officials of their unions? "Let the community get its own back." This "whole community" (another correspondent, 16 December) "has long been renowned for its patience and forbearance. But surely the time has come," etcetera. "We are sick and tired . . . " "the time has come," "irresponsible" . . . irresponsible *to us*!

What is, of course, "grotesque in its selfishness" is the time-worn hypocrisy of the bourgeois response to discomfort. Anyone familiar with the Victorian and Edwardian press cannot fail to detect, in these tones of moral outrage, that old bourgeois theme for moralisms: the "servant problem." But the servants now are out of reach; an electric light switch is impervious to the scolding of the mistress; a dust-cart cannot be given a week's wages in lieu of notice.

And anyone who has read his E. M. Forster or his Angus Wilson knows the old British bourgeois propensity to moralise his own convenience and to minister to his own comforts under a cloud of altruism. For 95 per cent of the bluster and outrage was the miasma rising from tens of thousands of petty material inconveniences. The electric alarm failed to go off, mummy fell over the dog in the dark, the grill faded with the fillet steak done on one side only, daddy got stuck for half an hour in the lift on the way to a directors' meeting, the children missed *Top of the Pops*, the fridge de-froze all over the soufflé, the bath was lukewarm, there was nothing to do but to go early to a loveless bourgeois bed. But, wait, there was one alternative: "Sir, Writing by candlelight . . ."

But to mention the *real* occasions might seem petty. It was necessary to generalise these inconveniences into a "national interest." The raw fillet steak became an inert kidney-machine, the dripping fridge an unlit operating theatre, the loveless bed became a threat to the "whole community." No matter: now the emergency is over, these moral fantasies will shrink back to their proper size. The shivering old age pensioners (many of whom will continue to shiver all winter through on their inadequate pensions), the imperilled invalids (many of whom will continue in peril from inadequate medical provision), will cease to obtrude themselves in the correspondence columns of *The Times*.

It has been a notable state of national humbug. It was concluded, as in an obligatory ritual, by David Frost, at peak

173

viewing hours on a Saturday night, bullying a few power workers, with a studio audience, handpicked for their utter insensitive self-righteousness, baying at his back.

Occasions were found, not only to express moral disapprobation, but also approval: the audience applauded to the echo nurses who, underpaid as they are, would never strike because of the needs of their patients. David Frost who, from what one has heard, does not face the same financial dilemmas—and the withdrawal of whose labour would scarcely induce even this government to declare a state of "national emergency"—was evidently delighted. The bourgeoisie has always been ready to acknowledge virtue in the servant class when it finds it: pliant, loyal, living patiently in the attic, carrying on dutifully a service to the "whole community." Aubrey Leatham, physician at St George's Hospital, Hyde Park Corner, saluted the same virtue among the cardiac technicians at his hospital (*The Times*, 16 December) who, earning "as little as £415 a year, would like to strike, but they do not, because they are humanitarian."

And how noble they are, indeed, to pace the hearts of emergency patients in the acute care area for only £8 a week! But, surely, if this is so, this also is an outrage, which we should have heard of before, and insistently, and not only as a stick to beat the power workers with? Has Mr Leatham taken up his pen before, to press the astonishing case of his cardiac technicians? Or will he, and the other militant correspondents to *The Times* and so many other papers, relapse into silence now that the inconvenience and discomfort is over?

The grand lesson of the "emergency" was this: the intricate reciprocity of human needs and services—a reciprocity of which we are, every day, the beneficiaries. In our re-ified mental world, we think we are dependent upon *things*. What other people do for us is mediated by inanimate objects: the switch, the water tap, the lavatory chain, the telephone receiver, the cheque through the post. That cheque is where the duties of the good bourgeois end. But let the switch or the tap, the chain or the receiver fail, and then the bourgeois discovers—at once—enormous "oughts" within the reciprocal flow.

But these "oughts" are always the moral obligations of other people: the sewage workers ought not to kill fish, the dustmen ought not to encourage rats, the power workers ought not to imperil invalids, and—this week it will be—the postmen ought not to deny bronchitic old age pensioners of their Christmas parcels from grandchildren in Australia. Why, all these people owe a duty to the "community"!

What the duty of the community is to these people is less firmly stated. Certainly, those whose lolly is the theme of the business supplements—those whose salary increases (like those of admirals and university teachers) are awarded quietly and without fuss, and which (it seems) create no national emergency and no dangerous inflationary pressures—have little need to compose letters to *The Times* as to their own moral obligations and duties.

It is the business of the servant class to serve. And it is the logic of this re-ified bourgeois world that their services are only noticed when they cease. It is only when the dustbins linger in the street, the unsorted post piles up—it is only when the power workers throw across the switches and look out into a darkness of their own making—that the servants know suddenly the great unspoken fact about our society: their own daily power.

[*24 December 1970*]

DEAD ENGLISH

Jeremy Seabrook

The language of suburbia—the language of the English middle class—is a dead language. It is dead because it has so few sources of contemporary enrichment and vitality. It is derivative and unoriginal, and it relies heavily on an imagery that stems from an obsolete popular speech. It is made up principally of set phrases and cliches. It embodies a petrified imagery from some very limited main sources: the natural world; the superseded crafts and skills connected with it; the human body; and warfare and combat. It is the language of an inert society devoid of imagination and inventiveness, living on a linguistic past that is not even its own.

The language is accepted by its speakers as uncritically as many of the values and beliefs implicit in it. Graphic and vivid when it was still relevant to the way of life out of which it arose, it has become ossified in middle class mouths. Of the many thousands of commonplaces which make up this dead linguistic heritage, I have been recording a sample—some of them set out under headings on pages 178 and 179—from conversations over the past few weeks.

The chief feature these survivals have in common is the fact that they postulate a world of elemental simplicity. Few of the actions to which they refer bear any relation to the preoccupations of middle class life. They have become figurative and allusive designations of something quite different. Not many people set hand to the plough, separate the wheat from the chaff, make a killing, make a last-ditch stand, sail near to the wind, pay the piper or find a hard nut to crack. These expressions have been extended to cover a wide range of human situations, which they indicate only obliquely. Their homely reverberations often conceal, rather than illuminate, the context in which they are used.

Their very vagueness lends itself to an (often tendentious) avoidance of calling activities by their right name. For instance, the borrowed imagery that describes economic activity attempts to modify the harshness of things that could be expressed in far more precise terms: "to feather one's nest," "to live from hand to mouth," "to keep the pot boiling," "to paddle one's own canoe," "to keep the wolf from the door," "to bring grist to the mill," "to stand on one's own two feet," "to get one's fingers burnt," "to be on one's uppers," "to save up for a rainy day," "to play ducks and drakes with," "to rob Peter to pay Paul." This is the language of *Daily Telegraph* leaders. It manages to evoke a world of primeval simplicity, of the farmyard and the chase, a life in close harmony with nature, a life of reassuring comprehensibility.

The language of politicians betrays the same devices. In recent years there has been a recurrence of picturesque imagery that modifies some fairly unacceptable realities: being blown off course, going cap in hand, drawing the teeth of, putting one's house in order, lame ducks and so on. Such expressions diminish and abate the actions which they are intended to represent. Behind the defunct imagery lies the same rural nostalgia that is evident in the manufactured Arcadia of suburban estates, the products of the garden-centre industry: storm lanterns and house names on rough-hewn varnished pieces of tree, cartwheels incorporated into front gates, wheelbarrows overflowing onto concrete driveways with lobelia and alyssum.

If the language expresses anything at all, it is a yearning for remote times when life may have corresponded to the imagery mummified in everyday speech. People long to go on wild-goose chases, to make hay while the sun shines, to beat about the bush, to take a horse to water, not to be able to see the wood for the trees and to sow their wild oats. It is a congealed urban dream of a sham rural life—for people who are trapped in commuter trains, immured in offices, clubhouses and private estates. It is part of the entrenched myth about struggling to survive, as though the speakers really were compelled to pit themselves against the elements. It is a fabricated game for people whose lives are safe and unassailable.

The dead imagery is a screen behind which to hide social realities. Despite their apparently vivid pictorial quality, the images make situations look homely and familiar; they eliminate moral complexity. The indefensible can be justified by recourse to a graphic cliche or proverb. It is reassuring to nip something in the bud, kill two birds with one stone, know you can't make a silk purse out of a sow's ear, not to stir up a hornet's nest, drive a coach and horses through something or to take the wind out of someone's sails.

But the familiar phrases do not only give us the consoling illusion that we understand, and can cope with, the world we live in and all its contingencies. Often there is also an implicit moral judgment. People shouldn't play fast and loose, blow hot and cold, be unable to see beyond their nose, make mountains out of molehills, have bees in their bonnets, fish in troubled waters, build castles in the air, kick over the traces. These phrases, which present themselves so readily, diminish the ability to assess situations objectively, because of their ready-made judgment.

THE NATURAL WORLD

bear fruit
let the grass grow under one's feet
leave no stone unturned
cut and dried
the apple of one's eye
nipped in the bud
no rose without a thorn
a shrinking violet
break the ice
a wild goose chase
in the clouds
make an ass of
sail close to the wind
be on thorns
draw in one's horns
a duck to water
a bolt from the blue

feather one's nest
throw into the shade
clip the wings of
hair of the dog that bit one
as the crow flies
a fish out of water
welcome as the flowers in May
a fair-weather friend
see daylight
root and branch
dull as ditchwater
weather the storm
move heaven and earth
salt of the earth
birds of a feather
a bed of roses
be in clover

CRAFTS AND SKILLS

grist to the mill
shoulder to the wheel
the thin end of the wedge
upset the applecart
hit the nail on the head
plough a lonely furrow
irons in the fire
put the cart before the horse
strike while the iron is hot

take the bull by the horns
bolt the stable door
off the beaten track
out of the wood
be in a rut
have an axe to grind
be in the saddle
hammer home

THE HUMAN BODY

more than flesh and blood can stand	fight tooth and nail
put one's back up	stand head and shoulders above
put one's best foot forward	wash one's hands of
lead by the nose	make one's heart bleed
get one's fingers burnt	cut to the quick
take the bit between the teeth	not have a leg to stand on
make one's blood boil	keep at arm's length
keep body and soul together	at breakneck speed
pull a long face	fall on deaf ears

COMBAT

stand one's ground	draw the long bow
armed to the teeth	keep at bay
ride full tilt at	take up the cudgels
show no quarter	up in arms
cross swords with	bite the dust
fall foul of	with flying colours
take by storm	wide of the mark

A whole philosophy, even, lies beneath the phrases and axioms, the (apparently) small talk and the obligatory conversational responses. The existing social structure perpetuates and defends itself most effectively with its words—evasive, adamant and impregnable. The spurious folk-wisdom creates a barrier against innovation and change. Proverbs merge into belief and opinion, the truth of which is felt to be just as self-evident as that contained in the ancient primitive imagery.

What is this philosophy? God helps those who help themselves. Don't upset the applecart, don't throw a spanner in the works. It's a rat race. It's dog eat dog. Don't swim against the stream/go against the grain. Everybody's out for number one. It's human nature. It'll all be the same in a 100 years' time. It wouldn't do for us all to be the same. We must have been put here for a purpose.

The middle class, perhaps even more than the working class, is at the mercy of the set phrase, the idea sanctioned by constant iteration. Words, maxims, proverbs, exercise a tyranny over our view of the world. Conflicting ideas have far more difficulty in finding expression. Conversations *generate* people's views,

179

instead of being a vehicle for them. In this way, opinions are formed arbitrarily, haphazardly.

Sometimes, if they are challenged on some especially illiberal idea contained within the cliches, people reply: "Oh, did I really say that? Well, of course, I didn't mean it." It is as though they see themselves as merely the passive intermediaries of ideas they bear no responsibility for—like entranced mediums, conveying messages from beyond the grave.

The strength of inertia and conservatism don't always derive from a conviction that tradition and the existing order represent the best form of social organisation. It stems from the failure of any of the complex or challenging alternatives to make any headway—locked away, as they are, in unfamiliar, threatening forms of expression.

[*25 March 1971*]

... in a plural world,

THE PATTERN OF CITIES TO COME

Peter Hall

Eight and a half million more people by 1980, 20 million more by the end of the century: for this cause alone, the need to build a town the size of Bournemouth, or Wolverhampton, or Bolton every four months to the year 2000. Smaller and smaller households: over 150,000 new households formed every year, demanding new homes. And on top, the remaining backlog of slums in the northern and Scottish towns. The housing programme now tops 400,000 a year; the National Plan promises 500,000 by 1970, the equivalent of a Leeds or Sheffield every four months. After that, perhaps a respite: estimates like those by the Town and Country Planning Association give an average of round about 400,000 a year up to the early 1980s. But if households go on showing fissile tendencies—if they go on fissing, as Dr David Eversley puts it—the total may go higher.

Only a few years ago, planners were still found who thought that all these millions could be squeezed into our existing conurbations, through ever grander versions of Corbusier's 40 year old *Ville Radieuse*. Now, few doubt that most new building will appropriate farmland. This is not just due to the size of the problem. There is the realisation also that very high densities can only give a big bonus in house-space by sacrificing open space, as was underlined by the Chelsea-LCC row about the World's End development. And there was the definitive contribution of Professor Gerald Wibberley, who showed that the loss of food production could be made up by more efficiency on the remaining farmland. Recently Wibberley made the most reasonable estimates he could about population and income growth, productivity and food imports, and concluded that by 1970 British agriculture could work efficiently with 5 per cent less average quality land than in 1960. That means $1\frac{1}{2}$ million less acres. And Wibberley's colleague at Wye College, Dr Robin Best, calculates that urban growth in England and Wales will need less than a million acres between 1960 and 1980, only two million up to the end of the century. By 2000, according to Best,

84 per cent of England and Wales will still be free of building. Even in the south east the figure should be about 81 per cent—though round London it will be much less.

This seems remarkable; it is. Best has shown that we use up less farmland every year for housing than in the 1930s despite a bigger population and a bigger housing programme. The United States uses up 30 times as much—or, correcting for a fourfold population, eight times. Landbound Englishmen, who spend their lives in suburbs, may doubt this; they should take to the air. Coming over the Atlantic, a city like Bristol appears astonishingly small compared with its American equivalents. All this stems from the national system of land use planning initiated by the 1947 Planning Act, which has allowed local planning authorities to keep urban areas within limits and to stop residential areas from sprawling too widely. New housing in Britain is commonly built at twelve, 15 or even more to the acre; in the United States the typical figure is one or two. Between Washington and Boston, Megalopolis USA is in danger of becoming a nightmare physical reality; between London and Manchester, Megalopolis England is a long way off yet.

That is no cause for complacency: a book like Lionel Brett's *Landscape in Distress* showed that on the outer fringes of suburbia, planning reality may be far from planning ideals. Researchers in the USA and Britain are hoping to start this autumn a comparative study of patterns of urbanisation in their respective Megalopolitan regions, which should yield useful lessons. But characteristically, the British programme lacks funds. This underlines a general point. If American planning suffers from a plethora of research and no action, British planning suffers from a surfeit of physical plans based on inadequate research data. And, in such a context, old ideas can survive after they cease to be useful.

Planning needs machinery and ideas. When in 1947 machinery was provided, the ideas had been maturing a half century. In 1898, against the background of Victorian slumdom, Ebenezer Howard wrote a book which influenced planners the world over: *Garden Cities of Tomorrow*. Howard's basic concern, as that of any good Victorian, was sanitary: in place of the dark, overcrowded, unhealthy Victorian city he advocated the self-

184

contained small town surrounded by farmland, where people would live and work in close contact with nature.

In the five decades between Howard's book and the 1947 Act, only two garden cities were built in England, and the idea itself froze until it found realisation in the postwar generation of new towns. Only two new concepts had been grafted on by then. One was the idea of twelve houses to the acre planning, established by the Tudor Walters housing report of 1918. Though Howard's original plan had much higher densities of nearly a hundred people to the acre, the report, like the book, was a reaction against Victorian slumdom. The other was the neighbourhood unit, borrowed from the American Clarence Perry in the 1920s; but even that was foreshadowed in Howard's own plan.

The new towns of the late 1940s, therefore, were conceived within an early 20th century context. The basic obsessions within them were sanitary (open space, nearness to countryside, sunlight, separation of homes and factories) or social (neighbourhoods, short journeys to work or to shop). They reflected a world which now seems to be passing away: a traditional, static, rather immobile world. But perhaps the truth is that the world of 1947 was really like that. We do not know, until we look back at the popular newspapers and magazines of that time, how different we were. Society then, for a great majority of the less prosperous, had moved little since 1914. It bore a greater similarity to the contemporary USSR than to contemporary Britain. Car ownership, for instance, was lower than in 1938: there were less than two million cars, compared with nine million today. Towns like Hemel Hempstead were built on the assumption that a small minority of the population would ever own cars. So lessons from outside were ignored. In the America of the early 1930s, when car ownership levels were near those of Britain now, Clarence Stein designed outside Paterson in New Jersey a township that gave its name to a principle of planning: Radburn. His principle—complete segregation of the circulation system for vehicles and pedestrians—was ignored in British new towns until the early 1960s.

Meanwhile, the early 1950s marked a moratorium on new town building: none were designated between Corby in 1949 and Cumbernauld in 1956. Since then, the number of designations has risen in an ever steepening curve, marking official

185

recognition of the challenge of the population projections. In the decade since Cumbernauld, counting in the major town expansions, well over a score of new towns have been born. Many of these are still on the drawing boards, and the future pattern of life for millions of people is being settled in passionate debates round planners' conference tables. Never in the history of British planning has such a ferment of discussion taken place. The new towns to emerge so far are not, like the Mark One towns of the 1940s, cast all in a similar mould. Instead they represent different, and in some cases violently opposed, responses to the twin challenges of continued population growth and universal car ownership.

Population growth means flexible planning. Designed in a static context of negligible population growth, the Mark One new towns made no provision for future expansion: and when a later generation tried to expand them, as at Harlow and, above all, Stevenage, a rich host of problems resulted. To provide simply for physical expansion of a town should lead to no overwhelming problem, given that the town is properly sited: the trouble is the extra strain on transport, on public services like colleges and hospitals, and above all on the town centre. A properly planned town will exist in a state of equilibrium, and one part cannot be increased without an effect on the functioning of all the others. For the future, it looks as if this will have to be met by reserving space for growth, either horizontally (reservations for extra lanes on urban motorways, ground level car parks that can be turned into shops), or vertically (extra floors on buildings in central area buildings). But the bigger problem is to accommodate the car.

The problem is not one merely of finding space for the moving or standing vehicle: it is that as American experience abundantly shows, under the impact of the car the city naturally explodes. Statistically it can be shown that in western North American cities, which developed almost wholly within the automobile era, dependence on the car is almost complete for most journeys, housing densities are very low (which alone makes effective public transport almost impossible) and town centres in the traditional European or eastern North American sense are almost non-existent. Los Angeles, the archetype of such towns, has a population almost as big as Greater London but a central

186

area workforce smaller than Glasgow or Manchester. The planner, whose historically based training gives him a profound respect for traditional European urban virtues, finds this outcome impossible to contemplate; and here lies his central dilemma today.

The first British planner to grapple with this problem, nearly a decade ago, was Hugh Wilson in his epoch-making plan for Cumbernauld. In a sense, all British new town plans since are responses to the challenge which Cumbernauld sets. Not merely in British but in world-wide terms, the intellectual impact of this bleak Scottish hilltop town can be set against the ideas of Howard, or Corbusier, or Sven Markelius's Stockholm planners of the 1950s.

For the first time in Britain, Wilson started to design a town on the assumption that every family would eventually own and use a car. His answer, which planners have argued about ever since, was to provide for completely free car movement on a graded hierarchy of roads, all except the most local of them built as motorways; but to encourage as many people as possible to walk to work and school and shop. Logically, this can only be done by pressing everyone close together. Wilson therefore puts 50,000 of his 70,000 people in a tightly huddled mass within walking distance of a multi-level town centre, at densities up to 80 or 90 to the acre, and without need for neighbourhoods. This inner town is then Radburnised in a very simple way: one inner loop swings through it, intersected by pedestrian underpasses.

Cumbernauld cannot yet be judged. The critical point will come soon, when the first part of the shopping centre is opened: will the people take the hard walk up the hill? Still more it will come when most have cars, and try to drive them to the centre—and that, for the many who came here from the slums of Gorbals and Anderston, is some way off yet. Yet again it will come if pressure arises to expand the town, for the *raison d'être* of the town is its compactness.

One thing though is clear: Cumbernauld is totally un-English. Architecturally, it is a north European town, whose affinities are with Hässelby Strand or Tapiola rather than with anything south of Carlisle. Socially, Wilson has brilliantly exploited a traditional Scots willingness to crowd together in towns. It can be forgotten that in Scotland the owner-occupied semi is a negligible force and that in their physical compactness Glasgow and Edinburgh are more like French towns than English ones. It would be a hard job indeed to adapt Cumbernauld to traditional English preconceptions about housing; and it is a tragedy that the only authority willing to take on the experiment, the LCC in its plan for Hook, was prevented at the last hour from carrying it out.

Cumbernauld then remains the only realised Mark Two new town. The English Mark Three towns that have been designed in its shadow—Dawley, Redditch, Runcorn and Skelmersdale—have taken a looser form, with maximum densities around 60 or 70 to the acre; and in all the neighbourhood unit reappears, though apparently no one cares give it its proper name. The new feature, compared with the Mark One towns, is the application of Radburn planning and the concentration of traffic flows on to a skeletal network of high capacity roads. Two of the Mark Threes—Redditch, designed by Wilson himself in cooperation with former Sheffield city architect Lewis Womersley, and Arthur Ling's Runcorn—are distinguished by special reserved busways, which are intended to put a high proportion of the peak hour flows (50 per cent in Runcorn) on to public transport. Critics already are arguing that this is an uneconomic solution because it does not provide necessary flexibility between public transport and the high flows of private cars which will increasingly be accommodated at evenings and weekends. Certainly the recent American study by Mayer, Kain and Wohl—*The Urban Transportation Problem*—comes out strongly on economic grounds in favour of a single pipe form of transport for most average sized towns.

One town design only so far can be said to reflect the influence of Californian views about the car. From the planning school at Berkeley, a couple of years back, Melvin Webber advanced the revolutionary hypothesis that European and American planners had been too obsessed with traditional forms rather than the way towns performed functions—in particular the essential function of getting people and goods about. Los Angeles, the traditional planner's nightmare, was in Webber's view at least as efficient as traditional cities because it provided for a multiplicity of high speed car journeys to and from a host of dispersed locations; its lack of centralisation, often dismissed as a vice, was in reality its great virtue. In Washington, County Durham, Llewelyn Davies, Weeks and Partners have created an interim plan for a town in the Webber image, with highly decentralised factory jobs and a uniform road grid which will take large numbers of crisscross car journeys without the need for elaborate intersections. This is the antithesis of Cumbernauld planning; but perhaps it could never have been designed without Cumbernauld's initial challenge.

But all these towns are traditional in one vital respect. They are designed within rigid size limits not much greater than those of the Mark One towns—generally between 70,000 and 90,000. Only in very recent years have planners begun to argue for a much larger size of urban unit. This is perhaps the most fundamental shift of all in our planning assumptions: and its long run implications are incalculable. It represents a complete break with the obsessions of an older generation of planners—the need for close access to countryside, the need to cut journeys to walking scale, the need to embrace a size and shape of town which any one of its inhabitants could grasp. It represents instead a new set of concerns with the minimum scale necessary for certain sorts of human activity: the minimum size of labour market necessary to provide choice of skilled jobs for the worker and choice of skilled applicants for the employer, the minimum size of shopping centre necessary to support a Marks and Spencer store (probably about 70,000 including the hinterland), the minimum size of labour force necessary to avoid dependence on one large factory (Stevenage with 55,000 is too small, according to Professor John H. Dunning), the minimum size needed to give a professional worker 20 interesting friends (a million, according to Professor Sargant Florence).

These questions are being asked, mainly because of a new planner's hunch about an obvious truth: counter magnets to London and other great cities must have the quality of magnetism. Because of the lack of a firm research base, it cannot be said that the planners are getting anything like adequate answers yet. Considering, for instance, the interest geographers have traditionally shown in urban hierarchies, it is astonishing to find that there is no comprehensive study of British retail centres and the sorts of shops found in them. Perhaps the answers will get better, given the money—for isolated studies of conurbations are now being made; but since geography departments are refused an allocation from the Social Science Research Council, it seems doubtful. Meanwhile, planners must plan.

And the trend in their hunches is plain. In the *South East Study* two years ago, the favoured size is just under 200,000. New cities at Bletchley and Newbury are to have 175,000; expansions at Ipswich and Peterborough and Northampton will be taken up to the same level. The idea in last summer's *West Midlands Study* for a development embracing Dawley and Wellington and Oakengates would have about 200,000 people and falls into this pattern; so does the proposal in the *North West Study* for a new town at Leyland. These would be towns which in size fall somewhere between Wolverhampton and Plymouth, and they should be able to provide an appropriate range of retail and other services.

But meanwhile the scale of thinking has escalated. Already the *South East Study* provided for a new conurbation to be produced by linking Southampton and Portsmouth, with over a million people in the future. The *Northampton-Bedford-North Bucks Study*, by Wilson and Womersely, proposes to put 200,000 into Bletchley new city, 100,000 more into Northampton and 60,000 more into Bedford; by the end of the century it suggests that linear growth between these centres, along communication lines, could provide another new conurbation with over a million people. Similarly, the *West Midlands Study* wants an immediate close look at the idea of a million people in a new conurbation between Dawley and Shrewsbury.

Since the British are arguably a nation of conurbation dwellers, the idea of planned new conurbations could be attractive to planner and planned. But again, the motor car presents the intractable problem. All previous experience shows that as urban areas get bigger it is progressively more difficult to accommodate more cars in their centres. The case studies in the Buchanan report underline this; so does a proposal like the Smigielski plan for Leicester, which would need £135 million to provide for very limited car access; so do theoretical studies like those of Professor Reuben Smeed, which show that to get everyone to work in cars along narrow streets and using ground-level car parks, in a central area employing a million, would require 77 per cent of the ground area to be devoted to the car. But cities like Los Angeles partly overcome this by decentralisation of function—though even there, over a half of the central area is devoted to roads and parking.

The moral would seem to be that new conurbations should be *polycentric* (on the model of the West Midlands or the Ruhr) rather than *monocentric* (on the model of London or Paris). Further, the central area functions like shops and offices should go as far as possible into new centres built round the car, on the model of American regional shopping centres (Roosevelt Field, Northlands) or Stockholm suburban centres (Vällingby, Farsta). But here conurbation planners will face a larger version of a dilemma currently faced by town expansion planners in towns like Ipswich, Peterborough or Northampton. Shopping and other services are firmly tied to existing congested central districts.

Unlike their North American counterparts, British shopping and property interests resolutely refuse to countenance flight from the city. They believe that the British housewife will continue to shop by public transport and they intend to stay where public transport is concentrated now. So the idea of tempting Marks and Spencer, or the big department store chains, out to a new centre in the early stages of construction, is not worth contemplating. But if the alternative is the reconstruction of a small county town to meet the demands of a conurbation of a million souls, that is not something the planner will willingly contemplate either. Here could be one of the major problems facing British planning in the 1970s.

If this challenge is met, the idea of the planned conurbation could well prove the most important concept in British planning since Howard's Garden City. (And in fairness it must be said that the germ of the conurbation idea was in Howard too.) It could provide for the diverse needs and aspirations of a society that is in many ways richer than ours today. It could embrace a great variety of urban forms and living conditions: the expanded town, the new city, the Swedish *Studentstaden*, the sort of planned new village Span is building at Hartley, the spec-built new town for owner-occupiers on the model of American towns like Reston and Columbia. Within such a physical framework, following the ideas now being developed by regional planners in

New York, people could have the choice of opting for what they most valued: nearness to transport (but higher densities), more garden space (but dependence on the car). But the realisation of this idea will demand two intellectual jumps on the part of planners.

First, it means an end to all the old, simple, all or nothing ideas about town functions, which docketed this as a commuter town, that as a self-contained town for factory workers. People —even members of the same family—can no longer be pigeon-holed so neatly. Secondly and perhaps even more importantly, it demands a new attitude to open space. Instead of *cordons sanitaires* of agricultural land many miles wide, protecting each town from the corrupting influence of the next, we need to think about setting the pieces of our new conurbations within a con-tinuous country park, of the sort foreshadowed in the new white paper on leisure. We need to think of whole suburbs wrapped round lakes, artificial if needs be, as the Swedes do so brilliantly at Hässelby Strand and the Americans at Reston. We need to think of active *conversion* of ploughland to high intensity recrea-tional use. We need to think of new types of planning and local government authorities, capable of the novel job of running a conurbation in a park. We need an end to the conservative atti-tude that rallies to the barricades every time a southern English town advances within six miles of another. In short, we need re-education in planning.

[*10 March 1966*]

SOMEWHERE TOTALLY ELSE

Reyner Banham

The desert is not diminished by the freeway; rather, it gains a new visual dimension from the twin streaks of black receding perfectly straight, perfectly parallel and in perfect perspective towards a notch in the bony hills on the far side of the basin. For the gasping ox-teams of the pioneers it must have been chiefly a serial experience in sweated time—from the shade of this rock, down into the bottom of that dry wash, up to the joshua tree on the other side, on to the salt stain beyond, and on, and on, the desert measured out in short successive stages, one after the other.

The freeway ignores such minor dramas, and offers instead a vision of instant and measurable immensity. As the car comes clear of one ridge, the eye can read, in the perspective of the carriageways, the distance to the next ridge: ten, twelve, fourteen miles. Checked against the mileage on the speedometer, the eye proves dauntingly accurate. It really was the estimated 14 miles—without habitation, help or human comfort.

For the freeway makes the desert no less hostile; 25 yards from the kerb it remains untouched, as it has always been. And all too frequently along the highway is inscribed the memento mori of the motor age—a pair of black wheelmarks looping and veering from side to side of the road and finally leaping the kerb into the desert, or, worse, ending in a circle of incinerated asphalt. A big Greyhound bus rolled and burned here recently; you wonder how it could possibly have happened: mechanical failure, boredom, hallucination?

The tyre marks always end in mystery, for the highway patrol and the towing services are more tidy-minded than vultures, which at least left the proverbial whitening skull as a memorial. But it is Unlawful to Litter Highway, and the remains have vanished. So you wonder; and when the sense of "There but for the grace of God ..." gets too strong, you pull off the road, even though it is Emergency Parking Only, to investigate.

The car humps over the kerb, and you feel the tyres bite into

193

the ancient unweathered gravel, that makes the steering handle as if on fresh wet snow, but with the sound of a small landslide. And you get out into the hard, grey sunlight, the heat, and the silence so utter that a sprig of dry tumbleweed (or something) hopping along the road in the wind can be heard clicking and tapping a couple of hundred yards away.

In the distance, beyond the cardboard saw-teeth of the nearer hills, a lake of dry soda gleams. Wet soda pools tend to be a putrid rusty yellow, but dried out soda flats reflect an almost fluorescent silver-through-blue glare. You feel you must be on the moon—until you ask yourself where on earth the early space-illustrators could have gone for visual analogues of the moonscapes described to them by the astronomers. Much as the smoking tar-pits of Mesopotamia gave horrible substance to Old Testament visions of Hell and Gehenna, the deserts of the south western us are the reality behind many science-fiction visions of worlds that do not support "life as we have known it."

Across this prospect of somewhere totally else, the town of Baker can be discerned at a distance of ten miles by the west-bound traveller. It cannot be discerned as a town; the glitter of its roofs and windows is seen as little more than an intensification of the flicker of the heat haze. But the map has shown it to lie by a bend in the freeway caused by a small mountain, and the bend and the mountain are plain to see.

In fact, Baker's main street is simply a road that goes on straight when the highway bends, and as you slow down to a decent urban speed, the sign by the roadside says simply: Baker, Calif; Pop 300, Elev 930. And what, in the name of humanity, are three hundred souls doing at this elevation in the middle of this wilderness?

What they are doing is manning a way-station, a relay, on the route from Los Angeles to Las Vegas; a plastic oasis of motels and filling stations and restaurants, whose boundaries are marked by two giant signs on the edge of the freeway—one, to the east, for the Bun Boy, and one to the west for Pike's restaurant. Each of these is a complete motor-age caravanserai, with its own motel and filling station and, at present, they seem to be most of the action in the town.

But an older oasis lurks underneath: unmodern buildings of uncertain age huddle in groves of dry, but well-grown, desert trees. Two dry washes, empty but bridged over to clear occasional flash floods, cross the main street, and between them another road comes in from the north, from Badwater and Furnace Creek and Shoshone, one of the escape trails from the infernal chemical beauties of Death Valley, beside which even the soda lakes must seem almost friendly.

It's a crossroads town, like a hundred thousand others in the US, and it even has a corner drugstore of sorts. But it is difficult to find another place which so blankly confronts man and desert, so shockingly spans backward through geological time from the sophisticated technologies of today to a condition of the earth's crust before men were on it, when raw chemicals lay about and the first accidental proteins had barely begun the game of life.

How can inherently damp and juicy creatures such as men survive in this almost totally arid environment? Baker's domestic water comes from three hundred feet down; I didn't see a single brackish drop above ground. And they are not merely surviving; they aren't even fighting back the desert, they are scampering about its surface, *playing* with it.

In the bottom of the wash, three generations of dune-buggy maniacs were preparing to move off. Their vehicles were neatly finished home-made improvisations; bare skeletons with two seats amidships and an air-cooled Volkswagen or Corvair engine stuck out the back between broad oversize tyres.

There were jump-seats for the kids set high ahead of the engines, and the youngest members of the party, who ranged down to about three and a half, were dressed in that international standard junior gear of striped T-shirts and very short shorts. The middle generation were dressed as for the garden or for Sunday car-washing. Only grandpop, who was wagonmaster and had a pennant on his radio aerial, was dressed in proper Western threads—heavy denim shirt and slacks, an old curly Stetson. He also seemed to have a genuine Western script-writer.

"Ah love thuh desert," he said. "Used to live on thuh coast, work for thuh State of Calafornuh, got muhself transferred up here. Wouldn't move 'way agin." Sighs, squares shoulders, ruminates. "Ain't no two ways 'bout it; yuh either loves thuh desert or yuh hates it . . . Ah love it!"

The sons finished tinkering with the carburettor of the newest buggy, the kids were strapped in, everybody got aboard and

195

they bumped away through a dust cloud that hung about in vertical curtains long after their exhausts had ceased to echo. Just as they vanished, the old man raised his hand in the kind of simple, manly and unaffected salute that Ronald Reagan could never quite manage, and threw me a strong leathery smile of teeth.

Every Sunday is an adventure for them—for real. On those tyres they don't have to stick even to the gravel roads, but can light out into really mean country. And if that carb should go on the blink again, there would have to be a real desert rescue operation. So it's Frontiersmanship of the Age of Fun, but don't be too quick to put it down. It's radically different even from skiing or trying to body-surf that ultimate wave down the side of the breakwater at Newport Harbour. Those are sudden-death sports, whose lure is that the rewards of error are instantaneous and very permanent.

But the desert and its addicts are something else. The fascinations have a slow burn, etch the mind with a value system of the enduring and contemplative type, however desperate the action may sometimes be. The beauty of the scenery is always mentioned, even by those whose puritan rationalisations are pass-storming or prospecting for minerals. They are hooked on some private, dry, pitiless Nirvana, and they are really *gone*— Arid-heads, I suppose. One was talking to me through the window of the car, and—in the flash of sunlight reflected from the windscreen of a lorry as it turned—his eyes appeared completely empty and golden, as if he had just foot-slogged in from the pages of Ray Bradbury's *The Illustrated Man*.

That kind of people are explicable up in the high desert, but there are quite normal-seeming inhabitants of Baker as well. One was behind the cash register of the Bun Boy; one of those unquenchable, bomb-proof, good-humour gals who makes the world go round instead of square—and by the look of her build, was going to make it Pop 301 in about a month. As she passed over my change, I asked if she could explain something for me.

"Sure; what is it?"

"Well, as I came into Baker today I got sort of lost, off the highway (a lie, but I needed a gambit, because I *had* to know) and round the back of the trailer camp (draws map with finger) was this weird kind of concentration camp, with a wire fence

196

around it, you know?" She gave me a funny look, but laughed. "It's not a concentration camp. The telephone company built it for its employees . . ."

"What's the fence for, then?"

"Keeps the rattlesnakes out . . . all those families with little kids . . . lots of rattlers out there in the desert."

"Ah, that's it, rattlesnakes. I couldn't work it out at all."

"Uh-huh. I wouldn't have known about it either, only my husband works for the telephone company and I, like, live there . . ."

Musing on the paradoxes of working for anything as plastic and domestic as the telephone company from behind a 6 foot snake-fence, I went out into the neon evening. The sky was black and a million miles deep between the stars, and the stars didn't twinkle because the atmosphere was too clean. The scent of charcoal-grilled steak hung on the heavy, cooling air, and the parking lot between the Bun Boy, the gas-station and the Golden Choya motel had suddenly filled up with sports cars on trailers —there had been a race meeting up at Vegas, and Baker is the first stop on the way back to Los Angeles.

Any motorised occasion of this sort is a kind of apotheosis for Baker, which largely lives by and for the automobile, mediates between it and the desert. And if the desert can break, burn or swallow a car, it is curiously tender with its metal parts. With age they are apparently transmuted into more noble materials for nothing really rusts up here in the normal damp sense. Old corrugated iron finally takes a powdery brown coating but the castings and forging of automotive technology will assume an antique patina or—since Ray Bradbury comes constantly to mind up here—take on the oblique gleam of rare Martian earths.

The raw elements of metal seem to preen themselves in the sun of this landscape where raw minerals are at home, where the beer-can by the highway gleams for many a summer in rustless impunity, while the exiguous and bitter tufts of vegetation have to space themselves out (to be sure of their share of the available traces of moisture) in a pattern that exhibits the concepts of both "territoriality" and "the struggle for existence" in a natural statistical diagram.

The pattern of these tufts is so regular that you know you are looking at the bare mathematics of survival, the odds that the

197

citizens of Baker are cheating with their access to subterranean water far beyond the reach of any creature but man.

And at the thought "creature," you know what's wrong, who's missing. Where are the camels? To any common English reader of my generation, brought up on T. E. Lawrence almost from birth, Doughty and Scawen Blunt from adolescence, a desert must almost automatically contain camels, and hawk-nosed figures swathed in the burnous. In the deserts of the Old World, the automobile has been preceded by Alexander the Great, Hannibal, sundry Caesars, the true and only Prophet of Allah, and by a whole culture evolved by the Prophet's followers; a culture which, for us, is as native and proper to the desert as Christianity to temperate north west Europe.

But here, hardly anything nor anybody preceded the Anglo-Saxon and his automobile. Even Indian and Spanish names—Shoshone, Amargosa—are few and very far between; most of the geography speaks English with painful directness: Good-springs, Furnace Creek, Chloride Cliff, Ash Meadows, Devil's Playground, and just plain godawful *Sands*. Hardly a breathing soul was here before us, and we have been here barely a hundred years yet.

There is no legend, history or myth between us and the desert to absorb the culture shock. Walk over a little ridge so the car is out of sight, and you are as spiritually unprotected as you are physically. Drive hurriedly back to Baker to the security of the motel. Security? Look down at the floor; the window comes right down to the ground, and where the carpet stops, the desert begins.

That's what the place is all about—in one step you can go from carpeted comfort to something so totally else that you have to wonder if that wire fence is to keep rattlesnakes out, or for something far worse—to prevent the normal amenities of civilisation seeping beyond control into the desert and being swallowed irretrievably in that unweathered and unforgiving gravel.

[*28 March 1968*]

TOKYO PASTORAL

Angela Carter

This is clearly one of those districts where it always seems to be Sunday afternoon. Somebody in a house by the corner shop is effortlessly practising Chopin on the piano. A dusty cat rolls in the ruts of the unpaved streetlet, yawning in the sunshine. Somebody's aged granny trots off to the supermarket for a litre or two of honourable saki. Her iron-grey hair is scraped into so tight a knot in the nape, no single hair could ever stray untidily out, and her decent, drab kimono is enveloped in the whitest of enormous aprons, trimmed with a sober frill of cotton lace—the kind of apron one associates with Victorian nursemaids.

She is bent to a full hoop because of all the babies she has carried on her back and she bows formally before she shows a socially acceptable quantity of her gold-rimmed teeth in a dignified smile. Frail, omnipotent granny who wields a rod of iron behind the paper walls.

This is a district peculiarly rich in grannies, cats and small children. We are a 60 yen train ride from the Marunouchi district, the great business section; and a 60 yen train ride in the other direction from Shinjuku, where there is the world's largest congregation of strip shows, clip joints and Turkish baths. We are a petty bourgeois enclave of perpetual Sunday wedged between two mega-highways.

The sounds are: the brisk swish of broom on tatami matting, the raucous cawing of hooded crows in a nearby willow grove; clickety-clackety rattle of chattering housewives, a sound like briskly plied knitting needles, for Japanese is a language full of TS and KS; and, in the mornings, the crowing of a cock. The nights have a rustic tranquillity. We owe our tranquillity entirely to faulty town planning; these streets are far too narrow to admit cars. The smells are: cooking; sewage; fresh washing.

It is difficult to find a boring part of Tokyo but, by God, I have done it. It is a very respectable neighbourhood and has the prim charm and the inescapable accompanying ennui of respectability.

Tokyo pastoral

I can touch the walls of the houses on either side by reaching out my arm and the wall of the house at the back by stretching out my hand, but the fragile structures somehow contrive to be detached, even if there is only a clearance of inches between them, as though they were stating emphatically that privacy, even if it does not actually exist, is, at least, a potential. Most homes draw drab, grey skirts of breeze-block walls around themselves with the touch-me-not decorum of old maids, but even the tiniest of gardens boasts an exceedingly green tree or two and the windowsills bristle with potted plants.

Our neighbourhood is too respectable to be picturesque but, nevertheless, has considerable cosy charm, a higgledy-piggledy huddle of brown-grey shingled roofs and shining spring foliage. In the mornings, gaudy quilts, brilliantly patterned mattresses and cages of singing birds are hung out to air on the balconies. If the Japanese aesthetic ideal is a subfusc, harmonious austerity, the cultural norm is a homey, cheerful clutter. One must cultivate cosiness; cosiness makes overcrowding tolerable. Symmetrical lines of very clean washing blow in the wind. You could eat your dinner off the children. It is an area of white collar workers; it is a good area.

The absolute domestic calm is disturbed by little more than the occasional bicycle or a boy on a motorbike delivering a trayful of lacquer noodle bowls from the cafe on the corner for somebody's lunch or supper. In the morning, the men go off to work in business uniform (dark suits, white nylon shirts); in the afternoon, schoolchildren loll about eating ice-cream. High school girls wear navy-blue pleated skirts and sailor tops, very Edith Nesbitt, and high school boys wear high-collared black jackets and peaked caps, inexpressibly Maxim Gorki.

At night, a very respectable drunk or two staggers, giggling, down the hill. A pragmatic race, the Japanese appear to have decided long ago that the only reason for drinking alcohol is to become intoxicated and therefore drink only when they wish to be drunk. They all are completely unabashed about it.

Although this is such a quiet district, the streets around the station contain everything a reasonable man might require. There is a blue movie theatre; a cinema that specialises in Italian and Japanese Westerns of hideous violence; a cinema that specialises in domestic consumption Japanese weepies; and yet another one currently showing *My Fair Lady*. There is a tintin-abulation of chinking *pachinko* (pinball) parlours, several bake-ries which sell improbably luxurious European patisserie, a gymnasium and an aphrodisiac shop or two.

If it lacks the excitement of most of the towns that, added up, amount to a massive and ill-plumbed concept called Greater Tokyo, that is because it is primarily a residential area, although one may easily find the cluster of hotels which offer hospitality by the hour. They are sited sedately up a side street by the station, off a turning by a festering rubbish tip outside a Chinese restaurant, and no neighbourhood, however respectable, is complete without them—for, in Japan, even the brothels are altogether respectable.

They are always scrupulously clean and cosy and the more expensive ones are very beautiful, with their windbells, stone lanterns and little rock gardens with streams, pools and water lilies. So elegantly homelike are they, indeed, that the occasional erotic accessory—a red light bulb in the bedside light, a machine that emits five minutes of enthusiastic moans, grunts and pants at the insertion of a 100 yen coin—seems like a bad joke in a foreign language. Repression operates in every sphere but the sexual, even if privacy may only be purchased at extortionate rates.

There are few pleasant walks around here; the tree-shaded avenue beside the river offers delight only to coprophiles. But it is a joy to go out shopping. Since this is Japan, warped toma-toes and knobbly apples cost half the price of perfect fruit. It is the strawberry season; the man in the open fruit shop packs martial rows of berries the size of thumbs, each berry red as a guardsman, into a polythene box and wraps each box before he sells it in paper printed with the legend "Strawberry for health and beauty." Non-indigenous foods often taste as if they had been assembled from a blueprint by a man who had never seen the real thing.

For example, cheese, butter and milk have such a degree of hygienic lack of tang they are wholly alienated from the natural cow. They taste absolutely, though not unpleasantly, synthetic and somehow indefinably obscene. Powdered cream (trade-named "Creap") is less obtrusive in one's coffee. Most people, in fact, tend to use evaporated milk.

Tokyo pastoral

Tokyo ought not be a happy city—no pavements; noise; few public places to sit down; occasional malodorous belches from sewage vents even in the best areas; and yesterday I saw a rat in the supermarket. It dashed out from under the seaweed counter and went to earth in the butchery. "*Asoka,*" said the assistant, which means: "Well, well, I never did," in so far as the phrase could be said to mean anything. But, final triumph of ingenuity, Megapolis One somehow contrives to be an exceedingly pleasant place in which to live. It is as though Fellini had decided to remake *Alphaville*.

Up the road, there is a poodle-clipping parlour; a Pepsi-Cola bottling plant heavily patrolled by the fuzz; a noodle shop which boasts a colour TV; a mattress shop which also sells wicker neck-pillows of antique design; innumerable bookshops, each with a shelf or two of European books, souvenirs of those who have passed this way before—a tattered paperback of *The Rosy Crucifixion*, a treatise on budgerigar keeping, Marx and Engels on England; a dispenser from which one may purchase condoms attractively packed in purple and gold paper, trademarked "Young Jelly"; and a swimming pool.

I am the first coloured family in this street. I moved in on the Emperor's birthday, so the children were all home from school. They were playing "catch" around the back of the house and a little boy came to hide in the embrasure of the window. He glanced round and caught sight of me. He did not register shock but he vanished immediately. Then there was a silence and, shortly afterwards, a soft thunder of tiny footsteps. They groped round the windows, invisible, peering, and a rustle rose up, like the dry murmur of dead leaves in the wind, the rustle of innumerable small voices murmuring the word: "*Gaijin, gaijin, gaijin*" (foreigner), in pure, repressed surprise. We spy strangers. *Asoka.*

[*11 June 1970*]

THE YOUNG ASIANS OF BRITAIN

Dilip Hiro

For a few weeks I have been talking in Urdu, Punjabi, Gujrati and English to various Asian teenagers living in the Home Counties and the midlands. Almost half of my 30 interviewees have been in Britain for five years or less; some have been here for as long as ten years or more. All of them, save one, attend or have attended secondary modern schools. The exception is Preetam, a boy of 14, who arrived in Britain four years ago from a hill station near Delhi, India, and lives in Hampstead where his mother runs an Indian dance school. He goes to a boarding school in East Anglia.

Akram, for example, is a youth of 19, who has been living in Maida Vale since he first came to this country 13 years ago from West Pakistan. Shiv, a 15 year old, left his home town in India four years ago, and has fond memories of his life there. He now lives in Birmingham where his father works in a bakery. Usha, a shy Hindu girl of 16, came to Clapham six years ago from a village in India; her father is a bus conductor. Deepak Singh, a tall Sikh, left Delhi five years ago for Southall; his father works in a plastics factory. Roop, 13, arrived in Ealing from a town in north India; his father now owns a stall at Shepherd's Bush market.

Talking to all these teenagers I followed a consistent line: what did they expect of Britain before they left home; what have been their experiences here; what do they think of their present environment; and what are their plans for the future?

Those who came when very young (four to seven years) had no idea of what to expect. Only those who were already ten or more had some knowledge, or tried to acquire it. "When I heard I was going to England I asked my friends about it," Rasheed, a 15 year old East Pakistani from Croydon, said, "but none of them knew, because they hadn't been to England." It was the same with the girl Usha. But Preetam's case was different because he was a boarder at a Jesuit school in India and had seen some films set in England. Shiv learnt about England from his grandfather who had, many years ago, visited England on business. "My granddad told me two things: the weather was very cold, and women were free and easy."

Recalling his arrival at Gravesend, Deepak Singh said: "Somehow it wasn't what I had expected. It was depressing. My mood was off. I wanted to go back." Rasheed, on the other hand, was quite impressed. "The airport was so big. And all smart people smartly dressed." Travelling by a taxi from Heathrow airport, Vallabh—another boy who was then eight and fresh from an Indian village—could not understand why the town of London did not "end."

The facets of life that impressed them most during their first days in Britain varied greatly. Town dwellers like Preetam, Shiv and Deepak Singh noticed the general quietness and orderliness that prevailed. Akram and Rasheed noticed that milk bottles were delivered at doorsteps, and that they were not stolen or broken. "You couldn't expect that sort of thing in Karachi or Lahore," Akram said.

Shiv was soon disappointed. "We came in winter. It wasn't very cold . . . no snow. I like snow. As soon as I returned home from school, it got dark. I got stuck in the house all the time. In Jullundur I was used to playing out in the streets until ten, eleven at night. It was a big change for me, here. Life was all boring. I had no friends. My sisters and I sat inside and watched television. We didn't understand what they were saying. We watched the photos." Deepak Singh, too, was disappointed, but in a different way. "My father had told us that he had paid 70,000 rupees (£3,500) for his house. I expected to see a bungalow for that price. But it was a poor house . . . no plaster on the walls . . . bare bricks."

An awareness of social differences usually came when they began attending school. Mehtab (an 18 year old girl who has lived in Wembley for 11 years now) recalled that her mother was opposed to her wearing a skirt; but when her father told her mother that it was the school "law," her mother yielded. However, neither parent liked the idea of school assembly or scripture class. "So I got exempted," Mehtab said. "There were other girls with me—Indian and Pakistani. Also some Jews. We'd sit out in a classroom." It was the same with Noor, a frail West Pakistani boy of 14 from Islington. But Preetam told

204

me that even if his parents had asked for exemption, he wouldn't have got it. "Mine is a grammar school," Preetam went on. "I don't mind assemblies or the bible class. But I call myself a Hindu. I keep reminding myself of the tales of Rama and Krishna that my mother has told me. I like Krishna the most. He was such a naughty boy: he'd steal butter and his mother would force him to open his mouth. Then she'd look inside and see visions . . . No, English boys are not interested . . . all they're interested in is sports."

I found that most of them hold tolerant views on religion. Deepak Singh, a turbaned Sikh, put it this way: "I've been attending assemblies since I joined my school. If my father asked me *now* not to attend them, I'd refuse . . . Religion is in one's heart." Roop, an unturbaned Sikh, agreed: "All religions are the same: love thy neighbour; don't kill; that sort of thing. Only they say it differently." Akram, indeed, was quite unconcerned about religion. "I've been to a mosque maybe half a dozen times in all these years in England. Of course, I'm a Muslim. I mean, once you're circumcised, you're a Muslim," he said. "Or a Jew," I added, smiling.

Their parents, however, are more particular. "My mother reads Sikh scriptures every day," Deepak Singh said. "But my parents don't force me to do so. I'm beginning to forget the Sikh prayers I used to know in India . . . No, I can't read Punjabi, nor write it. I speak it. At my *gurdwara* [church] they've started *gurmukhi* [Punjabi script] classes, but that teacher doesn't know much English. So? . . . I go to the *gurdwara* once in a fortnight, maybe." Roop, however, has stopped going to a *gurdwara*, because "I can't understand a word of what they're saying there. I know more of the bible than of my Holy Granth. The bible is no longer in Latin. Why don't they translate the Holy Granth into English? Sitting on the floor in a *gurdwara*, I get cramped. Why not use cushions, or something? And the service goes on all morning: five hours! They should modernise Sikhism. Look at the Christian churches . . . they're trying to attract the young—all those Salvation Army pop groups . . . I've been to Christian churches, both Protestant and Catholic. I like their services. At least I understand what they're saying . . . Yes, I speak Punjabi, at home, but I can't read or write it . . ."

Shiv's case is different because his father is a Hindu Brahmin. "So we have religious ceremonies at home . . . Well, there's no Hindu temple in all of London. I've heard they'll open one. When, I don't know." Usha's family has a simple Hindu altar over a mantelpiece at home: a few idols and pictures of Hindu gods and goddesses. "We celebrate important Hindu festivals and religious days with a simple *puja*," she said.

There are, of course, a few teenagers who feel strongly about their religion. "I read the Holy Koran as often as I can," Noor said. "There's a copy at home, in Arabic, with pronunciations in Urdu written under each line. I believe in the Holy Koran and the Prophet Mohamed. Our Prophet makes many references to Mary and Jesus and Abraham. I tell this to my religious teacher and English boys, but they don't bother. People don't care for religion in this country."

I often asked those who attended scripture classes which story or fable impressed them the most. Roop chose the Good Samaritan, whereas Shiv singled out Noah's Ark, because "it's like *Maha-praliva* in our Hindu books—the Great Flood."

Their generally tolerant attitude toward religion often extends to dressing and eating habits. Almost all the boys were wearing "knickers" at school in India or Pakistan. The switchover to trousers in Britain was expected, and was accepted without a murmur.

The crucial thing for a Sikh boy is the turban. It is no longer universal. My Sikh respondents put the number of those Sikh boys who have removed their turbans at 40 per cent to 60 per cent of the total. I asked Roop why he had removed his turban and long hair. "I was in a chain store once," Roop replied, "I was six then, and a sales lady thought I was a girl. That upset me. I wouldn't eat until they had my hair cut off. Of course, my father had removed his turban some time ago. In those days there was a lot of prejudice against turbans."

The girls' dressing problems crop up when they mature. When Mehtab recently joined a technical college, her mother insisted that she wear the Indian *salvar* because "she said that I was a grown-up girl, and that I was going to a coeducational college. I had to submit to her wishes." At one time Usha wanted to have short hair, but her mother thought it unfeminine. "Long hair is an object of beauty in a girl, she told me. I had to

206

go along with her views," Usha said. "After all, she's my mother."

As a rule, boys are less respectful of their parents' wishes and habits than girls. Akram found school lunches a "welcome change from the rich and spicy food I have to eat at home. Yes, I've eaten pork and bacon. I don't like it. It's too greasy. Of course, my parents don't know. They'd be appalled if they knew. They don't even buy margarine because someone told them it had pig's fat in it."

The parents of one Hindu boy feel differently. "They know I eat meat at school lunches," he said. "They don't mind as long as it's not at home. We are vegetarian—at home . . . I guess I must have eaten beef, because I eat what's given. It doesn't matter." But to Preetam it does. "I avoid beef," Preetam said solemnly. "All religions have some sacred animal or something. If Hindus have cow, I should respect it, shouldn't I?" Roop would not, or so he told me. "If I were about dying, I'd kill a cow and eat it. Religion did not make man. Man made religion. India could earn a lot by exporting those skinny things. Chop them off, and sell their skins abroad. My Indian friends don't agree; they get emotional . . ."

On the whole, Muslim students such as Rasheed, Noor and Mehtab tend to follow Jewish students on food restrictions at school.

Conflicts arise in schools on such subjects as history. Most of the older Indian students arrive in this country with some knowledge of modern Indian history. Consequently they find the British version of history, where it pertains to the Indian subcontinent, distasteful. The following example illustrates the situation:

"My history teacher was telling us how Clive the victorious went and conquered India," Deepak Singh said. "So I got up and told him that if it hadn't been for some of our clots the British would have been thrown out. He said, 'Get lost.' I was taken to the headmaster. I told him too. The history books here say all the good things the English did in India, not a word about all the bad things they did. What about that Jalianwalla Bagh in Amritsar? That orchard . . . they closed the gates and shot at our people . . . the English generals did. I've seen the bullet marks on the walls with my own eyes. Not a word about

207

that in English history books. Not a word about all the gold the English took from our country." In contrast, Akram had no previous knowledge of Indian/Pakistani history, and seemed unconcerned.

I scrupulously avoided any mention of colour, but invariably my respondent introduced the subject in our conversation. It seems to me that colour consciousness in an Asian child begins in one or more of the following ways:

1. Through parental experience: One boy told me that his father had made 200 applications for an office job during his first four weeks in England, and had secured one interview. (His father now works as a moulder in a Birmingham rubber factory.) Such parental experiences leave a mark on their children.

2. Through personal (or a close friend's) experience: This is the most common. On the very first day Deepak Singh went to the senior school, a white boy called him over, shouted "You fucking wog!" and punched him. Deepak Singh felt very bitter. Later on, when he found out that the white boy was, in fact, a Maltese immigrant, Deepak Singh's feelings against the white [English] boys did not change. "The point is that that boy had grown up in English society," Deepak Singh explained. "He had learnt their attitudes. Besides they're all the same: the Poles, the English, the Greeks. Same religions, same food, same customs."

Shiv had felt no distinction against being an Indian in a predominantly English school until the following incident happened. One morning an English boy pushed him on the way to assembly. So Shiv pushed him back. "The English boy hit me, and I hit him back," Shiv said. "And so it was going—until five-six English boys attacked me. I fell on the ground. Then I didn't know what happened. I was kicked from all sides by many English boys. I got very sore, bleeding all over my face. A teacher came and applied some medicine. Then I went to my class. Everybody said, 'Look, he got beaten, but nothing happened [to the boy who beat him].' After that I kept myself to myself. If English boys were playing on one side, I'd play on another. I had nothing to do with them."

A different norm exists in Roop's school: "If an Indian and English boy get into a fight, a teacher takes them to a gym to have a fair fight."

208

Girls' experiences are no different from boys'. "When I have a quarrel or something with a class mate, the first thing that comes out of her mouth is 'You black bitch!'" Usha said. "I mean girls whom you treat as friends. This colour thing is very deep."

Noor had had the worst experience of all. "One evening I was passing an alley and an English boy stopped me, and said, 'I want to fight with you.' I asked 'why?.' He said, 'Because you're a black bastard.' At once he drew a knife. I got scared, real scared. Then I just ran. He ran after me. I ran fast. After that, for many days I'd not walk alone in streets, not even in daylight."

3. Through indirect social reaction: Preetam's case illustrates this. "Everything is all right in my boarding grammar school. I'm the only Indian boy there. Every Saturday afternoon we watch sports on television, and then one of the pop shows. There's an Indian boy in the dancing crowd. When the camera pans on him, a cry of disgust goes up from the English boys in my hall. That's when I realise what they *really* think of me. It could be me on television."

I tried to gauge the reaction of my respondents to the white boys by asking them, "If you were a Negro in America, whose methods would you follow: Malcolm x's or Dr King's?" An overwhelming majority chose Malcolm x. "His method works," Shiv assured me. "After my beating I realised 'Why don't we Indians form our own community?' Our number in the school was growing. I made friends with Indians and Pakistanis. Then we began hitting back. Now if some English boy starts by bullying some small Indian boy, we get there and challenge him. We don't wait for him to accept our challenge. We hit him right away: that way he loses confidence. Now the English boys respect us." Roop preferred Dr King. "In the long run, non-violence will get you what you want."

Further, I asked if it were possible to be "neutral" about colour. Even the most anglicised, Akram, sounded pessimistic. "No," he replied. "How can you? I came here a long time ago. Ours was the only Asian house in the street. I was six or seven then. One day I was standing near a car in my street. Suddenly a ball hit the car. An English woman came rushing out of a house, and shouted, 'You black bastard!' I had absolutely nothing to do with the ball. It was some English kids playing

So, how can you be neutral? It's *they* who have to be neutral, not us. The working class adults are the worst. Not that others are any better. I went to an employment agency once. The woman there said, 'Yes, a department store in Oxford Street wants staff for their music shop.' Backroom job, mind you. Anyway, she picked up the phone. The next thing I know she's staring at me and saying on the phone, 'No, he's all right . . . he's not dark at all . . . he's very light.' "

The leisure activities of Asian teenagers—watching television, reading comics or novels, listening to music, visiting friends or clubs and cinemas—are not much different from those of their English counterparts.

Watching television is popular. Even the parents who do not understand English join in. "My parents pick up many English words that way," Noor said.

All of my respondents had read comics like *Hurricane*, *Horne*, *Superman*, *Captain America* or *Batman* at one stage. None of them does so now. Very few read any magazines like *True Romances* and *True Stories*. Those who read English novels tend to read thrillers. Most of them read Urdu, Hindi and Gujrati novels. They also read other Hindi and Urdu books, like the biographies of their national leaders.

Social visits among boys of the same group are very common. When large numbers of Indians or Pakistanis live in an area or go to the same school, there is a tendency for the same language group—Punjabi, Gujrati, Bengali—to congregate. Social contacts between Asian and English boys outside school are minimal; though Asian and English girls tend to develop closer relationships. Such sentiments as "Most of my friends are English" tend to be expressed with a false sense of bravado.

Almost all my respondents go to Indian/Pakistani films in Hindi/Urdu. The frequency varies from once a week to once a month. There are exceptions, like Akram. "I don't understand Urdu," he said. All my respondents go to English-language films as well. Their preferences vary. Some, like Shiv and Deepak Singh, feel that "Indian films always have a moral, but English films start off from somewhere and finish off somewhere." However, even they agree that "production standards of English films are very high."

Vallabh, 16, who proudly calls himself a "brown Brummie,"

prefers English to Indian films because "the majority of Indian films are based on love sort of thing. Not much variety." Roop went further, when he said, "In Indian films when someone dies there's a song, someone marries there's a song, someone falls into a pond there's a song. These songs and films bore me to tears."

Usha, however, is very fond of Indian film songs, because she thinks "there's so much feeling in them, the words are poetic, not like this *yé-yé* type." Admiration for Indian music and songs does not preclude listening and appreciating western music. Many names of western singers were mentioned: Elvis Presley, the Beatles, Billy Fury, Petula Clark. Tom Jones seemed to be the favourite. Most of my respondents were appreciative of "background" western music but derisive of the lyrics.

All of them have, by now, formed opinions about the British people and environment. I found nothing original in them. There were the usual remarks about the weather—its "constant changeability"—and the people—"cold and reserved." Most of them had some unjustifiable notion that the British people were "nice chaps, really cooperative"; but it had not turned out that way. As a rule, they find the British very polite. "In fact too polite. 'Yes, sir' and 'No, sir' in your face; and then read the letters they write in local papers: 'Send Indians back home; they smell'—that sort of thing," Shiv said. "I tell you they're dirty. They never bathe; they cover up their smell with all the perfumes and smelling salts."

Most of them tend to view the British political parties in terms of their policies toward immigration and immigrants. "My friend down the street tells me that if Tories came to power they'll chuck us out, but I said to him, 'The Tories were in power when my father first came in. They can't chuck us out like that. No'," Rasheed said. Once again Roop had an original idea: "We had both Tories and Labour. Neither of them is any good. So I say give the Liberals a chance."

Most of my Indian interviewees were familiar with the names of Gandhi, Nehru, Bose and Patel. They had either read about them in history books or had heard them being discussed by their parents at home. Parents form a vital link to their past: their religion, language and literature, and their attachment to—and continuing interest in—their "mother country." When

211

asked to choose the leader they most admired they chose Bose, Patel, Gandhi and Nehru—in that order. The Pakistani teenagers know Jinnah very well, but not Liaqat Ali Khan. I did not discuss present-day national leaders in either country.

Their plans for the future varied. "A girl's future lies in marriage," Mahtab said. "Right now my mother is in Pakistan, looking for a husband for me." Akram, on the other hand, has no desire to return to Pakistan: "I'll feel foreign there. I'm planning to be an actor. I've already joined a drama school. Acting is a serious business." Deepak Singh plans to be a fighter pilot with the RAF. "If that doesn't work out, I'll try the Indian Air Force. I'm in the Air Training Corps here." Vallabh is interested in business. "My uncle is minting money in shirt manufacture. He wants to take me on. This is the country for me. There's money here: pound-sterlings!" Roops is keen on education. "I'll go as far as I can in my education here. I've been back to India twice for holidays. I like it there. I'll go back." Noor proposes to be an electronics engineer. "Yes, in this country."

It is rare to find a totally orthodox or totally anglicised Asian teenager: in my sample, Noor and Akram come nearest to these two types. In between there are three broad categories: semi-orthodox, like Rasheed, Usha, Mehtab and Deepak Singh; the middle-zoners, like Shiv and Vallabh; and the semi-anglicised, like Preetam and Roop.

The major factors that bear on anglicisation are:

1. Time of arrival. The early arrivals (of the mid-1950s) were more prone to anglicisation because they arrived when very young and they were totally surrounded by the British environment. In contrast, the late arrivals were older in age, and found themselves surrounded more and more by their compatriots.

2. Period of stay: Longer stay helps anglicisation, but only up to a point. The change is swift in the beginning, but soon tapers off.

3. The racial composition of school and residential area: Concentration of Asians in schools and residential areas tends to retard anglicisation.

I am, of course, using the term "anglicisation" in a neutral sense; it is neither good nor bad.

[*1 June 1967*]

BEAT AND GANGS ON MERSEYSIDE

Colin Fletcher

Out of the unemployment, the endless two-up-and-two-downs with tin baths in the cobbled yards, among the smell of oil, salt and cattlecake, has come an adolescent phenomenon that culminated last week in the successful export of the Mersey product to the US. Between the age of 14 and 18 I was a member of two Merseyside gangs. At the age of 16 I became the singer and bass-guitarist of a "rock group." How the beat invaded the gangs and changed them beyond all recognition is one of the little known aspects of the Mersey story.

Gangs in Liverpool and Birkenhead took the same pattern as the adult association of men: a strict geographical delineation. Gangs developed with the same notion of territory as held by the men who gathered at the local every evening, but with an acceptable alternative to the pub: the chippy on the turf—a chip shop in the gang's area—or possibly a coffee bar.

The chippy was the centre of all action in the winter for the Holly Road gang—my first urban gang. It was always warm with a favourite smell and a Pepsi-Cola would legitimise a good half-evening. Parents and other adults used to scuttle in and out but being friends of the owner we were allowed to stay. The owner was very important to us as in return for a night's "protection" he would issue the evening's left-overs free of charge.

The chippy for the Park Gang—my second—was the climax of the evening. At 9 pm a long straggling line of boys and girls made their way up the hill. The fish cakes were ready and the bottles of orangeade waited. To a gang a chip shop was an essential prerequisite and a place to go regularly even after being out all evening. Looking back, I see now that what brought us into the gang and into the chippy every night was our feelings of insecurity. The epithet "teenager" implies that one has arrived at some stage in evolution but everything inside is jangling and jerking.

School, too, played its part in gang formation. At school we found out who lived near and who didn't. We discovered the different types of boys who made up the area. Most important of all we found the most reliable, tough and fair boy who was to become the gang's leader.

The Holly Road Gang was relatively small, though it was typical of those in an older working class urban area. Partly because of its size it acted as a buffer state between two stronger gangs who always thought that physical violence was the only way to solve their differences in opinion over which was the better gang. Holly Road had its fighters and thieves, its lovers and artists. In the Park Gang, which I knew better, it was the same.

As defence and warfare were high upon any gang's list of actions the "belligerents" were always considered important. These boys often fell into two categories; those who always wanted to fight and those who were always good at it. In every gang known there was a hard core. It was normally two brothers or "life-long" friends. In the Holly Road Gang there were the O'Haras and in the Park Gang were Bresso and Ronnie. These were the boys who could go in first and come out best. They had a social rank almost as high as that of the gang leader because, like him, they could go anywhere, across anybody's turf, and not be challenged.

When one of these boys left the Park Gang, Jack, our leader said, "I always felt safe with you." This was the biggest compliment that could be paid by a leader to a member because Jack, by nature of his job, had to be able to at least hold his own with any one person. Barnies (or punch-ups) were common but regulated. We fought for our status, not for fun. A fight was the result of consultations between the leader and his lieutenants; except when under attack. The Ferry Boys or the Tombstones (who were based at cemetery gates) had to disturb the balance of gangs or beat up a member or swipe one of the gang's girls before action came and then it was a concerted night's work.

Disturbance of the balance of gangs was infrequent. One such time was when the Ferry Boys laid into the Broadways and smashed their hut as well as everybody they found in it. This occurrence obviously worried every gang in the area. The Ferries would become too brash and rough with every gang and its

214

property if they were allowed to continue. The leader of the Tombstones came to see Jack and they met on the neutral territory of a border street corner. Both gangs were about ten yards behind just in case. The two leaders agreed that the Ferries could only be beaten badly by a combined force. Two members were sent to bring the remnants of the Broadways and we made our way by four separate routes down towards the station and the Ferry. We didn't thrash the Ferries on any principle of justice, but to reassert the positions of gangs in the neighbourhood.

The "criminals" were either gang-based or gang-supported. They were gang-based when the idea, which was their own, involved a great deal of risk, or the penalty of caught was likely to be severe. The gang-supported crimes were those annual—almost traditional—affairs to which the majority of the police force closed their eyes (cycle races through the park, letting ourselves in and out of the park-keeper's shed to make a cup of tea, and scrumping in orchards and gardens). Vandalism was not the aim of the exercise but there must have been some damage.

The most popular gang-based activity was prizing cigarette machines off the wall to obtain the money and weeds. It was not uncommon, also, for the local sweets and tobacconists to "get done" regularly. Many of the boys worked on newspaper rounds which gave them an intimate knowledge of the shop.

The police, however, were very well aware of the paper-round/breaking and entering relationship and a small number of arrests were almost guaranteed. Most leaders, too, were against serious crimes as the gang was then constantly under the strain of fear of arrest. The Holly Road Gang, because it had less fighting potential, turned very gradually to crime as its main interest. The leader was not a "criminal" and did his best to hold the gang together. Disappointed with his performance a large section of the criminal element left the gang and these boys then adopted a leader who had the glamour of "inside" experience. He led these boys through a long series of cunning petty felonies, getting more bold and less careful until various "stretches" split this little gang completely. The Holly Road Gang continued in a very much modified form which allowed new influences to have a greater effect.

Jack, of the Park Gang, was just as effective a regulator of crime as he was of warfare. He removed the criminal element's support by placing them very slightly out of the intimacy of the gang whenever they had a foolhardy scheme. The "criminals" were told to go and natter behind the shed if they couldn't talk about anything else. Many potential knock-offs were also averted by his refusal to allow "hot stuff" to be dumped in the gang's cellar. Jack looked after the gang by adhering to social standards when their contravention might have been detrimental.

The "romantics" helped themselves and the gang at the same time. They were the "good-lookers" who brought the birds to the gang by going out with them first and then, when the girl went out with another member they took to the sea of troubles again. They were seldom fighters and spent most of their time, as one "criminal" remarked, "standing in the chippy half looking at themselves in the mirror." Fred was a persistent romantic. Nobody knew how he succeeded but he always managed to find a girl from another territory and then just happen to be out with yet another when the girl's gang arrived to settle ownership.

Set apart from the gang was the "spiritual" element. Even if there was more than one person in it, it was still very small, though it could be very powerful. The "spiritual" boys could constrain the gang in the leader's absence. Its main functions were counselling for the members and advice for the leader. As the Park Gang was large it had two such members, who were both older and practising Christians. They were in constant demand in times of "rozzer rash" (when the gang was severely nettled by the police) and they kept the gang ticking over by just listening to troubles and advising the leader as to which members were directly responsible and who were the gullible youths.

The "musical" type was latent. In the Park Gang there was the boy who played a good harmonica; the one who was adept at a rhythm with knitting needles on a lamp post; the singer who never smiled and two harmonisers who picked up tunes readily but could never remember the words. There was a similar motley talent in the Holly Road Gang but they shouted more and took entertaining the gang far less seriously.

216

The leader of a gang needed to fit in with the unique arrangement of these elements within it. The Tombstones had a large belligerent section and so their leader was picked primarily for his physical prowess. The Park Gang had an equilibrium of types and Jack was chosen by the respect he had from each element, combined with the ability to control.

Pride in one's gang was high. Members always lived in the reflection of the group as a whole. If we had been beaten up then we felt rotten and listless. We all grumbled and blamed ourselves for a poor attempt. We believed we lost because we were not on form, rather than because the other gang had better fighters. We were all responsible for the gang's name.

Members looked upon the girls in the gang with an ambivalent attitude. For most of the time girls were supposed to be secondary: a mere accessory for living one's life in the gang. Sexual experience was of real importance only to the "romantics." A girl belonged to a gang because she lived on the turf. She did not have to join the gang, though most did, but it was ill-advised to join another. A girl was a drag if around too often or with the same boy too long. This idea of a girl being the property of the whole gang had great expression on gang outings. Every gang went every night possible to a visiting fun fair. The fair itself was considered neutral territory so the visit became a non-violent expression of talent. Girls fitted the bill. Their laughter and screams on the waltzers and dodgems, their appreciation of the gifts of bric-a-brac won by performing some feat and their physical attractiveness were all "notches on the gang's belt." Pride in the gang's girls and fighting record were central in its life.

The gang, between the periods 1954 and 1958, was not only a microcosm of society; it was relatively speaking the only society the adolescent knew and felt sure of. This was the situation when rock and roll arrived on Merseyside.

The arrival of rock and roll (words now consigned to the adolescent's scrap heap) in Merseyside was preceded by rumour. Almost every local picture house banned Bill Haley and his Comets, but there had been rumour that *Rock Around the Clock* had more effect on teenagers all over the world than any other film. The Bill Haley riots for the Holly Road Gang were on a traditional Saturday night in 1955. The queue outside the Palais

217

was large but quite orderly. There were many gangs present, but the pact of neutral territory held good.

Gangs filed in and filled up row after row. Unlike most of the films, this one had commanded an almost entirely adolescent audience. When the music started it was infectious—no one managed to keep still. It was the first time the gang had been exposed to an animal rhythm that matched their behaviour. Soon couples were in the aisles copying the jiving on the screen. The "bouncers" ran down to stop them. The audience went mad. Chairs were pulled backwards and forwards, arm rests uprooted, in an unprecedented orgy of vandalism. There were fourteen seats missing when it was "Queenie" time.

But the sound, new and exciting as it was, took some time to catch on. It was regarded as part of America. For the local adolescents and their gangs it was a little too polished, especially with that brass line-up, to be imitated.

Then the beat spread like a rumour; the interpretations were more important than the original. Saturday night had always been the climax of the week when boots were exchanged for polished shoes and a truce was called to allow free movement across town and city. The Saturday night meeting time had always been 7 o'clock but it was suddenly changed to 7.30 pm. This radical move was caused by BBC's new contribution to the passing craze, *6-5 Special*.

This show was very important, because it was more amateur-ish, as were all British attempts at the time, and this made copying very much easier. There were more "numbers" to choose from and the guitar started wholly to replace trumpets and saxophones. Elvis Presley's *Heartbreak hotel* realised the potential of a barrage of guitars. Slightly later Buddy Holly and the Crickets made the point eminently clear with their first record, *That'll be the day*. Ten members of the Park Gang bought this record—starting a habit that they were unlikely to give up—and the musical element found the hammering thrown-out beat easy and most enjoyable to imitate. Guitars and a set of drums were needed to succeed in a reasonable rendering but this idea was only a suggestion for four months.

All the local gangs fitted this new phenomenon into their lives with curiosity, and interest. On going down to Holly Street I found that this gang had a much more advanced interpretation

218

of the music. They were interested in the movement rather than the expression of beat. They preferred the numbers with "bags of body" in them. The more solid the noise the more they liked it.

For the next six months an increasing amount of the gang's time was taken up with listening to pop records. It was winter and the Park shed inevitably lost most of its attraction; the regular attendance of 50 members was decimated. Groups of friends broke away and were necessarily small as a record player could normally function only in someone's front room—the back room housed the rival telly. Members' attitudes towards listening to records varied greatly. The romantics obviously found the habit a good way of getting together and their parties became based upon jiving to the latest releases. Some of the "criminals" and "belligerents" found the new outlet a little hard to accept: it was "soft." For them there seemed to be nothing immediate, no virility-cum-violence in the records.

When the spring came and, without a signal, the Park Gang gradually reassembled, the beat and what should be done about it was foremost in our minds and conversation. This preoccupation with the new sound was usurping some of the old habits. There was no apparent decrease in violence but there was a great actual decrease in the desire to "rumble." The music, like the roughness, was gradually becoming "us." An additional attraction, especially as we were getting older, was the effect of the music on girls. They seemed to be "real gone"—another recently rejected term—over not only the sound but also those who made it. All these ideas slowly led to the formation of the gang's own group.

All over Merseyside gangs were giving birth to groups. Each gang had its musical element who had naturally become interested and then involved in the sound of rock. This natural affinity was encouraged by gangs and the musical boys needed little encouragement. They had been stuck with 1930s ballads too long to miss their chance. The group inevitably came from the gang as there were very few boys on Merseyside strong enough to resist joining one.

The Holly Road Gang had managed to acquire the help of a friendly woodwork master. This man gave them the active encouragement to "get off pipe-racks and on to something they could use" (his words). As there were a number of gangs

219

in that school the woodwork shop developed into a little factory for guitar-making.

In June 1958, following the trend, the Park Gang gave birth to the "Tremoloes." There had been excited anticipation when four of the musical element started to learn to play the guitar. The gang had no real notion of what a rock group looked like until these boys came down to the shed with their instruments one night and played for half an hour. The gang jived on the grass and clapped wildly after every item.

At this time I joined the group as singer and bass-guitarist. Soon the group began to practise regularly and some of the gang members pooled their knowledge and made two large amplifiers. The combination of terrific noise and regular practising soon made it impossible to practise in a front room. The gang scoured the turf for deserted houses, bomb shelters and finally church halls. Many church halls and youth clubs were glad to get the lads in somehow and the youth leaders were quite amazed at the number of people the group brought along.

Soon it became a regular thing for the gang actively to support every practice. The group was becoming the gang's totem. The gang had started to rival other gangs on a totally new level. As the process of producing a group from within a gang's ranks was cumulative one could feel the decline of tension in other forms of competition. What mattered now was not how many boys a gang could muster for a Friday night fight but how well their group played on Saturday night. By autumn there had been an almost total shift of interest.

[*20 February 1964*]

ULSTER'S CHILDREN OF CONFLICT

Morris Fraser

He was only twelve, but he sketched out his plan of campaign on my blotting-paper with the panache of a Montgomery. He drew a pair of parallel lines and added a row of dots on either side: "These are the lamp-posts," he said. "You fix your cheese-wire between them, about six feet high. There's always a soldier on the back of the Land-Rover; he can't see it in the dark. It's just at the right height to catch his throat. Then, when the jeep stops, we can come out and throw stones."

Jack, two years older, disagreed: "Only kids throw stones. Do like us; we put lots of stones in our pockets and carry hurley-sticks. If you put a stone down on the ground and swing the stick as hard as you can, you hit a soldier below his shield and cripple him. We once cut a squad of 36 down to 6 in ten minutes like this."

Peter, who was thirteen, but looked eleven, supported him: "Then," he said, "we come in with the petrol-bombs. If a soldier lowers his shield to protect himself against the stones, you can lob a bomb over the top and get him that way."

I pointed out that vertical wire-breakers were now welded on to all army vehicles.

We know all about that," said Jack. "Watch." He started to draw again . . .

The names are imaginary, but the boys are real. These are three of the youngsters who were in the national headlines only a few weeks ago—the child rioters, the nail-bomb throwers, the "mini-mobsters." Perhaps their behaviour is grossly disordered, but very few of these children ever reach the office of a child psychiatrist. When they do, it is usually because of some associated problem, such as truancy or school refusal, rather than for treatment of the aggressive behaviour itself. Indeed, in many areas, this type of activity is socially approved, openly by companions and tacitly by parents and relatives.

There is, however, one group of children who have so far received much less attention than they merit—children in whom

221

emotional problems, clearly brought on by the first-hand experience of violence, have been persistent and largely incapacitating. These symptoms have, in many instances, still been present long after the child's home area has become perfectly peaceful. I am still seeing children suffering from fainting attacks, irrational fears, even asthma and epilepsy, which had their onset during rioting in August 1969. Several are still unable to go to school, or even to go out in the street, alone. The symptoms which many of these children presented were striking; however the following cases are described not because they are unusual, but because they are typical.

Marie, aged ten, lives in Belfast's notorious "no-man's-land" —the area of tiny, interlocking streets between the Falls Road and the Shankill Road. She is the youngest of four children; her father disappeared without trace a year ago—it is believed for "political" reasons. Her mother has suffered from recurrent depression since the onset of disturbances in 1969, and suffers from insomnia, tremors and weeping fits.

Marie has been an epileptic since the age of four; until August 1969, her fits were adequately controlled by drugs, but in August, following serious trouble in her street, the frequency of fits increased sharply and she had to be admitted to hospital.

A rather small girl with a lively manner, she gave an animated account of her symptoms and their onset. She told me about the night, in August 1969, when a crowd of special constables (now disbanded) came up her street shooting at rioters, and when a factory nearby was set on fire. Her mother sent her upstairs, but forgot to pull down the blind. Marie sat at the window and stared out, as if "paralysed." But, she said, she was not frightened at the time. "It was just like the pictures."

"A couple of days later," she said, "we were going to school. We were late—and running. Suddenly, I thought of them all running on the street and my legs went weak and I fell. I woke in hospital and the policeman told me I'd had a fit.

"One day Mummy said, 'Light the gas,' and I thought of the CS gas and began to gasp and fell down again. I had to be taken to hospital with another fit. The next day in school we had our 'Sound Book'—you know, about different sounds. The teacher said, 'What goes ting-a-ling?' I thought of the fire engine and I felt my hand shaking. Then I woke up on the floor."

222

Marie continued to be severely handicapped by fits. Pre-disposing, or "triggering" stimuli, as well as those she described, included: bells ringing, the sight of an electric fire, seeing a crowd of boys running out of school, and an occasion when a friend said, "I'm as hot as a fire." She is still a psychiatric in-patient. In hospital, it has been found necessary to shield her from local news programmes on television, and also from refer-ences to the still troubled situation. In treatment, an early response to signs of anxiety, together with consistent support, has been the most useful approach. She is now more able to express her fears through talk and play and the number of fits has rapidly decreased. At the moment, she has been free from fits for several weeks and is about to be discharged. New accom-modation is being sought for the family.

Sean is also ten. During the few months before we saw him he had become increasingly irritable and tearful; he was also having frequent bouts of bronchial asthma. He is the middle one of eight children. Though always a timid child, he is of above average intelligence, and has a first-class school record.

This school record ended abruptly on a night in August 1969, when his street was the scene of a fierce gun battle. Sean, a small, pallid boy with dark rings round his eyes, remembers it like this: "I saw a big crowd coming up our street; they had guns. Some-body said, 'They're beating up all the children; they're going to shoot them.' I heard the guns and I felt sick and I shook all over and came out in a sweat. Then I started to wheeze and I couldn't breathe."

Even after the local trouble had subsided, Sean's symptoms continued unchanged. He lay awake for hours at night, listening for gunfire—and hearing some. He expressed numerous fears about fires and burning, and also marked anxiety for his parents' safety if they happened to go out. The cluster of symptoms he described (sweating, feelings of weakness, nausea and asthma) were repeatedly brought on by things like shouts, crowds, loud car engines, and, once, a quarry explosion. They would also follow any reference by his parents to their own anxiety about the troubled local situation.

His mother said, "I went into his room one morning and said, 'I see that a garage has been blown up,' and right away he went terribly pale, then he started to choke and his asthma came on. I shouldn't have said anything, but I had to tell someone."

It is difficult to treat a child whose fears are based in reality. In spite of psychotherapy and drug treatment, Sean continued to be very limited in his activities for several months, to the extent of being unable to go outside or to school. He improved only when his parents bought a new house in a quiet suburb. From the time that the deal was completed, even before the family moved, Sean's asthmatic attacks decreased, and he has now been discharged as symptom-free.

In some ways, Sean was fortunate; other children are less so. Margaret, again, is ten—a pale, under-nourished child. She is one of a family of twelve intimidated from their home in the lower Falls area during the latter part of 1969. Since then, they have been squatting in various unoccupied premises and are hopelessly overcrowded. They have had to move at least twice because of rioting and CS gas.

Margaret said: "The Protestants came to our street and shouted, 'Get out,' and the B specials were shooting at us. Then they burnt us out. I can't sleep at night for thinking about fires and burning. I sleep nearest the window so as my baby brother won't get hit with a bullet. Every time I hear a noise I shake all over."

Her symptoms—tremors, sleeplessness and loss of appetite—continued unchanged for several months. Although her home area had by then become peaceful, she still experienced the symptoms in response to sounds like cars back-firing, quarry blasting, or shouts in the street. Her activities became progressively reduced; she would not go out alone, and fantasies of burning houses kept her awake at night.

Treatment was initially unrewarding for her. Although Margaret clearly benefited from being able to come to the clinic to express her anxiety, she was still living in noisy surroundings that constantly brought back symptoms. An approach was made to the local housing committee, which was able to offer some accommodation in a quieter area. Margaret's symptoms improved somewhat, but she still has numerous fears, especially of being in a crowd or of being in the street alone.

Patricia is slightly older—13. Her family had to move house during the riots of 1969 when much of the property around them was destroyed by fire; and they lost most of their belongings. After a short stay in temporary accommodation, they obtained a small house in what was shortly to become one of Belfast's worst trouble spots. Here, for several nights in a row, the street was a battleground between troops and rioters, and the combatants frequently spilled over into their front garden.

On the first of these occasions, Patricia screamed, fell, lost consciousness and had to be taken to hospital. She was later discharged but although the area quietened down, she continued to have fainting fits, both at home and at school, symptoms of great anxiety, and disturbed sleep. She became afraid to go to school and her work deteriorated. These fainting attacks continued for several months; each attack typically followed an experience like seeing a crowd (an innocent one), hearing a loud noise or a shout, or any reference by her parents to local events. Her mother, for instance, mentions one fainting attack when she spoke, in Patricia's hearing, about a recent political murder.

Patricia claims to have complete amnesia about these episodes, but is now able to accept their link to anxiety. She has expressed many of her fears both verbally and through drawing and play media. She is now much better and is at last attending school regularly.

Sometimes the ways in which chronic anxiety showed itself were even more bizarre. Liam, eleven, was evacuated from his home in August 1969 following rioting and massive exposure of the whole area to CS gas.

He says: "There were twelve of us children in the house. We heard the shooting and saw men covered with blood. The gas was terrible. The lady who lived upstairs was very kind and gave us hankies with vinegar to put over our faces, but we still felt like we were going to choke. The lady said the Protestants were coming to shoot us all or burn us. We were very frightened; we were all crying."

Shortly after, Liam began to have vivid hallucinations of a "big evil man with frightening eyes." He decided that the man was a Protestant, because he "wore strange clothes, he looked different from us, he was bad, and he was trying to kill me." Night terrors, tremors, and fits of crying began. He started to have these hallucinations in the classroom and would run

225

outside. His school work greatly deteriorated. With psychiatric treatment, he was able to accept these hallucinations as a projection of his own fears and they disappeared. But the other symptoms remain, and he is still losing weight.

It is difficult to give exact figures, but each of these histories could be duplicated at least a dozen times. There is also Mary, aged twelve, who has epileptic fits precipitated by noises in the street. And Seamus (nine), who develops sweating and a tremor when he has to go out or when he sees a crowd.

Perhaps it is hardly surprising that the majority of children who were exposed to the kind of experiences recounted by Sean and Liam suffered from acute nervous symptoms at the time. From all accounts, indeed, disturbances in sleep and appetite, tearfulness, and separation anxiety were common. However, most of these children recovered as soon as the focus of violence had shifted to another part of the town. The children who, naturally, concern a psychiatrist most are those whose symptoms *even then*, persisted and worsened—children like Margaret and Sean. At the same time, a broad similarity between these and all other members of the group tells us something about prevention and treatment—as well as providing a fascinating insight into the mental mechanisms by which a child deals with this type of stress.

Behaviourally, the symptoms represent a form of "classical conditioning" after the Pavlovian model. Later experiences remind the child, either consciously or subconsciously, of the initial stressful events, and "trigger off" the same acute reaction —a process of *generalisation*. Sean's first attack of asthma, for example, followed gunfire; all subsequent attacks were brought about by almost any sudden and/or loud noise.

This is, of course, a gross over-simplification; all children from riot areas did not develop these chronic symptoms. Most major writers on phobic anxiety states believe that their causation is multiple, and I would agree, in that children's reaction to stress of this type is the result of three main factors.

First—vulnerability. Each affected child had at least one parent who was himself emotionally disturbed by the violence, and there was a previous lack of physical robustness, too, on the child's part. So that the important quantity here seemed to be the degree of emotional security enjoyed by the child up to

226

and during the period of acute stress, both in relation to his own resources and also to those of his immediate family.

Next, there was the psychodynamic role of the stress itself. In each case, the stressful occurrence brought about a purposive response which served as a defence against intolerable anxiety. The transient disturbances of consciousness that are represented by Margaret's fainting attacks, for example, can be thought of as a switching-off of the reality which had become intolerable. True, these responses persisted beyond the period of acute stress, but even then they could not be labelled "maladaptive," since they always continued until attention was drawn to the child's plight, and he was able to express his anxiety freely and to escape from the threatening environment. Then, their purpose fulfilled, the symptoms diminished or disappeared.

The nature of the symptoms also depends heavily on the child's own personality—his strengths and weaknesses. Susan, a chronically ailing girl, developed incapacitating gastric complaints; Margaret, a histrionic girl, developed fainting fits and screaming attacks; and Peter, shy and timid, developed double vision—thus effectively preventing his having to go out in the street.

It is as if each child has his Achilles heel—the point at which distress shows, following a failure on the part of the immediate family to respond adequately to the child's needs during the period of acute threat. Taking it another way, it seems from present evidence that a healthy, well-adjusted child in a stable family is unlikely to suffer from persistent psychiatric symptoms as a result of civil disturbance; also, that the attitude of the child's parents in the same situation is an important preventative. One ten year old boy said, "My parents were very calm, so I wasn't scared. If *they* had been frightened, it would have been awful."

This aspect may appear mildly heartening, but even more disturbing, just now, are the other child victims—the aggressive children, the hundreds (literally) of "street guerillas" in the eight to fourteen age-group.

Identification with rival factions begins early. A twelve year old boy from a Republican area draws a picture of himself in the traditional garb of an Irish warrior, sword in hand. In a poem underneath, he expresses his intention of fighting until

227

the British army is driven out of the country. A drawing by a Protestant boy, aged nine, shows his street with himself and a friend on the pavement, and streaks of red running between the rows of houses. This, he says, is "Fenian [Catholic] blood."

Two unrelated children who live in Unity Flats drew, at different times, pictures of the building. Unity Flats is a multi-storey block, occupied by Catholic families, but sited in a mainly Protestant area. It has frequently been the scene of bitter fighting. Intriguingly, each child depicted a fortress, having no physical resemblance to the reality. Do they see themselves as beleaguered, as among enemies?

The little man in Liam's drawing of his hallucination is called the "evil Protestant man." The figure is indeed portrayed in outlandish clothes, with garish colours and checks. Liam's drawing conveys, perhaps even better than words could, the total lack of contact between the two populations.

It would be easy to dismiss these drawings as childish fantasy —but the route from fantasy to reality seems to be a peculiarly short one in Belfast these troubled days.

In an atmosphere of total religio-political segregation, jealously fostered by the churches, opposing attitudes of bitter intensity have been building up for years, and it is not now very surprising to see these attitudes spill over into vicious street rioting. Young boys are easy prey for the "illegal organisations"; large numbers are at present being formed into semi-uniformed groups and being given formal training in methods of physical attack on those of the opposite set of beliefs, as well as on the security forces. The three boys I quoted at the beginning are members of just such an organisation.

Many observers believe that the breakthrough in community relations will not come until Catholic and Protestant children are being educated together from primary school age. While church leaders remain intransigent, hopes of peace can only be pipe-dreams.

[*15 April 1971*]

GESTURE GOES CLASSLESS

George Melly

In an autobiography I am unable to trace, the author speaks of an old lady who used to visit his family when he was very young. She would, when surprised, sit bolt upright, turn up her eyes and open her mouth, press her elbows into her side, extend her lower arms and raise her hands so as to show the palms. Much later the author recognised the identical gesture in Cruikshank's illustrations to Dickens, published during the old lady's youth.

Gestures stick to us like barnacles to the bottom of ships. Old women, even today, shield a teapot spout in order to mask the phallic simile. My parents' generation carry something of the twenties in the way they sit, drink or smoke. On a dance floor it is quite easy to spot the pre-twist, twist, and post-twist waves even though there is only a year or two between them. Gestures have always revealed our social and professional alignments, our class origin or aspirations, but significantly the sixties are developing a new way of running, jumping and standing still, and in the process the old clues to class are becoming harder to spot. It is increasingly difficult to "place" anyone under 20 by the way they move. Their gestures don't betray them anymore. On the contrary they signal their intentions and attitudes.

I have been looking recently at the way young people move and comparing it with the older generations. I shall attempt to describe these differences objectively, although any theories I propose are, of course, subjective. A difficulty is, that unless stone deaf, it's impossible not to hear what people say, and although a classless voice is also on the increase, it is advancing at a slower pace. Another factor which has to be taken into account is that a lot of people, due to psychological or physical singularity, move without reference to current mores. Very fat people for example adjust their movements to compensate for their weight in a rather acrobatic way. Obvious neurotics seem controlled from outside. Drunks, once past the point of no return, behave identically however old or young they may be.

It is necessary to choose examples for their normality within their frame of reference.

At the Tate Gallery, five art students talking in a group. The first noticeable thing about them was the lack of differentiation between the sexes. This was not due to the fact that they all wore a uniform, jeans and jackets, nor that one of the men had long hair and two of the girls short. It was because they all stood the same way. Heads craned forward, shoulders slightly raised, trunks off centre, but leaning either forward or to one side, never straight or backwards. Arms and legs were pushed out at angles so that there seemed no flow either singularly or as a group. When they moved, which was infrequently, everything seemed to jerk into new awkward angular shapes. The general effect was unsentimental and detached.

At a cocktail party, a middle-aged group, three men and two women, middle class and non-intellectual. Every gesture seemed designed to emphasise sexual differentiation. The women drew curves in the air with their arms and hands. The men, when they moved at all, described straight and jerky lines. They held their bodies stiffly and swayed a little on their heels. The women constantly shifted their weight from one hip to another, threw back their heads to laugh, and used their drinks and cigarettes as props. A feeling of formalised coquetry.

A lack of flirtatiousness in the young is almost standard. It's women over 35 who flaunt their femininity, men who are inclined to lunge and leer. The young play it cool.

Fashion photographs are a pointer. Today the poses of the models are clumsy, knees together, feet pointed inwards, shoulders hunched. This anti-elegance is comparatively recent. Brigitte Bardot marks the turning point. She instigated the shedding of gloves, umbrellas, hats, elaborately set hair, but she still used her body to provoke. She walked with an exaggerated wiggle, pushed her breasts out, and acknowledged the presence of men even when she rejected them. The new girls—the singer Sandie Shaw could stand as a prototype—are leggy, coltish, and seem completely cut off. This doesn't mean they have no sex appeal however. Compare the fashion photography in *Queen* with the trad pinups in the *Sunday Mirror*.

This coolness has penetrated every social level during the last few years. In the big chain stores, shop assistants who used to giggle and nudge each other exhibitionistically behind the long counters now moon distantly about their tasks. Secretaries emerge from their offices like somnambulists, and trudge flat-footedly towards their bus or tube. Only young barmaids remain flirtatious in their manners, but theirs has always been an old-fashioned profession.

The way the under-20s walk, leaning slightly forward and as if their feet were large and heavy, has cut right across class barriers.

In a street market I watched a working class mum and her daughter. The mother waddled as if her feet were playing her up.

Outside a Knightsbridge Hotel I watched an upper class mum and her daughter come out from a wedding reception and walk towards Hyde Park Corner, the mother on very thin legs slightly bowed as though she had wet herself. She controlled her body as if it might snap if moved too impulsively.

Both daughters walked identically.

In the *New Statesman* Paul Johnson included fashion photographers in a list of "social flotsam." Photographers are pertinent to this article because they are both obsessed with style and yet uninterested in apeing the upper classes. They have evolved, or at any rate display in its most extreme form, the male version of the new social choreography. I watched one at work the other day. While actually taking photographs he moved rapidly giving the impression that he was simply an eye, a camera, and a number of adjustable parts linking the two together, but between times he continuously stroked objects and furniture, and moved rarely and indolently. He could lounge, but was unable to sit. His gestures were the opposite of masculine in the old pipe smoking tweedy sense, but in no way effeminate. I should describe them as naturally sophisticated. Although modified by the exigencies of job or profession, this ease of manner is spreading. Just as the traditionally square chain store tailors are producing, with a decreasing time lag, less extreme versions of Carnaby Street gear, so young bank clerks, for example, are starting to project the unselfconscious physical ease of the more permissive world of showbiz and the near arts.

To observe the gestation of contemporary gesture there is nowhere more to the point than the discotheque; pop stars, fashion photographers, models and dollies, the whole cast in fact of Paul Johnson's list.

At the tables no conversation, no necking, no holding hands. When a couple gets up to dance they move with quiet resolution towards the floor. They dance expertly, even wildly, but essentially narcissistically.

Compare the traditional night club. The drunken fumbling gestures of the middle aged customers. The teasing movements of the girl employees. A cigarette girl in fishnet stockings pacing filly like between the tables. The hostesses leaning to display their breasts. Their greedy little girl gestures.

Of course the narcissism of contemporary gesture is suspect, and at its most extreme accompanies the diminished social responsibility of the mods who affect extreme refinement of gesture particularly when looking for trouble. On the Wardour Street pavements when they come up for air during the all night raves, they stand in tight self-conscious little groups as posed as waxworks.

Even so, and this I believe the other side of the coin, it suggests a refusal to accept traditional roles. A young married couple on a bus sit as equals and partners. There is no suggestion that they will turn into a comic postcard couple in middle age, the man deafening himself to the continuous grumbling chatter of the woman, the woman despising the man as a would-be lecherous and drunken worm. The young can exchange roles without diminishing themselves. The man can push a pram, the girl hang wallpaper. This sexual ambidexterity has even led to some direct reversals. It's the boys who move to show off their clothes.

There are, however, certain sections of society who seem to swim deliberately against the tide. Rockers, for example.

Rockers use brutalised gestures. They shove past each other, engage in rough horseplay, eat in great mouthfuls, and in relation to their girls, behave with aggressive masculinity. Most rockers come from poor working class backgrounds, and it is possible that their behaviour represents a last ditch protest against the classless style.

The same is perhaps true of the Oxbridge exquisites. These register their dismay by cultivating certain old-fashioned upper class mannerisms, and effecting extreme effeminacy. For example, they step back and forth, rapidly bringing their heels together, arrange their fingers so that none of them touch, and applaud speakers in the Unions by languidly banging their papers against their crossed legs.

Technicians, particularly those connected with television, remain on the whole faithful to a suburban philistinism, and exteriorise this through clumsy and unattractive gestures: arm-pit scratching, ostentatious winking and nudging, continuous examination of wristwatches, movements imitating the greedy drinking of tea to intimate the time has come for a refreshment break.

Advertising on the other hand would seem to encourage upper class but caddish gestures: obsessive bird watching; neurotic ticks as a proof of overwork; carmanship.

The county are unchanged, although this is genuine rather than assumed. The young men who never come up to London if they can avoid it, their pink and white sisters bulging through the season, haven't altered in 20 years. It's not that they reject the social revolution, they are unaware it's happening. But the smart upper class young are beginning to lose their mannerisms, or at any rate when sober. Whereas at one time they couldn't dance, and were in consequence instantly recognisable as "hoorays," they can now dance as well and sometimes better than their working and lower middle class contemporaries. When in their cups, however, they are still inclined to revert to a flushed arrogance of gesture. Their sisters, while still recognisable, usually on account of their height, are learning to conquer the hockey playing stride and toothy grin.

Lower middle class gentility and whimsy are also dying; the crook't finger sticking out from the teacup handle, the ballet steps in the presence of the first crocus, the hearty obtuseness of the saloon bar. Working class servility is dying. Cap touching, shuffling in the presence of social superiors, ugliness of movement. Compare, for example, young and old taxi drivers.

We are moving towards, if not a classless society, at least towards the establishment of a large classless area within our society. It has style, but lacks as yet direction. "Gesture without motion" Eliot wrote. That's the next problem.

[*17 June 1965*]

233

THE BODY TABOO

Sidney Jourard

To what extent will people let others see and touch their bodies? Little systematic research has been done into this; yet I suspect there is a connection between "body experience" (what someone perceives, believes, imagines, feels and fantasies about his body) and physical and mental health. Perhaps puritanical taboos about the body extend even into the attitudes of inquiring psychologists: the topic is not fit or important enough to study. Some research I have carried out attempts to make good the lack.

My approach was simple enough. I began my inquiries with some self-examination. "Whom have I let see me naked? Whom do I permit to touch me? Where do I allow them to touch me? How do I feel about this kind of intimacy? Are there some parts of my body I am embarrassed to touch myself, much less let someone else touch?" After I answered these questions, I was surprised, and (as an investigator) delighted to find that my attitudes and experience were very complex indeed.

I then asked students, patients, colleagues and friends to tell me their attitudes to body contact and their experience of it. I found fantastic variability. Some people reported that if anyone laid a hand on them, uninvited, they would become furious. Others stated that they liked nothing so much as to parade in the nude, and to receive a body massage at every opportunity.

There are also sharp cultural differences in the frequency with which inhabitants of different countries let their bodies contact others. In Mexico and Puerto Rico, for example, many people walk arm in arm—men with men, women with women—without anyone doubting their heterosexual integrity. People in conversation come close to one another, tap one another on the chest or arm to emphasise points. But Anglo-Saxon Americans, Canadians and British are more reserved and distant. They are uncomfortable if people "get too close."

I designed a simple self-report questionnaire, not unlike a butcher's beef chart. It consisted of an outline drawing of the

234

human figure, with 22 zones marked off and numbered. For example, the top of the head was No. 1, the hands were No. 15, the buttocks were No. 22. I prepared a little booklet with four of these drawings, one for mother, one for father, and one each for closest friend of the same sex, and closest friend of the opposite sex. I gave these booklets to several hundred college students in my class at the University of Florida, asking them to check which parts of their bodies had been seen, unclad, by each of the "target persons"; which parts had been touched for any reason whatever; and, which parts of these other persons' bodies they had seen and touched. I encouraged the students to be absolutely frank in their responses and said they could leave their names off the replies to ensure anonymity.

The findings rather surprised me. The "visual accessibility" scores were not very interesting, because almost all the students had seen and been seen by the other people in brief bathing costumes. But the touch data were a different matter. Both men and women students touched (and were touched by) their parents and same-sex friends on only a few areas of the body—the hands, arms and shoulders mostly. When the closest opposite-sex friend was considered, the data were striking. It was almost as if the floodgates were opened. There was a virtual deluge of physical contact, all over the body. But there was much variability in these findings. Not all the students enjoyed a steady relationship with someone of the opposite sex, and these poor devils reported that they were virtually untouched, and out of touch.

This research points up something important—that there isn't a great deal of body contact going on in these young students' lives, outside the strictly sexual context. It's almost as if all possible meanings of a touch are eliminated except the caress with sexually arousing intent. Not that there is anything wrong with the latter; but it does imply that unless a young American (or British?) adult is engaged in sexual lovemaking, he is unlikely to experience his body as it feels when someone is touching, poking, massaging, hugging or holding it. The exception, of course, is provided by physical-contact sports. These give devotees the opportunity to feel embodied in a personally and socially acceptable way. But not everyone takes part in these.

What other forms of acceptable body contact are available

to the average person in our contactless society? Physical massage can be purchased for a fee in most cities in the United States and Britain—but this is impersonal and professional. The physically ill may, if their nurse is not too busy sorting laundry, medications and papers, receive a skilful, depersonalised backrub, given either as prescribed TLC (tender loving care), or to prevent muscle stiffness and to relieve tension. Men's and women's hairdressers may provide a certain amount of touching and rubbing of the head without arousing anxieties or embarrassment in their clients. In the United States, many barbers use electrical vibrators strapped to their hand, to depersonalise the contact of hand on scalp. In American motels, beds are often equipped with "magic fingers"—a patented vibrator which, for a 25 cent coin, will shake a person into relaxation without benefit of human intervention. It seems as if the machine has taken over another function of man—the loving and soothing caress.

Thus, because of cultural norms in Anglo-Saxon countries, people are deprived of the most basic way to experience their bodies—through the human touch. Unless they have a sexual relationship going with someone, people in our countries are not likely to be touched after the years of childhood. I suspect that the dog patter, cat stroker and child hugger is seeking the contact that is conspicuously and poignantly lacking in his adult life.

Why the touch taboo?

I think it is part of the more general alienation process that characterises our depersonalising social system. I think it is related to the same source that underlies the dread of authentic self-disclosure. When people are committed to upward mobility, in competition with their fellows, everyone masquerades, and keeps his real self concealed from the other who is a potential enemy. You keep others at a distance and mystified by withholding disclosure, and by not letting them get close enough to touch, not letting them know how you feel.

In such a society, our bodies tend to disappear. Not from the other's gaze, or even from our own glance into the mirror. Rather, they vanish from our *experience*. We lose the capacity to experience our bodies as vital, enlivened and as the centres of our being. I think that the restricted experience of being touched is consistent with R. D. Laing's diagnosis of modern man as "unembodied." My own experience as a product of rather puritanical Canadian schooling, and adult life in the United States, has given me personal experience of the disembodiment middle class upbringing produces in these countries. My research and my experience as a psychotherapist both lead me to confirm Laing. I have come to believe that we give up the capacity to experience our body as enlivened, in return for the "benefits" of our increasingly automated and mechanised way of life.

We all begin life as sentient bodies, and then encounter the massive onslaught of repressive forces that aim at annihilating, or at least diminishing, the experience of pleasure and pain, sensuality, fatigue and energy, fullness and emptiness. The purpose of socialising is not only to control behaviour, but also to regulate experience. The capacity to experience one's body disappears—a victim of parents' and schools' efforts to transmute infants and children into respectable adults.

Children who touch their own bodies, as in exploratory masturbation, are punished, and threatened with predictions of insanity and depravity. Children who touch other things (children encounter the world by means of touch) are slapped, and told "mustn't touch." They are taught to keep their bodies at a distance from things and people: look, but don't touch.

Parents' and teachers' efforts to distract growing children from awareness of sexuality also succeed in distracting children from more general sensitivity to their bodies. By the time children reach adulthood, they have managed to set themselves at such a distance from their bodies, that their feet and hands, bellies and genitals, backs and backsides, are experienced as belonging "out there," away from the centre of self.

The diminuendo quality of the average person's experience of his body appears to be necessary, if he is to be able to subject himself to the increasingly automated and regulated styles of life offered him. A day which begins with the rush through breakfast, the hurry to go to work, and the mechanical, meaningless, fragmentary quality of work itself—anybody, anybody, would shriek in protest if he allowed himself to *feel* the violence to which he is subjecting himself. The "normal" state of being—numbness—seems essential for people to continue living in, and preserving social and economic status quos.

237

The body taboo

The devastated appearance of most adults' bodies when they reach their thirties and forties attests to the violence they have passively accepted. The ways of living life that earn money and respectability are the very ways that destroy the awareness and the liveliness of the bodies that we *are*.

When I lived in London, I used to pass the time on my daily trips to Piccadilly Circus tube station (beginning at Southgate) looking at people's bodies. One phenomenon that impressed me was the "vanishing lip." I would see a whole family seated side by side: the infants and the young children with soft, suckling lips. The adolescents already were getting the tight, disembodied look. The parents manifested what I called "the thin red line"— the lips had vanished, as if re-absorbed, replaced by a tight crack. So noticeable were the missing lips that, on a visit to Paris, I found myself standing in a Metro car, with a plump woman in her fifties to one side, a moustached policeman on the other. Both had such full lips, I felt like turning to right and left to kiss them.

A visit to a public beach, in the United States or Britain, is a sobering experience. The adults look hideous or pathetic. Mounds of billowing, pasty flesh, or tight bundles of piano wire.

I have a strong suspicion that a great deal of physical sickness arises because we have not noticed the early, all-is-not-well signals generated by the way of life that is not good for our bodies. If body experience is repressed, then the way of life is continued until stress and pain cross a very high threshold. Someone more tuned in to his body might have noticed the beginnings of malaise, and changed what he was doing to (and with) his body, in order to regain a sense of vitality and well-being. Indeed, much of the tranquilising and sedating medicine that is devoured aims at further annihilating body experience, so that destructive life styles can be continued, and the social system maintained.

Dancers and athletes necessarily have a keener sense of the condition of their bodies. They simply cannot perform when they are not warmed up, when they are cramped from inactivity, or depressed by an unsatisfying way of life. They can sense when muscles are stiff, when energy is at a low ebb, when they have eaten too much or too little. Likewise, Hatha Yoga devotees regain the alive, centred, organic sense of their bodies that they began life with. The *asanas* (special postures) undo the muscular

238

armouring that is generated by the usual way of life, and bring the body into a dynamic readiness and repose that is not available to the average person.

Smokers of marijuana and users of LSD regularly report that, when the drug begins to take effect, their mostly unused senses become enlivened. They hear sounds ordinarily ignored; smell odours that always have been present; and they feel their bodies with heightened awareness. Such psychedelic drugs seem to detach a person from his chronic projects, in pursuit of which he screens out irrelevant experience. Certainly, a keen awareness of our bodies would interfere with most of our daily or long-term aspirations. When the pull of our projects is suspended, as happens with the consciousness-expanding drugs, our awareness is inundated, as it were, with sense data that hitherto have been chronically screened out. It is as if all the channels on a television set were simultaneously turned on. The amplified consciousness of the body that occurs under "pot" or "acid" terrifies some over-repressed users, but is sought as a goal by others. The hippies—the new generation of non-violent revolutionaries— seek heightened experience of their bodies through drugs, or sensuous contact, as their form of social protest.

Increasing numbers of psychotherapists are becoming interested in techniques for awakening a benumbed body consciousness. In the United States, teachers of body awareness, like Bernard Gunther at the Esalen Institute in Big Sur Hot Springs, conduct classes aimed at undoing the repression of body experience. Alexander Lowen, a pupil of Wilhelm Reich, conducts classes and workshops in New York in which the students are run through exercises that undo cramped muscles, and awaken the possibilities of feeling in otherwise anaesthetic body zones.

In my own psychotherapeutic work, I have encouraged and guided patients into such Hatha Yoga postures that I have mastered myself, and in which I have found much benefit. And I have encouraged patients to learn the art of body massage, and to teach it to others so that this way of awakening body experience, and diminishing social distance, can be introduced into their lives,

I think that much could be done to make life more livable, and bodies more beautiful and healthy, through such reembodying procedures. Neglect of one's body through ignorance; avoidance of physical contact with others; loss of experience of one's body through repression; and misuse of the body in the obsessive pursuit of security or respectability—all these diminish life. As Bernard Gunther puts it (with tongue only partly in his cheek), "If everyone massaged somebody for an hour every day, there would be no war." Certainly, if people sought to regain the experience of their bodies through massage, meditation, exercises, yoga, and other means; and if they explored ways to keep their sense of their bodies alive, there would be much less illness. Finally, in a society which fosters the alienation of person from person, I can think of no more direct way to get in touch than by touching.

[*9 November 1967*]

THE VISIT

Tony Gould

Last night, during their party, one of the spastic girls broke down and cried; and went on crying although—or perhaps because—one of our students with a kind heart and strong maternal instincts tried to comfort her. They had to take her away, still crying, when all the spastics left early this morning by coach.

The spastics were at the Devon handicapped centre for a fortnight, on a course to test their aptitude for work; for they have all just finished their schooling. They did practical work, they painted pictures; they visited a castle, and a factory; they wrote mock-application letters for jobs, and had a discussion on the subject, "Why Work?"—"It's very simple," said Ian. "There's only one reason, and that's money." They spent what was probably the happiest fortnight of their lives.

The students of the art college gave a party for them and sang songs with guitar accompaniment. The girls, some barefoot with the long hair and paint-spattered jeans, and the boys (who are smart this year and wear ties) moved among the drably or brightly—but unfashionably—dressed spastics, brought them cups of coffee and encouraged them to join in—which they did, readily enough.

But the students only met them at parties; we, the staff of the college and centre, had every meal with them. We were their "friends," and as such were greeted on our entry into the dining-room and more or less told where to sit. Sport and the world of television were common topics of conversation. They organised their own session of *Juke Box Jury* and borrowed a bell to register hits.

It was Richard, our drama teacher and producer, who lent them the bell and did not complain when it came back cracked. Being popular, he was subjected to friendly physical assaults from both Ian and Philip. Philip could not speak coherently, but made noises when he wanted anything and smiled frequently; he threw his left arm back when he was excited and was usually the first to greet our entry into the room.

Judith often sat next to him and brought him his food; one of us would cut it up for him. Judith was a big Scandinavian blonde and herself severely handicapped. Both she and Philip wore deaf-aids and, though she could speak, her speech was very difficult to understand. But she liked to do things for others and would go and collect our food and coffee. She was so shaky, however, that most of the coffee would be in the saucers by the time it reached our table.

"I didn't go to school until I was eleven," she told me. "I'm backward, you see. I would like to have more education, learn more."

I sympathised and agreed. What had happened to my leg, she wanted to know. Polio. Had I had an iron machine on my chest? Yes, the iron lung. When was that? Seven years ago. How old was I then? Twenty.

At the next meal she told me I was 27. She was delighted when I appeared surprised that she should know my age. She explained how she had worked it out, and asked how far I could walk.

The night before last, as we entered the dining room for our evening meal, Richard said: "I can't face Ian tonight; we'll tell them we're having a business discussion and sit at another table."

We collected our soup and there were the usual shouts: "Over here, Richard," and "We've saved your seat, Tony." Richard made his excuses and went to another table. I followed, but Judith pulled out a chair as I was about to go past her.

"Sit here," she said.

"I can't tonight, Judith," I explained. "I have to talk with Richard—some business, you know. You must excuse me tonight." She looked at me and then her head dropped with a sudden spastic movement.

Yesterday morning at breakfast, she ignored me, walking past as if I were a stranger. I said, "Hello," but she did not reply. I sat at Ian's table and was relieved to find that I still had friends there. At lunch, Judith sat alone and I watched her from the next table; soon others joined her. By the evening excitement had reached high tide: the party was soon to begin. Ian was the comedian, his only prop a battered trilby; he ordered Richard, who had shown them round the theatre earlier in the day, to be there at the beginning, at 8 pm.

I arrived late. Everyone was seated along the four walls of the room and they were passing round a newspaper parcel. The one holding it when the music stopped stripped a layer of paper and had to perform a forfeit. "Kiss the girl with the most beautiful nose," read out the master of ceremonies, and there was general laughter—and embarrassment. The deed done, the package was passed on. The music stopped again and the girl who held it threw it on to her neighbour as if it were burning her fingers; her neighbour threw it back. It passed to and fro between them until order was restored. The first girl opened the package and there was the prize—a packet of sweet cigarettes.

"I hope she smokes," someone said.

For the next game, all the men were called to form a line in the centre of the room. The girls had to circle round, and grab a man's arm when the music stopped. Men were removed from each end of the line, and the girls went out one by one. Only one man remained—and two girls, one of whom was badly deformed. Chairs were placed at each end of the room for the contestants to go round. But the more crippled girl was so flustered that she began by circling in the wrong direction; then she caught hold of one chair and slid about, unable to control her movements.

"I can't do it. I can't," she said, with fear and excitement. Prizes were found for both.

Ian did his comedy act, but the others had seen it before and knew all his jokes. He had his revenge by calling out half-a-dozen of them to kneel on the floor as part of a shaggy-dog story involving a man in the desert looking for a camel.

Richard contributed impromptu limericks—or almost impromptu. They were much appreciated: "There was an old man called Dobby (Mr Dobson was in charge of the course), who had an extraordinary hobby . . ."

Then Dobby himself—for he was master of ceremonies—announced: "There's been a request for another performance from a young lady whom some of us saw dance the other night. For those who didn't I think it will be something of an experience. Unfortunately we have not got any ballet music here, so we're putting on the record *Tears*. Judith."

There was a round of applause as Judith walked to the centre of the room. I could not believe it. She began to dance. In all their terrible distortion the movements were recognisable as those of ballet: her hands met above her head, she kicked out her legs, and she bent forward and touched the ground with her sweeping hands. All this without self-consciousness; she even paused to adjust her right shoe. On her face a smile played, but she saw no one. I watched and listened, entranced and revolted. The grotesque sentimentality of the song might have been designed to emphasise the macabre element of the performance. The record would not end. I watched with horror the final shaky bow of the dancer and waited for her to fall on the floor. But she did not fall. Instead, she came over and sat down on the sofa in front of me.

"But that was beautiful, Judith," I said. I hoped we might still be friends, though I was glad she was going the next day. She turned round and stared at me. I was relieved that she smiled. She struggled for words. "You see, it comes from my soul," she spluttered.

I preferred facts of a different nature: "How long have you been dancing?" "A long time. I have dancing lessons . . ." The rest of the sentence I could not understand, so I nodded sagely.

Some of our students arrived with a guitar. They sang *We shall overcome* brightly and earnestly. The girl who had to be removed was weeping loudly. Carey sat by the young student, his arm around her as she held the head of the weeping girl against her breast. I moved to another seat. Judith brought over a bowl full of crisps and presented it to me as an offering, accompanied by bows and elaborate hand gestures. Then, as if suddenly remembering the prayers to Allah of Ian's comic act in the desert, she got down on her knees and raised her hands before bending forward with outstretched arms and lowered head. I pushed my chair back hard against the wall.

"Come on, Judith, get up—please. You must have some crisps, too." She shook her head, but she got up and then sat down beside me. "God will make you better," she said. "To-morrow morning you'll be better. You can bend your leg more than you could before, can't you?"

"Let's hope we all get better," I said weakly, aware of the pressure of her arm and thigh against me.

"Why don't you dance with the others, Judith?" I asked. But this was not her sort of dancing. She got up, however, and I saw someone stop to talk with her. I made for the staircase leading down to the bar.

[*20 October 1966*]

... where awkward questions crop up,

THE IMPORTANCE OF NATIONALISM

Douglas Johnson

There is a complex of ideas which are usually identified as nationalism. In this country the reputation of nationalism has undergone a number of interesting changes. There was a time when, apart from certain liberals and a few socialists, there was a general approval of nationalism as a European movement. Those statesmen in European history who had failed to recognise or to accept the power of nationalism were condemned for their blindness and for their obstinacy. Metternich was a monument of reaction and folly for believing that he could prop up any edifice against the attacks of the various nationalities; there was an exaggerated estimate of the extent to which British statesmen such as Palmerston and Gladstone had assisted certain national movements on the continent. It seemed natural that the 19th century should have been the century of nationalism, leading to the mutilation of old empires and the formation of new states, culminating in the principle of national self-determination at the Treaty of Versailles. Nationalism was associated with progress, with the voice of the people, with high ideals.

But this attitude started to undergo a change, mainly during the interwar period. With the realisation of the terrible nature of the 1914 war and the conviction that the next war would be even worse, went the belief that war arose from conflicting nationalisms. With the difficulties of international affairs went the realisation that the principle of national self-determination had not brought any harmony to Europe. With the growth of national aspirations in overseas territories went a reluctance to accept that there could be any similarity between the organised, sophisticated nation-states of Europe and the inchoate agglomerations of non-European peoples.

The experience of Hitler and Mussolini confirmed that nationalism was a bad thing. Nationalism was associated with racialism and persecution, with the suppression of the individual and of individual rights, with the destruction of moral and intellectual principles alike. Nationalism was an evil which had to be rejected; most forms of idealism became associated with internationalism.

Since the war, hostility to the ideas and principles of nationalism has been encouraged by the belief that nationalism as an ideal or as a political reality is on the way out. The demands of economic progress have underlined the inadequacies of national economies. The complicated technology of modern strategy causes national states to pool their resources and to combine their organisations. The rapidity of communications can only serve to break down national barriers. The whole nature of modern production and consumption can only bring national groups closer together, as they wear similar clothes, watch the same television programmes, listen to the same music, and lead lives which differ less and less from one country to another.

Therefore the resurgence of some form of nationalism, or the appearance of some articulate believer in the nation-state, such as General de Gaulle, is usually regarded as a step backwards and as something to be deplored. Such nationalism is either dangerous, and has to be opposed; or ludicrous, and one is assured that gaullism will disappear with its founder, who is the same age as the Eiffel Tower.

The nationalisms of Africa and Asia are not ignored, but it is claimed that they are radically different from their European predecessors. They have come about, either because of the weaknesses of European countries, or because they have been manufactured by an elite of European-trained intellectuals. Sometimes, the much vaunted nationalisms of Africa are conspicuous by their absence, as certain African states have not seized or demanded their independence, they have only had to whisper, or they have simply drifted into independence.

International organisation, thinking and culture, Europe, pan-Africanism, ideologies with a world-wide appeal and with supranational activities, negritude: it is these which supposedly hold the future. Professor Louis Halle has even maintained that the very interest which historians now show in the phenomenon of nationalism is a sign that nationalism is passing.

It is only when the old is about to disappear that we make it the subject of self-conscious study. It was not until 1890, when

250

sea power was on the eve of its obsolescence, that Alfred Thayer Mahan published *The Influence of Sea-Power on History*. Similarly, it could be argued that it was not until the process of European imperialism was slowing up that the Hobsons, Lenins and Schumpeters began to analyse what imperialism really was. It was not until the end of British India was already in the air that a writer such as E. M. Forster tried to grasp what it was and what it meant in terms of human relationships. So now historians try to come to grips with nationalism, rather than take it for granted, just as nationalism itself is becoming an anachronism.

There is a certain amount of truth in all this. But one has to ask whether the main assumptions are, in fact, true. Is one witnessing the disappearance of nationalism, or is one observing its persistence?

Since 1945 the world can hardly be said to have shown the decline of nationalism. Asia, Africa, and Latin America have exhibited different forms of nationalism, but one can usually find similarities between these nationalisms and those of the 19th and 20th centuries in Europe. Even when it is the contrasts which are most prominent, this only serves to demonstrate the richness of the concept. The idea that there is a specific group, whether real or imaginary, to which the population owes allegiance, and which is the nation, or the nation-state, or the nationally organised state, remains the dominant and persistent principle. The United States, for long a critic of narrow nationalism, has itself become a highly nationalist organisation. After the principle that there were "un-American activities" there came the message of the New Frontier—"Do not ask what your country can do for you, ask what you can do for your country." Communism, for long the enemy of nationalisms, seems to have accepted the idea of national communisms. And the supposedly remarkable idea of Europe has hardly had any effect on enthusiasm for the individual nation-state.

The successes of gaullism only arise because they correspond to genuine sentiments. Where there is a real enthusiasm for Europe, perhaps as in the case of Belgium, this arises because of the failure to create a Belgian nationalism, so that the state of Belgium is torn between two conflicting nationalisms. However fast the motor road between Liege and Aachen, when one

251

arrives in Aachen one finds that the beds are made in a specifically German way. The Tour de France is to return to the system
of being a competition of national teams, rather than a competition between manufacturers. Even in Great Britain a Welsh
nationalist is elected to parliament at a time of crisis, and whenever a British statesman wishes to call for greater efforts from
the population, it is the language of nationalism which he uses.
Neither Harold Wilson nor Duncan Sandys seems to find it out
of date to urge different classes and sectors of the community
to work for England and to demonstrate to the rest of the world
that there are qualities which are specifically British.

Bearing these things in mind, there are three factors which
are worthy of further consideration with regard to the problem
of nationalism. In the first place, we are bound to wonder
whether there is any general explanation for the phenomenon of
nationalism. It is easy enough to point to what is particular,
and to what is not of general application. But there is one
explanation which one can suggest as a generalisation: namely,
that nationalism seems to appear and to grow strong whenever
the other reference points of political loyalties weaken. When,
for a variety of reasons, religious, dynastic or feudal allegiances
as the justifications of political entities tend to be displaced,
then it seems that the natural right of the nation, however
exactly or loosely conceived, begins to grow and to thrive.

Therefore, if the consciousness of nationality or of belonging
to the nation-group is itself to decline, then it is fair to ask by
what is it to be replaced? We are told a great deal about the
difficulty of belonging to the community in which one lives, of
the sense of alienation or of anomie, of the need to establish
one's identity, of the need for security and fulfilment. Can one
suggest a religious or a political ideology which can confer
this sense of relevance on both the community and the individual?

It is difficult to think of one. A recent survey in France
attempted to discover what certain individual Frenchmen understood by nationalism. It was shown that individuals, while
claiming to belong to different political affiliations, to the right
or to the left, nevertheless were united in the importance they
attached to the idea of belonging to the historical entity of
France. It is the idea of the nation, more than anything else,

which can unite different political and social groups. Loyalty to capitalism or to communism, the desire of a particular group for economic and social progress, none of these is likely to be such a powerful cohesive force. The example of Vietnam has its relevance. One does not usually oppose American policy in Vietnam on behalf of the principle of the Asian revolution, but one opposes the Americans because one believes in the rights and in the future of the Vietnam nation. One does not usually support American policy because one believes in certain abstract constitutional principles, but because one believes that the entity of the Vietnam nation has to be defended and built up. Both viewpoints assume the existence of a nation in Vietnam.

Examples are only too common of communities which have opted for national identity rather than for economic comfort (the Germans in Danzig, the Greeks in Cyprus, many African and Asian nations). It has often been difficult for Europeans, with their national aspirations safely accomplished, to appreciate an apparent indifference to economic realities. An observer such as E. M. Forster was impatient with his Indian friends because they only thought of political freedom. They wouldn't, he said, "leave one fine impulse ungratified" (*The Hill of Devi*). It is difficult to see how all this, the functions of various types of nationalism, are to become otiose, or by what they can be replaced.

Secondly, one of the most striking aspects of nationalism is cultural nationalism. One of the best examples, naturally enough is to be found in France. "Since all French people know that there is a great part of the honour of France which is called Victor Hugo, it is appropriate to tell them that there is a part of the honour of France which is called Braque, because the honour of a country consists first of all in what that country gives to the world." So spoke André Malraux (*Le Monde*, 5 September 1963). As culture becomes more popular, is there any likelihood that it will become less national, or less nationalist? It is probable that as the individual is offered more leisure and greater cultural opportunities, he will above all seek the experience of the national culture.

Those who have the task of providing entertainment and information are above all preoccupied by the need to reach the masses, and they will meet their difficulties by insisting on national cultures. As state, municipal, or voluntary organisations

253

increasingly contribute to the cost of providing culture, it seems probable that they will support national culture most readily. Possibly J. B. Priestley was wrong when he spoke of us all being "Home Service types," but perhaps in the long run he may be proved right. It is sometimes said that there is no more revealing culture than sport. In the recent World Cup, although everyone could applaud the skill of the best players in the world and appreciate the sport in terms of its intrinsic values, yet it seems that enthusiasm and appreciation were invariably national. The future holds the prospect of more world cups, as it holds the prospect of more national participation in international competitions, more encouragement for national sportsmen and artists, and more national news bulletins.

Thirdly, there is the great problem of the relations which exist between the developed (or overdeveloped) societies, and the developing (or underdeveloped) societies, the Third World. And here it is relevant to European nationalisms to consider the concept of "neo-colonialism." Supposedly invented by Sartre in 1956, and popularised particularly by Dr Nkrumah's most recently published book, this theory betrays the profound disappointment of many Africans and Asians with the consequences of their independence. Colonial governments have been removed, but their economic power and privilege have remained. European and American investors and capitalists still exploit the populations of the *Tiers Monde*. What has been effected is a limited, bourgeois revolution, which has given a certain prosperity to a minority, while the majority remains condemned to misery and lasting ignorance.

In this, African and Asian thinkers join with those from Latin America who claim that the independence of their states is a myth, within the reality of economic control by the United States, but the real hero of these theories is Patrice Lumumba. It is Lumumba who represents the African Revolution; it is those who have overthrown him who represent the betrayal of the revolution and the power of neo-colonialism. One is likely to see a further emphasis on nationalism linked to socialism, and a search for a new identity, that of all the oppressed nations together. Such moves are likely to be opposed by various particularist groups, those who are privileged or those who have other means of asserting their identity.

What concerns us here is not so much the reality or otherwise of neo-colonialism, but what this concept tells us about the developed nations. One of the constants of nationalism is the need which national groups often experience—the need to feel, or to assert, their superiority. The present relations between the developed and the underdeveloped countries seems to satisfy that need. The whole idea of aid and assistance to the backward and starving (and usually coloured) populations, underlines the technical and moral superiority of those who are rich. Whether the aid is received with gratitude or not, the sense of superiority remains. It is not simply that politicians, parsons and do-gooders find an easy theme; it is not that the Lady Bountifuls are in the OXFAM shops; nor that young people can find a sense of purpose by spending a year working overseas. It fosters the sense of being privileged and of being successful, sometimes in a more complete way than imperialism did.

In the days of empire there was a sense of frustration. One knew that there were indigenous institutions and customs which were bad and which should be abolished; but often one was governing through, and thanks to, those very institutions, and one was powerless to change the customs. In some ways, neo-colonialism is more attractive to us than colonialism.

The attitude of the British public towards Lumumba, or towards the overthrow of Nkrumah, is well worth investigating. The language concerning Lumumba was particularly violent (and he was referred to in a Historical Association pamphlet with a bitter hostility which must be unique in these publications). The unanimity with which Nkrumah's downfall was welcomed was also impressive. Is it not likely that both Lumumba and Nkrumah were men who did not fit easily into the picture of a benevolent west, helping others to stand on their feet? Therefore they were offensive to a certain British sense of identity, which is something which stands near to what one means by nationalism.

Political thinkers these days are self-consciously prudent. They approach both abstract concepts and political decisions with an equal caution, and we are all influenced by this. It seems reasonable then to suggest that rather than dream of the disappearance of nations and nation-states, we should find out more about nationalism and how it affects us. Paley once wrote,

255

The importance of nationalism

"Although we speak of communities as of sentient beings; although we ascribe to them happiness and misery, desires, interests and passions; nothing really exists or feels but individuals." Historians, like others, are becoming more community-conscious. It is hard to agree with Paley.

[*1 September 1966*]

THE DETROIT RIOTS

Nathan Glazer

Everyone feels that the Detroit riots of 1967 mark a turning point—either that the country from this point on descends more steeply into a nightmare of destruction and anarchy; or that there will be a violent, fearful, and vengeful reaction by the people and their governments; or that by some miracle we will find a way to overcome this spiral of looting, burning, and killing. And one feels it will take a miracle, for the worst aspect of Detroit is not the fact that it is the most destructive of the riots— 37 lives, 1,700 businesses, $200 million or more in damage— but that it demonstrates to us how little we know and understand about what is happening in the northern ghettoes, and thus weakens our will—already too weak—to undertake the programmes and the actions that might overcome the crisis.

Actually for a few weeks before Detroit, it was clear that something new was happening. For three summers now, city after city has undergone the same pattern—an incident, generally involving the police, a gathering crowd, the beginning of window smashing and looting, a more or less swift and forceful response by the police, some killings, many more arrests, perhaps fires, all too easily started in a country where every filling station and automobile is a potential arsenal of Molotov cocktails, and eventually peace.

And then the newspapers and the civic leaders and the politicians begin to ask: why Rochester, or Cleveland, or Philadelphia, or whatever city has been hit? And in response, some palliative measures—a job programme, in which the businessmen offer more of the jobs that the unemployed youth don't want, or in which the city makes some work, a recreational programme, a community relations programme involving the police, to teach them how to behave in a less provocative manner, and how to keep their cool and hold their fire to prevent bad incidents from building up and getting worse.

To see merely the continued development of such a pattern would be to seriously misunderstand what is happening. First,

257

since the beginning of the summer the disorders have been hitting more than one city at a time. In fact, the disorder is now endemic in every Negro area in the urban north and west. We hear of only four or five cities at a time—or, in the worst cases, about a dozen, as in the last few days—but in other cities too, Negro youths are gathering, breaking into stores, throwing fire bombs. Perhaps there are only three or four incidents, not enough to make a full-scale riot, because of luck. Perhaps the Negro youths do not have a really daring leader, the police are more skilful (though in what the skill consists it would be hard to say), or the area does not have enough traffic to collect a crowd to observe the arrests.

If you talk to a sociologist who has been working in the ghetto, he will say: when is breaking a few store windows and grabbing the stuff inside simply another Saturday night in the ghetto—and when is it a riot? There is no question that Newark and Detroit are full-scale riots—but there are a lot of marginal cases. But I am convinced that overall the pattern of disturbance has changed—there is less of breaking, grabbing and running by a single individual or a group of furtive youths, and more of open and arrogant looting. But in any case, the pattern has spread—and that is ominous in itself.

Second, the riots have increased in nastiness. One of the hopeful aspects—if one can find any hopeful aspects—of the rioting of the past three years has been that it has not involved direct physical attacks by whites on Negroes, or Negroes on whites. The shops and stores have been the targets, rather than the shopkeepers. This has contributed to the carnival aspect, which from one point of view is grisly, but from another point of view has suggested that perhaps the passion for goods outweighs the hate of the white man. And on the other side, whereas the riots that followed the first world war and accompanied the second world war often consisted of ferocious attacks by white men on Negroes, in which Negroes were hunted through the streets and killed, in the present spate of riots there has been very little of ordinary citizens killing each other. Rather, the deaths have been the result of police shooting and, even more, National Guard shooting.

But with Newark and Detroit, things have got nastier. Shooting at firemen trying to control the fires has now become a standard part of the scene (firemen were killed in Newark and Detroit)—which is why the fires have become so much more destructive. In Newark, the snipers also shot at the emergency room of the main hospital, and pinned down the hospital staff a number of times. In Plainfield, New Jersey, a policeman was killed by a Negro mob, after he had been disarmed. In Newark, the National Guardsmen shot out the windows of Negro businesses that had been spared by the rioters. In Plainfield, the National Guard carried out a house-to-house search of doubtful legality in a Negro housing project, looking for arms, and in the course of it left the homes a shambles. Up until now, some have said, these are not race riots but uprisings of the poor, because the races are not ranged on opposite sides—except for the fact that most of the policemen are white. (But Newark has 400 Negro policemen out of 1,600.) It is no longer possible to minimise the race aspect.

Third, up until now the riots have been confined to the ghettoes, and while the ghettoes have burned, the rest of the city has gone about its business. Even in Los Angeles, despite the enormous area over which the destruction and shooting raged, most of that widespread city was unaffected. There were fears that Negroes would invade the white areas, and threats too that they would. But these were not realised. There was a scare; many people 20 or 30 miles from Watts bought guns. But the riot was confined to the Negro areas.

The change here is partly an ecological matter. In Newark, which is more than 50 per cent Negro, it is inevitable that the Negro area abuts the downtown—and the downtown closed down, because employees were afraid to come to work, customers were afraid to come to shop or to do business. In Detroit, the impact on the city has been worse. Thirty per cent Negro, with the Negro areas consisting of a number of wide belts, reaching out to the city's borders, and with large parts of the city integrated—more so perhaps than any other large American city—it was inevitable that the disorder affected almost the whole city.

The great headquarters of the auto companies could not open, the factories were closed. Governor Romney himself, in Detroit, expressed fears for his wife, in their home in the northern suburb of Bloomfield Hills. In New York, stores on Fifth Avenue have been looted for the first time. Unquestionably, in the next riots, the plateglass windows of the great downtown stores and banks will be smashed, and the pathetic stores of the Jewish shopkeepers of the ghetto will have grander company in distress.

Fourth, the disorders have now spread to cities that break many of the normal stereotypes of ghetto. Does the violence hit the cities with the densest concentrations of Negroes, the largest ghettoes? Minneapolis, with the smallest Negro population of any large city in the country (3 per cent) has had its riot, occasioning the calling out of the National Guard to supplement the local police. Does it hit only the large cities? Waterloo, Iowa, and large numbers of other small cities, with tiny Negro communities, have also had their outbreaks of looting and destruction. Is it that it hits cities with conservative administrations that do not take advantage of federal programmes of public housing, urban renewal, job training? Newark and Boston, with programmes more extensive than most, have had serious riots.

It was perhaps possible to ascribe some of the problems of Cleveland to its conservative Mayor Locher, some of the problems of Los Angeles to its conservative Mayor Yorty. It was possible to argue that it was Mayor Lindsay's heroic efforts last summer in New York to provide jobs and facilities in the ghettoes, to demonstrate personal concern and to show his presence on the hot streets, to institute intensive training of the police force in community relations, in riot control, in keeping things from blowing up—that all this had paid off, for New York did not have any major riot last year.

But under the impact of the most recent developments, every generalisation has crumbled. We know nothing; and this is perhaps the most frightening thing; for we do not know what to do. Or rather, we know what to do, for justice dictates many measures. But we can have no assurance it will prevent anarchy in the cities.

Consider Detroit. Thirty per cent Negro, it is true. Unemployment among Negroes is high, much of the housing is poor. But here is the city in which Negroes, on the average, make the most money, in which the gap between Negro and white income is among the smallest, in which Negroes have the most important role in government and in the affairs of the city. Mayor Jerome

Cavanagh was elected with Negro votes, and in recent months has been fighting the efforts of a white backlash group to recall him. He is one of the most intelligent, informed, liberal mayors in the country. He has sat on federal task forces on urban affairs, is close to the great foundations, and consults and is consulted by the leading experts on urban affairs. He has been aware of both the short-range and long-range measures that the best intelligence of the country thinks are necessary to deal with the problems of the ghettoes.

Thus, special measures have been taken to make sure that the residents of the ghetto have direct access to government to express their grievances, that government is aware of what is going on. The police have been educated in human relations. The school system has been among the leaders in integration—to the extent that is possible in a city like Detroit—and in developing new materials for the ghetto schools that speak specifically to these children and their problems. It has been among the most aggressive cities in taking advantage of the various federal programmes in training, child care and the like, made available by the poverty act.

All this may not amount to much, but there is more that should have made Detroit the least likely candidate for the most destructive riot. Its Negro community is represented in city, state and federal government on a scale that perhaps no other city can match. It sends two Negro Congressmen to Congress—which means that Detroit's Negroes are perhaps the only ones in the country that have representation in Congress equal to or surpassing their numbers. The United Automobile Workers are a power in the city of Detroit, and Negroes are integrated into the UAW, as workers, sharing in the high wages of the auto industry, and as leaders. It has what is perhaps the most fully integrated urban university in the country—Wayne State University. And one can say the same for the industrial cities of Michigan that have also been plagued by riots. Two of them—Flint and Saginaw—have Negro mayors.

In New Jersey, Paul Ylvisaker, formerly of the Ford Foundation, is State Commissioner of Community Affairs. In Minneapolis Art Naftalin, a former Professor of Political Science at the University of Minnesota, is now Mayor of Minneapolis. If one gathered ten top urban experts to consider what to do about the crisis, Ylvisaker, Cavanagh and Naftalin would very likely be among them. What could they say?

In Detroit, Negro businessmen and community leaders bitterly attacked Mayor Cavanagh and the police—because he had given the police, in the first few critical hours, instructions not to shoot, and the looting and burning then raged out of control. What lessons will be learned from Detroit? The one that will be learned most clearly, I am afraid, is that the police should begin shooting faster.

Thus the most serious change is that it may already be too late for the liberal and progressive response to social problems. We may be facing in the United States the kind of situation that comes up in world affairs and in revolutionary situations, when two antagonists are ready to destroy each other, when nations and groups decide that no accommodation is possible, when every resource is committed to conflict, even though rational men can demonstrate that conflict will destroy more than even victory can gain.

One does not measure costs when one knows that the enemy is so evil that he must be destroyed, when one knows that he is not to be trusted at all and that every promise is a ruse, when one is convinced that one's own existence is at stake. One knows that such thinking and such attitudes exist in the Negro community. The question is—how widespread are these attitudes, and do they have really any direct connection with the riots?

Just after Newark, and before Detroit, the Black Power conference convened in Newark. Adam Clayton Powell was one of its co-sponsors (though he stayed in the Bahamas in view of the danger of arrest if he came to the United States), well-known leaders such as Floyd McKissick and James Farmer attended (though they withdrew before the end), but it nevertheless represented more than the extreme fringe in the Negro community. Those who take African and Muslim names and dress were present in large numbers, but well-known Negro political leaders and officials were also there. A great number of resolutions were passed, and if they were compiled they would serve as a compendium of the kind of talk that has been heard ever more frequently in the ghetto: that white America is irredeemably racist, irredeemably malevolent, irredeemably committed to the inferiority and even destruction of the Negro. And many things

262

followed from this: freedom and equality for the black man would have to be achieved through his own power alone; no white ally could be trusted; force and violence were necessary; and ultimately the blacks would have to be separated from the whites, in their own nation.

Thus, by a roundabout route, the communist demand of the thirties for a separate Negro nation in America has been resuscitated. It seemed like a comic fantasy when a year and a half ago a Negro group in San Francisco attacked birth control programmes (birth control information and supplies are now being made available to women on welfare in many communities) as genocide, designed to decrease the numbers of the Negro race. One of the resolutions at the Black Power conference, however, subscribed to this belief.

We can interpret what is happening in two different ways. The first would be to emphasise the real conditions of the ghetto —the poor jobs, the unemployment, the dilapidated housing, the inadequate schools and health and recreational facilities, the prejudices of the police, the indifference or remoteness of the teachers and social workers. And we can insist that these conditions cause the riots, and until they are modified, the riots will continue and grow worse. Objectively, there has been a good deal of change in the northern Negro communities. There are somewhat more good jobs, and considerably more aid in getting them and getting training for them; the quality of housing is slowly improving as Negroes move out of the oldest slums; schools are improving physically, and unmeasured numbers of programmes try out new approaches to training teachers and teaching children. Free legal services are becoming available to help in dealing with the police and the welfare and housing and educational agencies.

It is very unfashionable to refer to what has been, and is being, done. And one is almost embarrassed to do so. The liberal, rational, meliorist interpretation of these events would be to emphasise that not enough has been done, that more must be done, and that objective improvement in the situation, if it comes fast enough, will restore peace.

But one can adopt quite another interpretation of what is happening. Whatever objective changes have occurred or are even conceivable in the near future, may be no match for the

263

revolutionary change in expectations, in demands and, even worse, in the conception of American society, its nature and how changes in it take place, that is now taking place in the ghetto. Perhaps a revolution in rising expectations can be dealt with, in a country as rich as the United States. But how does one deal with a revolution in the prevalent view of society, which emphasises its incapacity to change, even under the impact of violence? If it is racist, malevolent, and corrupt, can any of its actions be good, and is anything aside from fire and destruction therefore adequate to its enormity?

Thus one interpretation of Detroit is that a truly revolutionary mood has seized enough Negroes in the ghetto, one that is no longer concerned with reform, gradual change, concrete and objective amelioration, but with destroying existing society in the revolutionary hope—which is rarely fully explicated and developed—that something better must succeed it.

Certainly, as I have said, some Negroes think this way. How many? I would guess this is the prevalent mood of the militants who seized control of the Black Power conference, of Stokely Carmichael and his successor in the leadership of SNCC (the Student Non-violent Coordinating Committee), H. Rap Brown, who called upon the people of Cambridge, Maryland, to burn down the city, including their inadequate school, which they promptly began to do. Unfortunately, in the atmosphere of the racist south, the volunteer fire company simply stood by, despite the pleas of Negro citizens and state officials, and let the *Negro* part of the city burn down.

Cambridge reminds one of the one very large generalisation that one can still make in the light of the fact that liberal cities burn, as well as conservative ones—that up to now the riots have been pretty well confined to the north and west. One assumes that the Negroes don't riot in the south because they know the southern police will have fewer compunctions in shooting them down, the southern firemen will act as they did in Maryland. Or perhaps because southern Negroes are not yet dominated by revolutionary hopes and illusions, as the Negro militants and their followers in the northern and western ghettoes are.

The main question remains, and no one has any convincing answers—what is the dominant mood of the Negro ghetto? Do the Negroes believe reform and change is still possible? Are the riots the work of small groups of revolutionaries, visionaries, malcontents, and criminals? After all, it takes very few snipers in a city to turn it into an uproar, very few to start the shop smashing and the burning—there will be plenty later to join in the less demanding task of hauling the goods away.

Or has the unbridled language of the last few years already created a mood which nothing that the cities do can change, and which will turn the American cities into jungles that will be dominated only by brute force? This is a very serious question indeed at this juncture. Responsible leadership, white and Negro, can only accept the first interpretation—reform will work, improvement will work, the revolutionaries and criminals are only an infinitesimal proportion of the Negro community, whatever has been done up till now is too little, and greater imagination and greater resources must be thrown into the task of making the Negro a full part of the American people.

But having said that much, one must add that there is no guarantee that Congress will see it that way. Its majority may have already adopted, along with the Negro militants, the second perspective. All that men of good will can do is to insist that we must expand old reforms and experiments, and devise new ones, and hope that the definition of the American people can still be expanded—to take in the Negro.

[*3 August 1967*]

ENOCH POWELL'S POSTBAG

Diana Spearman

Enoch Powell has received about a hundred thousand letters in support of his speech on immigration, with an approximate eight hundred in disagreement. The letters in support must contain a considerable amount of information which might throw light on colour prejudice and attitudes to immigrants. I therefore asked to be allowed to examine them.

Reading a hundred thousand letters or even a sizeable proportion of them would require a large amount of time and skilled labour. But random sampling is a satisfactory procedure. Before I saw them the letters had already been divided into the following categories:

For: with signature and address
For: anonymous or lacking an address
For: special
For: from Wolverhampton (Mr Powell's constituency)
Against: both signed and anonymous

From the point of view of social and political attitudes the most interesting thing to discover appeared to be the reasons given for supporting Powell. For this purpose the only letters that were significant were the "for" group. I decided not to take a sample of the letters from Wolverhampton because a member's own constituency is likely, to some extent at least, to reflect his personal views. I looked at the special category which seemed to consist of letters from personal friends, prominent people, letters written in Latin and Greek, etc.

I took a sample of 100 letters from the anonymous pile but it contained so high a proportion of letters pledging support but giving no reasons that it would have been a waste of effort to continue with them. They are also a small proportion of the total, and the only point of interest in connection with them is that eleven, which is of course 11 per cent, asserted that they did not sign their names from fear of persecution under the Race Relations Act or of intimidation by immigrants.

This article is based on 3,537 letters. A problem immediately appeared because a number of letters contained more than one signature. Should one regard the "population" (the statistical total) as consisting of letters or of signatures? It is obvious that it is the number of signatures which is relevant, otherwise the opinion of one person would equal that of 152 or 133. The population therefore consists of signatures, husband and wife counting as one person.

The views gleaned from these letters were not given in response to a questionnaire, so similar opinions were expressed in a variety of ways. A considerable number also were written by fairly unsophisticated people. For both reasons it was not always easy to decide in what category to place some of them. Each letter was read twice. The writers—as far as one could see from the paper, address and style—came from every social class and from every part of the country. I split the letters analysed into nine categories. The first category expressed support for Powell's views, but gave no reason.

Racialist
Before putting any letters into this category it was clearly necessary to arrive at some definition of racialist. I first defined it as contempt or dislike of coloured people, connected with some theory, however crude or loosely expressed, of their inherent inferiority. There were, however, so few of these, 17 to be exact, or approximately 0.3 per cent of the total number of signatures, that they were without statistical significance.

The theories on which they were based were also varied: four believed that God had created the human races different from each other and did not wish them to mix, six expressed a strong faith in the virtues of Saxon or Norman blood, and one based his view on a life-long study of the performances of racehorses. I therefore extended the term to cover general accusations against the immigrants, the use of words generally considered offensive to them, such as nigger or coon, unless they occur in letters in which a specific complaint is made and letters which said "send them all back." With these included the total is 71. All the 71 were letters with single signatures.

The behaviour of immigrants
There are 66 letters mainly or solely concerned with complaints

at the behaviour of immigrants. (Such complaints appear in other letters, especially in those concerned about the future of English society, but in more general terms.) Thirty relate to housing, "turning districts into slums, deliberately over-crowding their own houses," etc. Two make detailed accusations of intimidation of white tenants in order to get them to leave. Twelve complain of insanitary habits, defecating in gardens, streets, etc, summed up in the question, "How can we integrate with people who don't even know how to use a lavatory?" (This comes from a letter saying, "I have read your speech and you are 100 per cent right. People who don't *live* in the areas don't know" and giving no other reason for support.) Eighteen object to arrogance and rudeness, ranging from trivial incidents through to street fights and a case of stabbing. They include three references to black power utterances and two to Tariq Ali. Complaints are made of coloured men saying that "they would soon take the town over." Four complain of the immigrants' disloyalty to the country and that "they're talking England down."

THE BREAKDOWN OF THE POWELL SAMPLE

number of letters	3437
number of signatures	5570
no reason given	2608
racialist	71
complaints of behaviour	66
fears for British culture	1128
fear for British culture with special emphasis on liberty	*839
strain on social services	204
fear of repetition of events in USA	64
over-population fears	59
financial fears	52
total reasons given	1444

*This figure is included in the 1128 of the general fears for British culture

Most of these complaints come from people living among immigrants and obviously not very used to putting their ideas on paper. The expressions used are sometimes vivid, though never obscene. The most extreme word in the whole range of letters is bloody. It is possible that other readers might be inclined to put some of them into the category of racialist. On the other hand some of the letters described as racialist might be unskilful attempts to express concern about the future of the country.

British culture and traditions
Signatures expressing fear that the continuation of immigration would be a threat to British culture and traditions numbered 1,128, one of whom was a distinguished academic economist. In expression they range from considerable sophistication to great simplicity. Their attitude is best shown by quotations: "No Briton wants to see his traditional way of living, the country he has loved and fought for, lose its identity, and particular character through the over great acceptance of too many peoples of quite different cultures and ways of life." "The whole British way of life is in jeopardy." "To change the name of our great country to no man's land." "A non-British population which cares nothing for our traditions."

One hundred and thirty-six members of an important profession signed a declaration as follows: "Every contributor has been asked whether they hold any particular racial prejudices and I am glad to say, none have. We all feel what you have said is of paramount importance to the security, social, and economic well-being of Great Britain."

Thirteen business executives referred to "the dissipation of our heritage and the alteration of our rights" involved in the continuation of immigration. Other letters stated: "My friends and I have no intentions of bringing up their children in a multi-racial mish-mash." "I want above all else an integrated society and I am convinced this can never come about if a large racial minority is allowed to build up. In my work as a town planner I come across the problems posed by too hasty immigration."

"No reasonable man would hate another just because he has a darker skin, but it would be blind to pretend that coloured immigration on the scale we now see does not endanger the Englishness of England. It is not ignoble to wish one's children and grandchildren to grow up in the English traditions and way of life which our forebears fostered. Nor is it ignoble that we should wish to avoid the danger that these traditions and beliefs would be distorted by too many of alien origins and 'ethos'."

What a large influx of immigrants means to a working class district is shown in a letter from an elderly working man. After

269

explaining that the district he lived in had become a slum, he added: "Before the war we never had much money . . . but all the time it was our little part of England with a clean face to the houses, nice little pubs and streets."

Among this batch of letters are some from men who feel convinced that no amount of goodwill can produce genuine integration. An ex-colonial civil servant, while he expresses admiration and respect for the Sikh, Moslem and Hindu cultures, says that "the Hindus never integrated and never will integrate with any other race." An ex-missionary from Africa takes the same attitude to Africans, declaring that although he has respect and love for the people among whom he worked, they cannot be assimilated into English society in any large numbers.

Worries about liberty were expressed in 839 of these letters, chiefly about the interference with individual freedom, especially free speech, inseparable from the Race Relations Act 1965 and the Race Relations Bill now in committee. Many regarded Powell's removal from the shadow cabinet as interference with free speech and some thought he was going to be prosecuted.

A letter from 359 postal workers: "We fought a war for freedom, including freedom of speech." From 30 members of the staff of a branch bank: "We believe in complete freedom of speech, whether considered inflammatory by some or not."

"Even people like Colin Jordan and the most rabid communist should have freedom of expression, for what is said openly can be combated openly." Extreme bitterness is expressed in many of the letters. "I must not voice an opinion in my country for fear of persecution." "I have served in HM forces for four years in order to defend my right . . . to decide with whom I shall live, with whom I shall or shall not be friendly, to whom I shall or shall not sell my hard earned property." "It is almost a sin in England now to speak my mind."

This bitterness extends not only to the actions of the government and opposition but also to the press, television and radio. "We are Labour supporters . . . The reaction to your speech gives us great cause for concern because we feel that to penalise or prevent any from speaking the truth is contrary to the British justice that we hold so dear." "Obviously the service which I and my three sons have given to the forces has been wasted."

270

"It is a poor show that the people who fought the fascists to remain free will not by law be free to sell their house to whom they please and employ whom they please." "If action is taken against you then the authorities must also prosecute myself." "Does this law mean that people who form an opinion based on experience cannot speak the truth?"

The strain on the social services
Signatures mainly about the strain on the social services numbered 204. Typical of this attitude is a statement with 39 signatures: "We believe that the time has come to end all further immigration into this country until such time as we have properly integrated the present immigrants into our society and have solved our present economic, educational, housing and social difficulties."

Another, with 150 signatures, stated: "We as a small section of the community without question of colour, creed or class, but fearing the breakdown of our democratic way of life, call upon the government to introduce a temporary ban on all immigration, to allow time for the necessary and proper arrangements for the housing, health and education of those already resident in the country."

Others are less concerned about the immigrants and more about their own prospects, especially education for their children. Their letters do not reveal anything that is not already known about the difficulties in schools and hospitals.

Repetition of the events in the US
Fear of a repetition of the race riots in the USA is mentioned in 64 letters. The writers were clearly horrified by the action of the American Negroes. These 64 are all letters with one signature.

Over-population
The plea for a complete cessation of immigration on the view that this country is already over-populated and that no avoidable increase should be allowed is put forward in 59 letters. Their attitude is adequately summarised in the following quotation:

"I think it is tragic that publicity should have treated this

271

problem as a racial one when it is merely one of overwhelming numbers." These letters were signed by one person only.

Financial
Fifty-two letters express worry about the burden caused to tax and rate payers by the immigrants. The taxpayers are small taxpayers. It is felt to be unfair that, while people who are too old to have acquired the requisite stamps are denied an old age pension, the immigrants can claim family allowances as soon as they arrive here. There is also an impression that a Muslim can claim tax allowances for more than one wife. The frauds on the Inland Revenue reported in the press also find a place here.

Even if one assumes that anyone who voices a complaint about the behaviour of the immigrants is inspired by racial prejudice and that those who fear a repetition of the events in the US are neurotic, and the financial complaints are wholly selfish, the number of letters which could be called ugly or vicious is only 361.

The impression given by the numerical analysis is borne out by the tone of the letters. None of them, with the exception of some "racialist" ones and of those containing complaints about immigrants' actions, shows any rancour towards the coloured people already here. Anger is frequently expressed at being called racialist or evil for saying immigration should stop.

A typical letter states: "To prevent any more race ill feeling for God's sake let's see that those who are already here are looked after, that no more come and that those who want to return can be helped to do so."

Others state: "We are Christian people not racialists, and friendly with our coloured neighbours, but immigration must be stopped." "We all accept we must have some coloured people but with a reasonable limit. Those immigrants that are here should be treated as *us*." "All immigration should be stopped to give us a chance to settle in harmony." "We left South Africa a good six years ago at risk of financial loss to ourselves because we could not accept the nationalist government's racial policy. I see no incongruity with this and the acceptance of every word you had to say in your speech."

The words foreign or black or coloured invasion are freely

used. A sense of being overwhelmed by an unforeseen, un-planned event is expressed. There is no suggestion of expulsion; even the racialists wish to pay the immigrants to leave rather than force them.

I considered introducing another category: "alienation" to describe a distrust of the political parties or the "Establishment." Most of the letters which went beyond a simple message of congratulation included phrases like "at last an honest MP," "the only man who has spoken for us," "a man who puts country before party."

Examples of such views include: "I realise that the 'Establish-ment' would consider my opinion to be that of an ignorant nonentity." "When we think of all the hypocrisy that is written in the press and spoken on radio and television we despair and feel contempt for the leaders of state and church": 21 signatures. "Over the years my contempt for MPs has grown from year to year principally for the arrogant way they ignore the wishes of the people who put them in power." "I was pleased to hear one MP have the courage of his convictions to speak out." "What is appalling to us who love our country, and have not been in the past afraid to show it, is the fact that the wishes and views of the vast majority are completely ignored by their elected rep-resentatives." "It is quite obvious that the two leading parties are merely a government unto themselves and no longer fail to make this apparent by their galling legislation which contravenes the will of the community." "If it weren't for people like you important issues wouldn't even be discussed. Thank you sir."

The letters reflect the feeling that *they* by their actions have produced problems for *us*, which do not in any way affect *them* and which they are not doing anything to help us solve. *Their* idea is to tell *us* what we must and must not do.

[*9 May 1968*]

LIBERATION BY ORGASM

R. D. Laing

It is as though he had never existed. Few medical students in 1968, if any, will have heard his name so much as mentioned in medical school, and will never come across him in their textbooks. It is not that his views are less scientific than many of those taught today—which are no more scientific than those clinical dogmas of even 50 years ago that we are now pleased to ridicule or patronise.

Reich's proposals as to the *social* influences on the functions of sympathetic, parasympathetic and central nervous systems, and on our biochemistry, *are* testable, but are never tested, as with much else that is really important—Lemert's work on the conspiratorial nature of the social field of people who think there is a conspiracy going on; Scheff's work on admission procedures to mental hospitals; Jourard's work on bodily contact, for instance. Exciting to "laymen," perhaps noticed by professionals, seldom pursued. If one insists on referring to them, one is becoming tiresome.

Not one person, as far as I know, in any institution in this country is doing a single piece of research even to disconfirm any of the detailed findings or hypotheses of the above gentlemen, including Reich. Professions institutionalise ignorance, and turn ignorance into a claim for status. Reich was arrested by the FBI as a suspected Nazi spy. He was actively persecuted while alive, and is conspiratorially ignored now he is dead. More ought to be done on the sociology of attempts to destroy heretics without trace. *How can we tell when they are successful?* Many psychiatric textbooks are largely concerned to screen out information that only advanced students can be trusted to know about, when they, it is hoped, will be so brainwashed theoretically, or hooked to professional practices, that no one can do anything about it (if we had more staff, more money, etc). The textbook becomes a burial ground. Intellectual ancestor worship. Seldom read after a few years, but there are always new ideas that are dying or can be killed and buried.

Reich has been written off professionally for years. But—somehow or other—patients, perhaps, who must be as daft as him, keep on reading his books. Suddenly it is going to be discovered that we have all known all along everything that is worthwhile to know of what he said. The rest can easily be consigned to the convenient dustbins of psychotic ideas. The true dustbins of history are the textbooks. Try reading the textbooks of 30 to 40 years ago and compare them with Reich's work of that time. Reich is still *alive*. There is no a priori reason to suppose that what survives through history is the truth. More likely we have not much else to go on than the lies that those who win the power game pass on.

The true story of Reich's split with the inner psychoanalytic circle is still a closely kept secret, and will now probably never be known. Why? The dynamics of that group are likely to be as instructive as the theories that emerged from it. More than 50 per cent killed themselves or allegedly went mad, or both. Ernest Jones's official story is less credible than many fairy stories. Reich has penetrating insights into the European patriarchal family but, like Groddeck, he seems to have formed a primitive transference to Freud, without fully appreciating the whole group scenario.

Although Wilhelm Reich's presence still hovers—ridiculous, menacing, pitiful, according to projection—walled off "outside" the orthodoxy of psychiatry and psychoanalysis, there seems to be a quiet re-evaluation going on among the younger people of all ages. Even his later work on what he called biophysics cannot be so glibly consigned to cranksville as it was even ten years ago. The more I know at first hand of what Reich was talking about, the more seriously I take him.

Reich began in the twenties as a psychoanalyst, with a particular interest in sexology. He was a distinguished member of Freud's circle in Vienna. Gradually his views took shape out of his own clinical experience. They ran the following course, as recounted by him.

He formed the impression that *all* his patients suffered from a disturbance of genitality. This was not always manifested in obvious frigidity or impotence, but always entailed an incapacity for total orgasm with full gratification. This was not obvious because many people did not (and do not) know what total orgasm is, so they did not know what they were missing. Orgasm, as Reich describes it, is a serpentine undulation of the whole body, a giving in, a surrender, reaching an acme followed by complete dissolution of pre-orgasmic tension.

It is generated through a free flow of bioelectric energy, and is resisted by practically everyone to some extent by means of chronic tensions in the skeletal muscles. From head to foot, according to Reich, we are all encased in a sort of muscle armour, that *is* our character. Its main function is to avoid pleasure. It kills gratification and life. We have developed this lethal anti-gratification equipment in childhood, learning to keep a stiff upper lip, holding our head high, chin up, back arched, shoulders rounded, diaphragm rigid, pelvis dead, afraid even to breathe freely, especially to expire.

After some years Reich gave up the techniques of psycho-analysis. He came to regard the exclusive use of talking as often a collusive way for both analyst and patient to remain trapped in their character armour. He moved to direct efforts to dis-armour the person by various methods of relaxing the muscles.

In doing this, the imprisoned serpent-power was mobilised— sometimes, as he describes it, in ways that would frighten anyone who did not have real trust in the basic forces of life. Character armour maintains in frozen preservation all through life the original conflicts which occasioned its formation in the first place. When loosened, the first impulses to be released may not look too nice.

The biopathy of this state of affairs leads directly to many physical functional and structural ills, and the latter, especially cancer, gained increasing attention from him towards the end of his life. The culmination for Reich of his life's work was the discovery of a type of biological and cosmic energy, and the investigation of its particular energy field.

Whether or not one agrees or disagrees with this or that of Reich's theory and practice, it is inescapable that he was a great clinician, with an unusually wide range. His account of his therapy with schizoid and schizophrenic patients will enlighten in some ways anyone involved in this enterprise. He understood the mess we are all in—hysteric, obsessional, psychosomatic, *homo normalis*—as very few have done. Yet one will look through a hundred journals in the Royal Society of Medicine without coming across one mention of him. Why is he *never* mentioned?

He assaults our narcissism in almost unforgivable ways. Freud was cool. Reich is uncool. He tells us that *homo normalis* is a sort of bladder, often dried up, sometimes overtaken with convulsions, longing and terrified to burst, whether through penetration from outside, or explosion from within: terrified to live freely, which would be to love; with an insane fear of being destroyed and at the same time with a senseless readiness to die, to destroy what he fears; fearful of almost everything, most of all, himself; psychically turned inside out, persecuting righteously his persecutors outside himself, none other than his own projections of evil.

It is easy to dismiss statements of this kind as wild and untestable by the canons of science, which Reich claims for them. I do not think it is justified. The signs and symptoms of what Reich called the endemic emotional plague are as evident as the signs of the bubonic plague would be. The extent to which Reich is ignored cannot be explained rationally, and invites an explanation along his own lines—viz, the plague is no respecter of professional boundaries, and psychiatrists suffer from it as much as anyone else. One of its symptoms is an inability to see that one suffers from it.

Some people do see it, but are still subject to it. They are liable to be diagnosed as schizophrenics. "There must be a potent reason why the schizophrenic is treated so cruelly and the cruel *homo normalis* is honoured so crazily all over this planet." Indeed. "The neurotic and the perverse are to the schizophrenic, as far as their feelings of life are concerned, as the miserly shopkeeper is to the big scale safe cracker." "A few cases of the schizophrenia, well understood instead of 'shocked,' would, in the long run, save society countless millions of dollars.

"It seems too much to expect such foresight. It is known that mental institutions are, in reality, jails for psychotics, with little medical care, scarce funds, and in most of them, no research at all." Written in 1948, true today, as the more enlightened and honest superintendents, staff, and patients of mental hospitals continue to testify.

Reich asks us to imagine a parliamentary debate on puberty, to suggest to us how divorced from the facts of life politicians are, who at the same time make it their business to regiment even our biochemistry. He would not have been disappointed in the debates in the Commons and Lords last year on the new dangerous-drug legislation. Political and war correspondents are possibly pretty tough, but they still seem to get frightened when a general or leading politician seems actually to believe his own nonsense. Then watch out. We have got used to the idea that the majority of people will believe what they are told. The danger is that the politician might *stop* being cynical.

Freud felt there was nothing to be done about it. Our civilisation was founded on repression, and societal repression was interlocked in alliance with part of the biological constitution of each of us. Reich was more optimistic. He does not explain why man has turned against himself in the first place, but his work contains rich detailed documentation of how he has, and he did seem to be able to disarm a number of very heavily armoured characters. He has left us a vivid record of part of his adventure. We would be wise to study it with care. I for one have been instructed.

[*28 March 1968*]

REVOLUTION IS PURITAN

E. J. Hobsbawm

The late Che Guevara would have been very surprised and acutely irritated by the discovery that his picture is now on the cover of *Evergreen Review*, his personality the subject of an article in *Vogue*, and his name the ostensible excuse for some homosexual exhibitionism in a New York theatre. We can leave *Vogue* aside. Its business is to tell women what it is fashionable to wear, to know and to talk about; its interest in Che Guevara has no more political implications than the editor's of *Who's Who*. The other two jokes, however, reflect a widespread belief that there is some sort of connexion between social-revolutionary movements and permissiveness in public sexual or other personal behaviour. It is about time someone pointed out that there are no good grounds for this belief.

In the first place, it ought now to be evident that conventions about what sexual behaviour is permissible in public have no specific connexion with systems of political rule or social and economic exploitation. (An exception is the rule of men over women, and the exploitation of women by men which, at a guess, imply more or less strict limitations on the public behaviour of the inferior sex.) Sexual "liberation" has only indirect relations with any other kind of liberation. Systems of class rule and exploitation may impose strict conventions of personal (for example, sexual) behaviour in public or private, or they may not. Hindu society was not in any sense more free or egalitarian than the Welsh Nonconformist community, because the one used temples to demonstrate a vast variety of sexual activities in the most tempting manner, whereas the other imposed rigid restrictions on its members, at any rate in theory. All we can deduce from this particular cultural difference is that pious Hindus who wanted to vary their sexual routine could learn to do so much more easily than pious Welshmen.

Indeed, if a rough generalisation about the relation between class rule and sexual freedom is possible, it is that rulers find it

279

convenient to encourage sexual permissiveness or laxity among their subjects if only to keep their minds off their subjection.

Nobody ever imposed sexual puritanism on slaves; quite the contrary. The sort of societies in which the poor are strictly kept in their place are quite familiar with regular institutionalised mass outbursts of free sex, such as carnivals. In fact, since sex is the cheapest form of enjoyment as well as the most intense (as the Neapolitans say, bed is the poor man's grand opera), it is politically very advantageous, other things being equal, to get them to practise it as much as possible.

In other words, there is no necessary connexion between social or political censorship and moral censorship, though it is often assumed that there is. To transfer some kinds of statement of behaviour from the impermissible to the publicly permitted is a political act only if it implies changing political relations. Winning the right for white and black to make love in South Africa would be a political act, not because it widens the range of what is sexually allowed but because it attacks racial subjection. Winning the right to publish *Lady Chatterley* has no such implications, though it may be welcomed on other grounds.

This should be abundantly clear from our own experience. Within the last few years the official or conventional prohibitions on what can be said, heard, done and shown about sex in public —or for that matter in private—have been virtually abolished in several western countries. The belief that a narrow sexual morality is an essential bulwark of the capitalist system is no longer tenable. Nor, indeed, is the belief that the fight against such a morality is very urgent. There are still a few outdated crusaders who may think of themselves as storming a puritan fortress, but in fact its walls have been virtually razed.

No doubt there are still things that cannot be printed or shown but they are progressively harder to find and to get indignant about. The abolition of censorship is a one-dimensional activity, like the movement of women's necklines and skirts, and if that movement goes on too long in a single direction, the returns in revolutionary satisfaction of the crusaders diminish sharply. The right of actors to fuck each other on stage is palpably a less important advance even of personal liberation than the right of Victorian girls to ride bicycles was. It is today becoming quite hard even to mobilise those prosecutions of obscenity on

280

which publishers and producers have so long relied for free publicity.

For practical purposes the battle for public sex has been won. Has this brought social revolution any nearer, or indeed any change outside the bed, the printed page, and public entertainment (which may or may not be desirable)? There is no sign of it. All it has obviously brought is a lot more public sex in an otherwise unchanged social order.

But if there is no intrinsic connexion between sexual permissiveness and social organisation, there *is*, I am bound to note with a little regret, a persistent affinity between revolution and puritanism. I can think of no well-established organised revolutionary movement or regime which has not developed marked puritanical tendencies. Including marxist ones, whose founders' doctrine was quite unpuritanical (or in Engels's case actively anti-puritanical). Including those in countries like Cuba, whose native tradition is the opposite of puritan. Including the most officially anarchist-libertarian ones. Anyone who believes that the morality of the old anarchist militants was free and easy, does not know what he or she is talking about. Free love (in which they believed passionately) meant no drink, no drugs and monogamy without a formal marriage.

The libertarian, or more exactly antinomian, component of revolutionary movements, though sometimes strong and even dominant at the actual moment of liberation, has never been able to resist the puritan. The Robespierres always win out over the Dantons. Those revolutionaries for whom sexual, or for that matter cultural, libertarianism are really central issues of the revolution, are sooner or later edged aside by it. Wilhelm Reich, the apostle of the orgasm, did indeed start out, as the New Left reminds us, as a revolutionary marxist-cum-freudian, and a very able one, to judge by his *Mass Psychology of Fascism* (which was subtitled *The sexual economy of political reaction and proletarian sexual policy*). But can we be really surprised that such a man ended by concentrating his interest on orgasm rather than organisation? Neither stalinists nor trotskyites felt any enthusiasm for the revolutionary surrealists who hammered at their gates asking to be admitted. Those who survived in politics did not do so as surrealists.

Why this is so is an important and obscure question, which

cannot be answered here. Whether it is necessarily so is an even more important question—at all events for revolutionaries who think the official puritanism of revolutionary regimes excessive and often beside the point. But that the great revolutions of our century have not been devoted to sexual permissiveness can hardly be denied. They have advanced sexual freedom (and fundamentally) not by abolishing *sexual* prohibitions, but by a major act of *social* emancipation: the liberation of women from their oppression. And that revolutionary movements have found personal libertarianism a nuisance is also beyond question. One of the big issues in the American SDS (Students for a Democratic Society) is today whether militants should take drugs.

The whole business is really part of a much wider question. What is the role in revolution or any social change of that cultural rebellion which is today so visible a part of the left, and in certain countries such as the United States the predominant aspect of it? There is no great social revolution which is not combined, at least peripherally, with such cultural dissidence. Perhaps today in the west, where "alienation" rather than poverty is the crucial motive-force of rebellion, no movement which does not also attack the system of personal relations and private satisfactions can be revolutionary. But taken by themselves, cultural revolt and cultural dissidence are symptoms, not revolutionary forces and not very important.

The Russian revolution of 1917 reduced Dada to its proper social and political proportions. When the French went on general strike in May 1968, the happenings in the Odeon Theatre and those splendid *graffiti* ("It is forbidden to forbid," "When I make revolution it makes me feel like making love") could be seen to be forms of minor literature and theatre, marginal to the main events. The more prominent Dada and similar phenomena are, the more confident we can be that the big things are not happening. Shocking the bourgeois is, alas, easier than overthrowing him.

[*22 May 1969*]

ACQUISITIVE DISSENT

Philip Hanson

"Is Russia the only country in the world where nobody thinks about anything but money?" This question from a Soviet student seemed to me, six years ago, to prove only one thing: that travel broadens the mind. Now that more travelling in the Soviet Union has broadened my own mind, I am not so sure.

The conflict between state-imposed economic controls and the acquisitiveness of people is sharper in the Soviet Union than in other industrial countries. As a problem for Soviet economic policy it has almost certainly been growing. While Soviet consumption levels have risen a great deal since the 1950s, they are still well below those of the west, and Russians now know more about the gap. The result is that, among younger Russians in the main cities at least, you can get an impression of almost ceaseless wheeling and dealing. The acquisition of consumer goods—particularly western consumer goods—has now become something between a national sport and a form of dissent. It is one of the ways of being bolshie in the world created by the original bolsheviks, and the preferences behind it are almost an exact inversion of the American drop-out philosophy.

To a large extent this conflict is due to the "demonstration effect" of western consumer goods, a subject which western sovietologists have neglected. In all countries except the very richest, people's expectations and behaviour are affected by what they know about the wealth of richer countries. In Soviet conditions, however, the demonstration effect works in a peculiar way. In non-communist, underdeveloped countries, sophisticated western goods can usually be seen by all, and bought by those who can afford them, in shops in the big cities. In the Soviet Union this is often not so. Information about the goods tends to get through, but for many things legitimate supplies are not available at any price. In Mexico City you can buy a pair of jeans, for example, in a shop, and in Moscow you can't. (Imitation, non-denim jeans were in the shops earlier this year, but were not popular.) To get a pair of jeans you have to operate on the black, or grey, market. In other words, they must be bought directly or indirectly from foreign visitors or on trips abroad. The unofficial price (in roubles converted to pounds at the official exchange rate) currently ranges from £15 to £50. Anyone who sees how many of the young Russians on Kalinin Prospekt in Moscow, or Georgians on Rustaveli Prospekt in Tbilisi, are wearing jeans, can also see that there must be a lot of such dealing going on. The same sort of thing can happen in non-communist countries with import controls, but it is usually less extensive and has quite different political and social side-effects.

Unofficial trading with foreigners has been going on for a long time. Small boys have been swapping Lenin badges for chewing gum since the 1950s. (This, the Lenin centenary year, has probably brought a bumper chewing-gum harvest.) More sophisticated characters, including *agents provocateurs*, have been offering to change dollars at appetising rates and buy the more fashionable clothes off one's back for at least as long. What has happened since the 1950s is that the unofficial market for western goods has grown.

The old westward-looking acquisitive dissent of the *stilyagi*— the Soviet teddy-boys of the late 1950s, has become a less stridently expressed but much commoner attitude. The sharp dividing line between *stilyagi* and conventional youth has gone, together with the word *stilyagi* itself.

To the well-brought-up Anglo-Saxon intellectual it is all a little shocking. He finds two intelligent young journalists, for example, discussing Philip Morris cigarettes instead of Warhol movies. A research student proudly displays to him a James Bond wrist-watch. Another friend presents him, on parting, with a list of gifts he would like to receive: a cassette tape-recorder, corduroy sneakers and even a peculiar, obscene pen-holder which this intelligent young Russian clearly assumes no fashionable western home would be without. Students are distressingly familiar with the least progressive kinds of pop. The visitor returns with either less disdain for the trivia of his own society or less respect for his Russian friends.

The belief that western consumer goods are better and more varied has developed into a snobbery. Many Russians assume automatically that all western consumer goods must be better than their Soviet or even east European counterparts. A columnist in the *Literaturnaya Gazeta* satirised this attitude recently with a story about a Russian who goes to Paris determined to bring back some exotic trophy. Seeing a queue in a shop ("In Paris, of all places!"), he reacts in the normal Russian way and joins it. The queue turns out to be for woollen sweaters. He buys one and exhibits it proudly to his friends on his return until one of them examines it and finds a label saying "Made in USSR." The moral is a fair one, but for the point to get through to the readers, the attitude satirised must itself be widespread. My own impression is that it certainly is common—and, among younger Russians in the big cities, has now become almost universal.

The snobbery about western consumer goods spills over on to other things. There is little evidence that it convinces many Russians that a general return to private enterprise would be a good thing. But it is certainly a source of grumbles about the present system and the people at the top of it. Complaints about the quality of Soviet goods are compounded by complaints about their availability. There is even a paranoid belief that the government deliberately engineers shortages to keep people on the hop. (The rationale allegedly is that if people are kept busy hunting for flour, meat, razor blades and lavatory paper, they won't have time to make a fuss about other things.)

The importance of these everyday grumbles to the Soviet leadership is considerable. In an economy of the Soviet type, the top party/state leadership is clearly, directly and in considerable detail, responsible for production.

The result is that both bouquets and brickbats for every aspect of economic performance seem to be concentrated on the political leadership even more than they are in western countries. In trying both to keep up with rising expectations and chase the moving target of western affluence, the Soviet leadership has its work cut out.

The demonstration effect of western consumer goods also tends, along with quite a few other things, to make official doctrines look rather silly. Nobody pretends that Soviet products must be best buys here and now, but they are supposed to be catching up in quality and variety as well as quantity. In some cases this is happening, but it is not obvious overall. Almost all new and improved products originate in the west, and the embarrassing fact is that Soviet consumers and, more sluggishly, Soviet industry, follow western fashion.

Imports are often sold only to a privileged elite. Others are confined to the special "dollar" shops, for foreign tourists and Russians with legitimate hard-currency earnings only. All this seems calculated to make people cynical both about the technical level of their own economic system as well as about its moral superiority in removing privilege. One way of thumbing your nose at high-minded official rhetoric is to be as materialist as you know how. This, I think, is why many unmistakably high-minded young Russians will strenuously insist that money and a good time are all they want in life, and flourish the oddest western merchandise to prove it.

Government policy can neither ignore nor easily cope with the western demonstration effect. The demand for more private cars is a good example. Khrushchev resisted it. Since his fall, his successors have tried to meet it. This has meant considerable balance-of-payments costs, though the Fiat deal was arranged to minimise direct hard-currency expenditure. It also means heavy investment in roads and service facilities. The start of mass production of the modified Fiats at Togliattigrad has now fallen behind schedule, with rumours of big organisational errors. Already in 1969 people were having to wait to get on the waiting list for the new Fiats.

If the gap in quality and variety between Soviet and west European goods could be substantially reduced many people, I suspect, would be less alienated from the regime. But the traditional system of tight central controls is ill-equipped to do this, and the economic controls are closely connected with the regime's political controls.

In a non-communist country new consumer goods and technology tend to be assimilated from abroad willy-nilly. Tariff, quota and exchange controls are used to keep down consumer imports, but they are usually much less effective than the Soviet-style state monopoly of foreign trade, in which the state planners' control of import decisions is direct. Foreign firms usually set up subsidiaries in the country more readily than the Soviet government can buy western equipment and know-how. Competitive pressures force domestic firms to try to match foreign-owned production.

It may be that in very poor countries the costs of this open-ness to western influence can outweigh the benefits. But the result in countries like Italy, Spain and Greece, with average consumption levels roughly equal to or a bit below Soviet levels, is that the quality and variety of goods bought by a large part of the population tend to be rather better than their Soviet equivalents. Although the distribution of income is probably much more uneven than in the Soviet Union there are at the same time fewer administrative barriers to the spread of new buying habits from richer to poorer people.

In the Soviet Union only a relatively small quantity of western consumer goods come in as official imports. Some are sold only to top people and do not appear in the ordinary shops. Some are sold only for hard currency. Of the supplies to the general retail system, many are allocated only to Moscow and Lenin-grad. They are usually sold at state prices at which demand exceeds supply, and disappear quickly from the counters. Domestic production is usually under no competitive pressure to match new products or improved quality since shortages and sellers' markets prevail and production is still largely determined by central plans.

The Soviet system needs different mechanisms of its own to get the innovations in consumer products and technology which competition can produce in a market economy. Various methods have been tried but within the present system none of them seems to work very well. Tight central control pushed through the basic industrialisation of the country very quickly and has just about kept on terms technologically with America in the top-priority military sectors. But it seems that creating the frills of western affluence with the present planning system is like trying to build a nicely-crenellated sandcastle with a bulldozer. Exactly how much change is needed to do it, nobody knows. Many east European economists—for instance, Ota Sik and some others in Czechoslovakia before August 1968—have argued that direct state control over imports, exports and the domestic price level should be sacrificed, very largely for the sake of achieving more rapid technical change (in non-consumer as well as consumer goods).

Meanwhile, the popular pursuit of western consumer goods continues to be a nuisance and an embarrassment, and is one

287

of the pressures for economic reform. It has some affinity with overt political dissent in the Soviet Union. Both are reactions against centralism. The unofficial market is a way of voting with one's money against an authoritarian system of controls over production and foreign trade.

Like the opposition over freedom of speech and the rights of religious and nationality groups, it is something that can be understood in terms of old-fashioned liberal doctrines, and is in many ways the direct opposite of radical dissent in the current western sense (and therefore very congenial to western academic specialists past their first youth).

Perhaps all advanced industrial systems will at some date and in some sense converge, but Russia is still a very different place from the west, in which old battles have still to be fought. One of these battles is for laissez-faire, though it seems almost certain to be for a kind of socialist laissez-faire. It is one measure of the difference between Soviet and western society that Soviet economists are still discovering Adam Smith. The essence of Soviet and east European economic revisionism for some time has been that an automatic market mechanism can (sometimes) harmonise the interests of the different members of society better than state control. Another measure of the gap between Russia and the west is that so many young Russians are still turned on, rather than off, by western affluence.

[*29 October 1970*]

. . . like ''Who Whom?''

DOWN THERE

Jane Alexander

People in Britain smell less than they used to, on the whole. Is it the effect of education, affluence—and launderettes? Or have advertising and deodorants brought it about?

Deodorants are big business. More women use an underarm deodorant than don't and men often use them now. How far should elimination of body odours be carried, with the common implication in advertisements that the *smell* of sweat, and so on, means that you're dirty and prone to infection?

Certainly, there's doubt about the need for and the efficiency of a booming new type of deodorant—the genital one (the "other one" as some of the ads coyly suggest). "Vaginal" deodorants were available in this country as early as 1961, without being notably successful. In the past two years they've leapt ahead and more brands are coming out all the time.

As anxiety-makers, vaginal deodorants are tops: not only a fear that you may smell but a fear that you're *sexually* offensive. They rouse terrible wrath in some people—notably sensualists and women's liberationists and people who are concerned with human dignity. They're usually greeted with distaste or derision by the educated or firmly middle class woman ("A daily bath and a change of underclothes is a fairly good genital deodorant"). And even their devoted users tend to show a sort of complacent scepticism when asked to explain their reasons for using them: "I suppose it's partly psychological," they say sagely—from Dalston to Kensington, Boots to Harrods.

What's truly mystifying is the continuing advertising theme used: *"Are you offending, unawares?"* There's really only one of your body smells you can't smell yourself: your breath. The others you can smell as well as the next man. Yet, "What a girl's best boyfriend won't tell her," reads an ad for Alberto-Culver's FDS (Feminine Deodorant Spray): "You know what it is. But maybe you think you haven't the problem. Perhaps you don't. But it's surprising how many girls do ... We only

291

mention it to you, because we wouldn't want anyone else to. Especially your husband."

At least advertising in the seventies makes calm assumptions that a woman may go to bed with her "boyfriend." FDS portrays a naked couple embracing (cut off at hip level) and some of their ads leave the "Especially your husband" line out of the copy. Fresh'n Dainty shows a girl from the waist down, in rose-embroidered panties, legs wide apart. Between the legs, the copy: "Nature made you to be loved. Fresh'n Dainty was made to help you be a little more lovable."

Advertising has given agents and manufacturers some trouble. In America, they described it first of all as a deodorant for "the most girl part of you"—but thankfully women showed signs of being irritated by this, so they started using the "outer vaginal area" bit. There must often have been a harsh contrast between the sometimes healthy facetiousness of agency chat and the resultant ads. Another American ad read: "Unfortunately, the trickiest deodorant problem a girl has *isn't* under her pretty little arms." Who could resist finishing it?

Manufacturers, advertisers, publishers and some women's journalists are still nervous about speaking about vaginal deodorants at all, for fear of offending people. Commercial television, both here and in America, has lifted bans on advertising them only within the past year. Here they may not use the word "vaginal"—though if that's to prevent telly-watching children from being corrupted, it seems that little girls might well be more attracted by the word "feminine" than by the other. Some people in the trade seem to think that Avon, which sells at the door, has an advantage because it can sell the new deodorants in the privacy of the home. But, in fact, people seem perfectly ready to talk about them. It may be partly the result of all the market research and the media surveys—making people readier to indulge in public introspection—and it may apply more in London than most places: but people of both sexes, of no great sophistication and a wide age-range, talked happily to me about sexual smells, vaginal discharge, washing habits, possible sexual hangups resulting from overdeodorising; and the power of advertising and their response to it: helplessness, indifference or sturdy resistance.

The thing it was more difficult to get them to talk frankly

about was the frequency of their baths or washes. The poor British get the worst of all worlds in this. The class system says that anyone worth tuppence baths every morning. Washing the body doesn't count: that's done by parlourmaids (which dates it nicely) and continentals (who also have that dirty thing, the bidet). And Americans, through films and telly (where every goody is always taking a shower), and in their very considerable numbers living here, keep telling us what a dirty lot we are: baths are dirty in any case, they say, but the English don't even take *them*. Estimates seem to support them: the average Briton is even now supposed to bath only once every three days. But if you want to find a Briton who will admit to this it seems necessary to preface your question with a face-saving blurb, like: "Busy people often don't have time for a daily bath. In the days in between baths most people have a wash, if they have time. Sometimes, if you're late for work, you may not have time for either." Some users of vaginal deodorant sprays would then admit that this was about right.

It's obvious that some of the most enthusiastic users are using them *instead* of washing. It's the woman who gets her confidence from her morning bath—and is bright enough to know that she can tell if she smells—who will reject vaginal deodorants outright. If you're fastidious you don't use them. This may change, of course, but the same pattern was perceptible several years ago when the Tavistock Clinic did some research into vaginal deodorants.

The Tavistock research did indicate that the miniskirt had made girls more conscious of genital odour or the possibility of it. And girls who don't wash much concentrate on the underarms because, pre-mini, this was a more social area (and one or two people suggested this to me). The mini may have been the making of vaginal deodorants: will the fast-increasing sales level off now that the mini has died? A lot of the advertising is aimed frankly at the young. The makers of Femfresh produced a separate one, Elle, for the young market. IPC's 1970 Young Spending Survey investigated the spending habits of single women and estimates the disposable income of 15–18 year olds at a weekly average of £2 14s, and 18–20s at £5 12s and the 21–24s at £6 17s. "Even one of the youngest-appealing titles in the [Young Magazines] Group, *Fabulous 208*, can claim readers with a disposable income of £40 million per annum—£40 million to be spent virtually wherever they want, on whatever catches their eye," the survey says.

Most vaginal deodorants are advertised in the younger women's magazines, like *19* and *Petticoat*, rather more than in sophisticated magazines or those for older women. But a lot of teenagers begin using a vaginal deodorant because their mother has one in the bathroom and they want one, too. One sickened product manager told of a mother who amusedly allowed her six year old daughter to use one regularly because the child wanted to imitate mummy. Perhaps the child was too young to get hooked, or to be affected by the "cover up your sex" element, but she could be affected by the spray—at least one manufacturer has a warning on the can to keep it away from children (and eyes, broken skin, direct heat). And some people have come out in a rash as a result of using the sprays.

The girl I met who was most hooked on aerosol deodorants was a 17 year old who reads magazines like *Petticoat*, works on the cosmetic counter of a department store, and has a father who owns a small chemist's shop. She gets most things free and uses three aerosol deodorants: underarm, vaginal area, and foot. Her 13 year old sister is now using them, too. The young and intact female can hardly need more than a daily wash, and 13 year olds feeling some anxiety about "unsuspected" sexual odour just doesn't bear thinking about. Elle, advertising in magazines which assume a readership of 13 upwards, calls itself "the adult deodorant." "If you're afraid underarm deodorants are inadequate anywhere but under arms, you're right. The basic feminine deodorant problem begins where you are most basically feminine . . . But you needn't worry. All you need is Elle . . . Make Elle a daily deodorant habit. Starting today. You'd hate yourself if you waited till tomorrow . . . Elle. A part of your makeup."

Makeup is just how many users seem to regard it. Encouraged to talk about their body's past smells, women often said something like: "No, I don't ever remember noticing that I did smell. Except during my period, of course, if I wasn't careful. But they say you don't always know." Having started using a spray, they went on using one, partly from indifference to the truth of the ads, and partly because "It's like makeup. You know you don't really need makeup: but you use it because other people do and so it gives you confidence—the ads are right, there." The makers want you to get the daily habit, of course. For this, they have to convince you that you smell unawares. (If you *do* suffer daily offensive vaginal odour, in spite of daily bathing, you might be advised to see your doctor.)

Charles Anderson, the Bidex account director at J. Walter Thompson, said first that most people are not really capable of recognising their body odours—other people do it. Later, however, to prove how much women wanted and needed genital deodorants, he said that many women, when the news of vaginal deodorants finally was broken to them, immediately said, "What a good idea!" And the Bidex product manager said that: "37 per cent of women are aware of vaginal odour." He didn't say how often any given women was aware of it, or what steps she'd previously taken to avoid it. The various advertisements list a lot of occasions when odour is likely to overtake you: Freshette says, " . . . when you have your period. When you get nervous. When the weather's hot or you're over excited." FDS adds, ". . . when the nights heat up."

The beauty pages of the young magazines are on the side of the advertisers. Before Valentine's day, *Petticoat* listed the sort of girl who would get a Valentine. Among other things. "They smell sweet and always use a vaginal deodorant and a foot spray."

Understandably, old wives' tales about genital deodorants are already about: but it's reassuring to see that the advice pages don't echo the easy virtue of the beauty pages. Celia, of Cardiff, writes to the *Petticoat* adviser: "I have been told by friends that feminine deodorant sprays can ruin your chances of conception if used too often. They say that twice a week is sufficient. Please could you advise me as I use them daily, often twice a day." Claire Rayner's reply: "Let's be logical about this. Do you really think a little scent is going to act as a contraceptive? If it did, believe me it would solve a lot of people's problems." And a 15 year old wrote to the *Petticoat* doctor: "Have I got VD? I think (I am not sure) that I had sexual intercourse when I was about twelve and my periods had not started. I have an itchy outer vaginal area which is occasionally sore, between periods, and I have a fairly thick, yellowish discharge. I am worried about this and I have tried using Nivea cream and Bidex spray every day, but nothing seems to help." The reply: "All thick discharges should be reported to your doctor . . ."

The naivety of these letters—and they're not at all untypical—show how vulnerable younger teenagers are. It's obscene to think of them as a market. It makes one sympathise with the view expressed in the militant women's liberation paper, *Shrew*: "To me, the growth of the vaginal deodorant trade is a specific instance of a very successful, cold-blooded, current commercial exploitation of women . . . Most women would be too embarassed to talk about their private sexual areas to all and sundry, yet somewhere, a panel of admen and probably women, must have sat down and worked out a campaign about us. The campaigns are in themselves an invasion of the special privacy of women . . . aimed at the younger women and adolescent girls . . . So at the very time in their lives when girls are painfully adjusting to being women, when they should be learning to be proud of their bodies: they are encouraged to believe they will give offence in the deepest human relationship if they don't buy that magic spray in its phallus-shaped container . . ."

To a lot of people, implanting a compulsion to deodorise your vaginal area would not be as offensive if the deodorants weren't scented. It's obvious that it's smelling the scent of the deodorant that reassures a lot of women. The scents are usually described as delicate or refreshing (Dorothy Gray's has "a cooling hint of green woodland ferns") and seem to have the same insipidly sweet powdery quality that you get in the aerosol air "fresheners" with which cinema usherettes, sometimes nauseate audiences. The women who use several differently scented sprays—like the chemist's daughter—on different parts of their body, can have no sense of smell at all (which proves that there is an advertisers' market). Eliminate the scents, and sophisticated women might be more tolerant of them—although the trade seems to be doing all right without the sophisticates.

It's the spray form that sells best, both here and in America. In France, a liquid version sells well—they're used with bidets: for *washing* with. Another type which cleans you, but which doesn't sell well here, is a tissue impregnated with the deodorant and contained in a small sealed package. It's useful, and amongst the women I talked to, it's the only kind used by reasonably intelligent women—except those in the trade, which doesn't count. Its poor sales probably reflect the repressions the average woman feels about touching her own body. Some of the makers think they're not quite nice, too: so they call them "sachets." The young, articulate, female manager of a modern chemist's shop, when I asked what the "sachets" were, said calmly: "You wipe yourself with them." She used them sometimes when she had her period or was travelling. But one of her assistants—bleached and back-combed—who had admitted quite happily to using a spray several times a day (going to the lavatory for a quick respray sometimes if the shop was empty) got a bit dainty when I asked about the sachets. "I know what you *mean*, but I don't fancy them myself."

The sprays are used, "from a distance of six inches," which is probably no more than a functional instruction (even though the spray could never reach into the crevices unaided), but certainly comforts those who are most likely to get sexual hang-ups from constantly spraying their genital area.

Some of the advertising is clearly aimed at making women nervous that they'll "offend," just as their loved one is about to take them to bed. It assumes that he would be horrified at such a moment to scent your sexual odour. One woman I talked to said she always sprayed herself (without washing) when she and her husband were going to make love. "I like it," her husband said staunchly, "I think it's smashing. The average man is no longer stimulated by sexual odours."

Another man seemed to think that sex would be unconfined if we didn't cover up our sexual odours—because men find them so stimulating. Novelists and poets increasingly include conventionally unmentionable smells in their accounts of sensual joys; and Henry Green once said that perfect happiness could be defined as sitting up in bed in the morning eating buttered toast with cunty fingers.

"Vaginal odour is your problem. Don't let it become his," says a Bidex ad showing a naked couple. The aim, Bidex says in a press release, "is primarily an educational one—ie, to explain the problem and make women aware of it, and to provide the remedy." Ad agency people often talk as though the gratification a product gives to the consumer is heaven-sent. Just as a lot of consumers speak placidly about the "confidence" they are buying, so the men speak virtuously of physical assurance and even sexual assurance. Charles Anderson, an American, kept trying me out with Thoreau in case I was a nature nut. And more than one adman introduced the subject of prices, and the trade supposition that people won't trust your product unless you pile on the price.

There's confusion about the length of time a genital deodorant is supposed to give you confidence/protection. The anti-perspirants which make underarm deodorants effective all day cannot, it's said, be used on the more sensitive genital area. Not all makers claim all-day protection. One which does, Bidex, claims to have done substantial research and testing of its product. (Most claim this.) Originating in Switzerland, Bidex has a patent pending here. A report was made of the Bidex tests —the final one is affectionately known as "the sniff test"—but the report is confidential and the product manager was unable or unwilling to produce any kind of verification of the claim. Although many people would assume "all day" to include the evening, and the Bidex ads show a couple from getting-up time to bedtime—all day to Bidex means twelve hours.

Charles Anderson, director of the account, says that proof of the truth of the Bidex claim is that the firm is allowed to say it; if it had been untrue, (a) the Trade Descriptions Act would have got Bidex and (b) magazines would not have accepted the ads. This is a little disingenuous, since the act is as often as not implemented (by local weights and measures inspectors) on a complaint. And the mind boggles at the woman who would claim that this particular claim was untrue: what would she offer as evidence? And, in practice, not all magazines are wary of possible false claims in advertisements they accept. Femfresh, in its Lui and Elle ads, said: "It also reduces the risk of infection for you and her." The ad was to be placed in several IPC young magazines and in *Nova, She* and ABC *Film Review*. The advertisement director of the IPC group, William McIntosh, objected to such a sweeping and ambiguous claim and it was changed in the young magazines. But the ad still appeared in its original form in the others.

The latest genital deodorants on the scene are male ones. Where Femfresh's young female one, Elle, is for "the most feminine part of you." Lui is merely for the "most sensitive area of your body." The formula for all three is basically the same. The things which cause embarrassing odour in the male: "Fear, excitement or any emotional stress." Lui has a "subtle woody fragrance that is fresh and masculine." And everyone I spoke to fell about laughing at the thought of male genital deodorants—except those men who think them a sexual insult. "They can be used upside down!" spluttered the people who had heard of them. But this only means that genital deodorant containers, unlike most aerosols, can be used upside down: and indeed need to be. The sprays are rather cold on the flesh, especially after a hot bath: and the male genitals could hardly be efficiently sprayed without a certain amount of manoeuvring: all of which gives rise to some humorous conjecture. "Cocksure" is the popular name for them.

One male deodorant is called Below the Belt. Revlon does one, at 45s, called Private, which it doesn't advertise; the only ads seen here are in American magazines. There's apparently a unisex one called Cupid's Quiver, which comes in flavours—but not here, yet; not even in the sex shops.

Very few places stock any male genital deodorants, yet, except Lui, which has a fair distribution. The charming, elderly proprietor of an old-established West End barber shop, was very amused to hear about them. He really should stock them, he thought; he stocks some expensive underarm ones. But they wouldn't sell well with him, he was sure; a regular customer wouldn't want it known that he was buying one. "He'd go to a chemist, instead. Though he'd probably wait until a man was free to serve him; he wouldn't want to buy one from a woman." Just like contraceptives used to be, I said. "Exactly. Of course we sell those. That's different. If a customer buys, say, a couple of dozen of those; well!" he threw up his hands in the happy continental way so many Englishmen have: "His barber would be pretty impressed."

He thought there was a need, not so much for a deodorant, as for a harmless scent, "After all," he said nostalgically, "most men, when young, have—when they're going out on an important occasion—burnt their Hampton Wick, their John Thomas, their *how d'ye do*." he looked whimsically at me to see if I caught his meaning, "by dabbing cologne on it!"

Down there

The oddest thing about the male ones is that they're advertised principally in the women's magazines. This is because the trade believes that 70 per cent of men's grooming aids are bought for them by women. So they assume the same will happen to this product. In twin ads with Elle, Lui is being advertised in *Honey*, *19*, *Petticoat*, *Woman's Own*, *Nova*, *She*, and *Rave*— with only *Club* and ABC *Film Review* to redress the balance.

Glints, the trendy men's toiletries shop, says that the (few) men who buy genital deodorants are in the 30–45 age range. But it's early days: younger men may yet want in. With a new product, it seems that thousands are distributed free as samples to people in the advertising and retail side. Even with the female ones, it sometimes seems that almost everyone using them got the first one free from someone they knew in the trade. But since there seems to be no case for the male ones, they seem doubly offensive.

There's no doubt, however, that there are going to be a lot of sexual relationships busted this way; a lot of laughing girls have hit on this absolute giggle of a present to give their men. Will the men be laughing? That *would* take sexual confidence.

[*21 January 1971*]

MARRIAGES ON PROBATION

Geoffrey Parkinson

Most probation officers feel uneasy about their work with matrimonial cases. Such recent and reasonable studies as have been made suggest that we are not very good at it and are left to do the work mainly because no other professional body is willing or in a position to take over the responsibility. "Mats" are in many respects regarded as an irritating duty added uneasily to a probation officer's caseload.

At first glance this may seem curious since, unlike most of our clients, "Mats" come willingly, they seek help, they have generally recognisable problems and they are thus eligible for "casework." Quite a few probation officers in training get excited at the prospect of treating damaged marriages; the idea of learning about other people's sex lives, of hearing men and women squabbling is not without its attractions, especially when, after treatment, emotional wounds may be healed, sexuality enriched and the probation officer gratefully recognised as the doer of good. Yet, once in the field, the young probation officer's enthusiasm is all too often blighted. He may even join the growing ranks of colleagues who feel "this is not really our work."

Why should this be? Dr H. V. Dicks, the doyen of professional matrimonial workers, held generations of probation officer trainees enthralled by his brilliant case studies of broken and unhappy marriages. We sought to imitate his ways, which to my memory involved assisting husbands and wives to see the errors and inaccuracies of their Oedipal ways by methods so subtle and sensitive that even the most painful of insights came as creative experiences.

Once in the courts we were to learn a hard lesson. "Mats" were no more open to traditional casework than were delinquents even though they entered our offices voluntarily. "Mats" proved stubborn. They did not want to look at the personality of their marriage or their own personalities. They didn't want to see any of the complications or subtleties of their

301

own reactions or the reactions of their spouses. They seemed generally to be fixated to the present; the only feelings that had any meaning for them were the feelings they felt at that moment and these were usually as blind as they were overwhelming.

We tried to give interviews a sense of depth but in the end all they wanted was a summons or a letter ticking their husbands off. They ran to us as children run to teachers in a playground to settle some dispute, swiftly and with authority, and we for the most part sat benign and neutral, fiddling around with our insights. We soon came to feel, certainly I felt, that our role for these clients was closely prescribed and that to break out of the set limits was not only difficult but probably quite pointless. For a while I joined the ranks of those who believed we should get rid of the work.

The dilemma of "Mats" in the probation setting is either assisted or handicapped by the situation in which the work is obtained, according to one's viewpoint. Magistrates' courts in London usually carry out their matrimonial duties by a routine which involves directing applicants in the first instance to the scrutiny of a probation officer. The aggrieved wife—and it usually seems to be only the wife we see—can't get a summons against her husband for persistent cruelty, desertion or any other matrimonial offence, without a *prima facie* case, and this often becomes the officer's major quasi-legal function. He usually assesses the situation and may apply to the court on her behalf.

The yardstick for matrimonial offences is rather crude to middle class eyes and was at one time, in my opinion, unpleasantly rigid. Persistent cruelty, for example, had in practice to be three blows to the body during the previous six months, in the presence, if possible, of a witness, and I can never remember making an application on the grounds of mental cruelty. If only two punches were readily recalled, the officer might scratch around his client's uneasy memory, even asking such curious questions as "Do you mean to say that when your husband got drunk at Christmas he didn't come home and punch you?"

Frequently applicants do not pursue their original intention of summonsing because, after a chat, they decide they want to "make another go of it"—and leave after requesting the officer to write a letter to the husband telling him to behave himself.

302

From this sort of situation an axiom arises; many clients think they want to end their marriages but unconsciously they wish to make a go of things and this is their way of seeking help. On such a cunning psychological principle I often used to send a wife back to the slaughter of her marriage, taking with her one or two unhappy children. She believed I was helping; that adds to the irony of the situation. I think the essence of the matter is in many respects the reverse of this axiom: many women want to end their marriages on a conscious level but are unconsciously committed to a sado-masochistic drama.

Our case files show the same monotonous repetition of detail. Sometimes one feels the unhappy histories follow a few stereotyped lines and only the clients' names and faces are different. Mrs A with three children has a husband who drinks heavily at the weekends, takes most of the housekeeping money and punches her when she protests. Mrs B who loved her naughty husband until she produced naughty children whom she preferred and thereafter thought her husband should be good. Mrs C who sits up into the early hours of the morning fascinated and fearful while her workshy, drunken husband goes into rages about her imagined infidelities.

One knows the stories behind such marriages are complex and their drama serves perverse needs for both husband and wife. One is, for example, familiar with the unconscious problems existing in a drunkard's wife and one knows that individuals may often avoid disturbance in themselves by living in a disturbed marriage. Many traditional casework methods would attempt to reveal such truths to these unhappy women. They would theoretically be expected to understand their choice of partner, their need for a depriving angry male, part child, part monster. All this might be fine except that it doesn't often work. Insights are largely useless except to the worker who may use them as psychological amphetamines, keeping him interested and alert during depressing sessions.

A large percentage of the women visiting us are highly masochistic. Most of them have never reflected upon themselves or the nature of their behaviour and they are thus both the innocents and slaves of their unconscious conflicts. The men they married may have once delighted them with their heavy drinking, their half-playful anger, their irresponsibility in work, their

303

abuse of feminine qualities and their aggressive, though not always effective, sexuality. When the marriage reaches our office all this has crumbled into moans, violence, economic deprivation, partial desertion and meaningless intercourse, with the husband finding such satisfaction as he may in light ales, and the wife with such pleasures as she can from her small uncontrolled and anxious children. If the officer is aware of anything from these situations, it is that the clients need action not insight.

The psychoanalytic morality and motives of some caseworkers, however stimulating, are useless unless they can be blended with traditional methods of mending marriages in a neighbourhood. In the East End, and the body of my experience is in that area, the probation officer has now to some extent to fulfil the role previously played by fathers and brothers. Thirty years ago a daughter would ultimately have gone back to dad with her complaints about her husband and dad would have either made it clear that she had "made her bed and must lie on it," or, if the complaints were persistent and her parents sympathetic, possibly send one or two of the men in her family to see the defaulting husband and show him the error of his ways, if necessary by a swift punch-up.

This happens less and less frequently as the function of the family in the East End diminishes and the environment becomes more complex and generally less threatening. Thus now, instead of dad, the court and the probation officer are expected to deal with things. A gently phrased letter inviting the husband to discuss his difficulties may be all therapy and light to the officer who sends it. The husband, however, when he notices the printed notepaper "Probation Service" knows his wife is putting the pressure on; he is going to be ticked off at the best and dragged into court at the worst. Invariably he feels he does not want to answer questions put to him by some clever middle class official and, partly from a sense of guilt, he probably believes that only his wife's side will be believed. The letter is usually torn up and the husband either proceeds to fortify the wife's *prima facie* case or for a time gives up his bad habits and promises to be better.

My present approach to "Mats" is based upon solving one central problem, the apparent lack of sincerity of clients in their search for help. By lack of sincerity I mean their inability to decide between contradicting forces both within themselves and within the marriage. Though matrimonial clients rarely admit to faults, all agree that they vacillate insofar as they find it difficult to take appropriate steps in dealing with their marriage problems.

It is of this that I most regularly and persistently accuse them: "Well, maybe your husband does hit you, but why are you there to be hit?" or, "Why shouldn't your husband think you like being kicked around? You have never done anything about it until now. You may not do anything about it even now." I have often elaborated on this more extensively and personally: "You are young and attractive and you can still make a go of life. If you let things drift, in ten years time you will have four or five kids and you will be stuck and nobody will want to help you very much." All the time I repeat my central theme: "You must make him realise you are serious about this. Things must either get better or you must end it." I am often accused in my approach of being biased on the wife's side. In a sense this is true. The wife, not the husband, is usually the client and the wife rather than the husband suffers most physically and financially.

Our clients lack beautiful middle class egos and come from depressed uncreative backgrounds. Frequently if the husband is a drunk so was the father; if the client is knocked around so also was her mother. And if I am "on the wife's side" it is not through a failure to grasp the husband's position or any lack of sympathy for his viewpoint; my approach often implies a considerable understanding of his aggressive feelings since I deal with aggressive feelings the wife provokes in me by making comments and requests containing a high content of anger—like "You must . . ." or "It is no good your . . ." For me the sure guide to a masochistic wife is my desire after ten minutes to get up and hit her.

My methods, by making me happy, make me more useful to the client, and the client feels this. In earlier days she liked the irresponsible brashness of her husband, now she can enjoy the more responsible brashness of the caseworker. Since I am seen as being on her side, I can say things to her which she would not accept from someone more "impartial."

I frequently use the court, or the threat of the court, as a technique. Husbands must see the limits, and the law is often the best way of achieving this. For years Mr x has hit Mrs x in front of the kids; now suddenly this is challenged by the disappearance of Mrs x and the kids, and the appearance of a summons to explain to a judge why he, Mr x, is behaving like this. His wife now becomes a person with ideas and an identity of her own. He now, summons in hand, knows he loves her.

Whether at this point the wife continues to proceed against her husband or returns to him must depend on a whole variety of factors, but provided she is clear in her own mind that the situation must never be allowed to deteriorate in the same way again then all may be well. In her intention to establish a different type of relationship she must know that the probation officer will play the role of her supporter expecting her to report at the earliest point any signs of deterioration. By a different relationship, incidentally, I mean only one thing: no more extreme violence or financial deprivation or whatever the offences may be. Just as with delinquents, the central focus must be around acts of crime, so with matrimonials the central focus must be around the ending of specific acts of cruelty. To be sidetracked in any way from this is exceedingly dangerous. Husbands may give subtle reasons for hitting their wives but in the end they hear from me that they must either put up with their wives more or less as they are or they must get out. They can't have it both ways. Incidentally, I now always make a point of regularly sending reminding letters to wives offering them further appointments, and these are used by wives to show their husbands when things get a little difficult. They are quite effective.

The probation officer is probably wise to seek very limited objectives and abandon any attempt at an extensive "cure." If punching is the complaint then the cessation of punching is probably the aim. In seeking this the officer will indirectly alter many aspects of the marriage, some in a positive, others inevitably in a negative way. The central problem posed by most matrimonials is their inability to act effectively and in this they are ably assisted by the housing shortage and poor economic conditions; therefore the officer should probably spend a great deal more time than he has in the past helping complainants to places of refuge from violent and defaulting husbands.

The probation officer has an important role to play with matrimonial clients, utilising and transcending the quasi-legal function given to him by the courts. The starting point must be the abandonment of therapeutic methods and goals so persuasively argued by those whose matrimonial work is effected in a more genteel sociological and casework atmosphere.

[*22 May 1969*]

GOING BAIL

Colin MacInnes

The Home Office is worried about whether bail is too difficult to get, and police spokesmen say magistrates and judges give it far too easily. The chief arguments for, and against, granting bail would seem to be:

For: 1. "Innocent until proved guilty." 2. To enable the accused to prepare an adequate defence. 3. To prevent a defendant, who may eventually be acquitted, spending possibly months in prison without trial. 4. Not further to congest crowded prisons.

Against: 1. The accused may jump bail and abscond. 2. He may intimidate prosecution witnesses. 3. He can more easily fake his defence with false alibis and other testimony. 4. He may commit a second, undetected, crime to finance his defence of the first.

Having myself gone bail some 20 times in the past two decades, my chief impression—admittedly, haphazard and subjective—is how very capricious and unpredictable the whole process is. For whether bail is granted depends not just, as one might expect, on the gravity of the charge, but on such factors as the individual attitudes of magistrates who can withhold it; of police officers who can oppose it; on whether or not a lawyer is applying for it on your behalf; and on the very various opinions each of these may have about yourself as a possible surety.

To illustrate the process at its most bizarre, I would recall a case—initially of Grievous Bodily Harm, though subsequently the charge was reduced to malicious wounding—of which my mate was eventually acquitted. Two applications for bail were opposed by the police, and refused by magistrates at successive remands, after which the police back-tracked and advised me to appeal for bail again, which was granted without their opposition. When the case finally came to be tried, the detective in charge asked me to go bail as well for another defendant, who was a complete stranger to me.

Perhaps we should begin at the beginning; and, before describing the sort of thing that can happen, I should make it clear I am altogether omitting the very simple kind of charge for which the police can grant bail directly, usually for just one night, before the case comes into court in the morning. The more usual, more serious, and more tricky situation is when bail has to be requested in open court before, initially, a magistrate.

The first point to grasp is that a person, when asked to stand bail, usually has to make a snap decision. It is true that a man remanded in custody, through no one turning up to try to bail him, can ask a friend, later on, to make application for bail on his behalf. But often a person will approach you immediately after arrest—that is, if the police allow him to telephone, if he has the right money, and if he can remember your phone number. Sometimes, for various reasons, the police will telephone, or actually call upon you, on his behalf.

Such appeals rarely come during the day, more often in the small hours; and the request is always that you should not only stand bail, but be ready to do so when the accused comes up in court next morning—or the day after, if he happens to be arrested on a Saturday evening. He wants a quick "yes" or "no" answer, preferably "yes," of course, since if you refuse, he must try to find someone else.

Four snap decisions you have to make (on being awoken, say, at 2 am), are these: first, whether to go bail for him at all; second, whether prior commitments will enable you to get to court; third, whether you will have time to get a lawyer along as well, since this helps enormously in *all* legal proceedings; fourth, if your friend can't afford a lawyer, can you pay for one yourself, if legal aid isn't granted.

To these factors—that must be decided in a matter of minutes, before the coppers at the station tell your friend the phone's needed, or he runs out of the right coins—I would add a fifth, which happens in a surprisingly large number of cases. Many men, on arrest, give a false name; conversely, they may be known to *you* under a false name or nickname, and have given, for various reasons, their real name (or another false name) to the police. Now, even when you hear your friend's own voice—

difficult enough to identify on a telephone—and he firmly says he's your old pal Ferdinand (of whom you've never heard), it's hard enough to decide who he is; but if the police phone on behalf of this mysterious Ferdinand (who may well, of course, really be your dear old mate Jimmy), the complexity of reaching a correct decision is even greater. For if there's one thing nobody wants to do, it's to go bail for someone who *is* a complete stranger.

If you've agreed, and had some experience of this sort of situation, the first thing you do is see if you can get a solicitor, however junior, down to the court to help with your application. Trying to get bail for a friend without one is infinitely more difficult. No one around the court will tell you a thing; the police officers don't want to meet you—unless, for some reason, they wish the prisoner to be bailed—and you have not, as a solicitor has, right of access to the accused.

In any event, be prepared for a long wait. Courts, unlike any other institution in the nation, have no sense of time whatever. Prisoners, officers, witnesses, jurors, advocates and sureties all wait on the court's pleasure. Your friend may not come on for charge and remand that morning at all: it may be in the afternoon, it may even be tomorrow, after another night in custody. So take an air cushion, a hefty paperback, and a packet of mints in case they're strict about smoking, to help your endless wait in those drear halls—so aptly named in France *la salle des pas perdus.*

While you're waiting it's quite possible a copper will come and check you over. He will be unfavourably impressed if you are not a householder, and have no employer; persons living in flats, and self-employed, seem somewhat suspect. He will also get enough personal information to see if his computer comes up with anything about you.

If bail is not opposed by the police, and *is* granted by the magistrates—not necessarily the same thing, for sometimes magistrates overrule both police objections and non-objections —you take the oath, state you are worth so much, and the prisoner is delivered into your hands. If, however, he has not been able to contact you prior to his first appearance in court, but has appealed to you from prison by letter or through a lawyer, you can apply for bail without him. If successful, you get a release order (one hour), travel down to Brixton (another), and wait till he's handed over to you (usually two more).

Let's hope, for your sake, your friend is granted "continuing bail," for then you don't have to turn up at each weekly remand, of which there may be almost any number. If he gets "once only bail," you may have to spend two or three days, or longer, waiting around in different courts in successive weeks, for cases get switched from place to place, and it's not always easy (if you haven't a lawyer) to find out where the next trial after remand, will take place. Note, too, that when the final trial does occur, it is by no means certain it will be over in one, or even two days of the same week.

If the police don't oppose bail, your actual appearance in court—once you get inside it, from that lost feet saloon—is usually a quick formality; but if the police do oppose, the tussle over bail can last for quite a while. You may find yourself cross-examined by the detective in charge (if he's prosecuting); by the prosecution lawyer; by a single magistrate; or by a bench of them. These questions are mostly simple to answer, until they shoot the great unanswerable one at you, which is how can you be *certain* the prisoner will turn up for trial?

It's a silly question, really, for the only true answer is that, short of handcuffing yourself to the defendant, and even then, no one can be positive he'll be there. I've personally been stood up only once—or rather, my friend did turn up, but late and in custody—because, correctly anticipating his conviction on the morrow, he'd had a farewell party the night before, got drunk, and been charged and sentenced for that in another court, before arriving at the one where we were all awaiting him.

Individual attitudes to going bail, or not, seem to vary enormously: surprisingly, the most respectable people will agree to it instantly, considering it a "citizen duty," while others you'd guess would have no objection at all, will suddenly turn coy. I think it's a mistake to agree to do it too often, because word gets around you're an easy touch; and the police are apt to say, "Not *you* again!" when you arrive in court several times in the same year.

I would like to end with three mildly controversial comments. The first is, that while the American system of professional "bondsmen"—who get you out, if they can, on a purely

311

commercial basis—is considered rather disgraceful in England, I think myself there's a lot to be said for it. Readers of this article would doubtless find no difficulty in getting sureties, if they needed them. But a lot of underprivileged people do find it hard to get anyone, and, to them, a professional bondsman would be a godsend. For not only is it nicer to be outside prison than in it, but it's extremely difficult to arrange a legitimate defence from prison.

The next thing is that I don't think anyone ought to go bail at all, unless they leave their friend entirely free to skip it, if he wants to. I don't mean a surety should encourage his friend to do so, or connive at it. But I don't think the surety should be surprised, or resentful, if his friend absconds.

Regarding the arguments over whether bail is granted too much or too little, although I well appreciate the police viewpoint—who doesn't?—I disagree with it. After all, real villains never get bail or hardly ever. It's the marginal, minor cases, which most of us come in contact with, where bail is still too hard and, above all, too complicated to get. The granting of bail, like the jury system, is a valuable civil liberty; we've seen the second eroded in recent years, and I think we should try to preserve the former intact.

[*30 September 1971*]

WEEKEND JUNKIES

Sheila Yeger

"Greytown" is rather a strange town, an ugly industrial blot on the typically English landscape which surrounds it. The town grew up round the railway works at the end of the last century; the works are in the slow process of closing down and releasing the strong hold they have had on the way of life in the town. The streets are long, parallel, uniformly grey. It is an almost totally working class community, with a strong distrust of the newfangled, the weird, the beat. It is a secure environment, to which people return time and again, although they are always talking about escaping from it. It is an immensely boring place in which to live and an immensely difficult one to break away from.

In this community, not surprisingly, there is very little in the way of the "beat scene," with which drug taking is normally associated in the eyes of the general public. Those young people who wish to make their rebellion *that* apparent would tend to leave Greytown and gravitate towards a nearby university town, where nonconformity in dress and way-out behaviour are more easily tolerated, In this, they act as individuals, rather than as members of a group, and their interest in drugs seems to centre on pot-smoking, with occasional use of "acid," methedrin and morphine, depending on availability. When they return to Greytown, they are easily identified by the adult community as "beatniks" or "junkies," because their entire appearance—long or freaked-out hair, colourful clothes, even beards—is so totally at variance with what is accepted in this tightly conformist community.

Meanwhile, a different drug "scene" has become a way of life for a much greater number of young people in the town. The "mod set" take a great pride in their appearance, their hair-styles, and so on. At the moment, most favour a modified skin-head look in hair and a smartly casual line in suits. Not a kaftan in sight. They follow all the latest fads in music, but prefer music you can dance to, "Reggae" is top favourite at present. In

313

contrast to the self-styled beats, these boys do not consider themselves to be rebels, though they do seem to regard themselves as a group apart—"sharper" in all respects than those denied membership. Drugs are as much a part of the culture of this group as their mode of dress and the music they prefer. Yet the great majority of them use drugs only at the weekend, or perhaps once during the week when they go to a discotheque or a party. They are almost all pillheads—ie, they use drugs in pill form. Some smoke pot occasionally, or have done so in the past, but most say that it's "no good," or "useless, compared to pills."

They experiment with different combinations of amphetamine and barbiturate in such preparations as "blues," "dubes," "decks," "bombers." The slang names are used almost with affection. Recently these youngsters have also taken to using the various pill preparations of LSD now available. Another commonly used pill—which is not actually illegal, though there are moves afoot to remedy this—is playfully known as a "Mandy" (Mandrax). This is a particularly virulent sleeping pill, which, when taken in conjunction with a pint or two, can affect behaviour quite drastically.

They buy their pills on the black market, usually through the services of one member of the group, who acts as go-between. He will travel as far as London if necessary, to meet the "connection" (my word, not their's) and buy a large supply of pills, which he then brings back and sells at a profit to the rest of the crowd and any hangers-on who may want to try "just a few." Regular customers are preferred and get preferential treatment. Even so, there is a great deal of fiddling, even among professed mates. People are prepared to pay as much as 2s per pill (very much more for LSD-type pills). As many of them are using, say, 40 blues at a time, it is obviously a very expensive business. Yet they seem to regard it as a top-priority expenditure and willingly go penniless for the rest of the week. The fetching of the pills, their distribution often blatantly in public places, the haggling over prices, the inevitable cheating, are all part of a weekly ritual, which, one feels, is every bit as important to these young people as the pill-taking itself.

These youngsters are not, on the whole, layabouts. They work hard during the week as apprentices or on the railways. Perhaps their jobs are monotonous, but they get through Monday to

Friday in eager anticipation of the weekend, and in particular of Saturday night. They will begin to take the pills as soon as they get them, but they save the bulk of them for Saturday night. That is the climax. Everybody, or so they will assure you, *everybody* was blocked on Saturday night.

They leave Greytown on their scooters, often not going far afield, but going where there's their own kind of music and their own kind of people exclusively. They stay awake throughout the night on Saturday, taking more pills as the effects of the first batch begin to wear off, comparing their feelings of wellbeing, analysing their symptoms—"My back keeps tingling, does yours?" "My eyes keep going funny." It doesn't matter if the experience is unpleasant as long as it is there, as long as everyone knows about it, as long as everyone can talk about it afterwards.

As Sunday morning dawns, they are into the less attractive stages of the proceedings: comedown. When the effects of the massive overdoses they have consumed begin to wear off, and there are no more pills to restore the sense of wellbeing, they experience a kind of nightmare hangover. Throughout Sunday, no one can face either food or drink; conversation, which was non-stop and scintillating the night before, becomes stilted; bodies are draped all round the room; faces are pale; eyes have a fixed, bloodshot gaze. Everyone keeps looking in the mirror, as if to make sure that the night's excesses have not left too dreadful a mark, or is it to reassure themselves that they still exist?

This, too, is all part of the ritual, not to be forgone. In the week, the group will be fortified, will reestablish its special identity, with tales of how "bad" John was on Sunday, of how Mick fell down the stairs at the Disco, "blocked out of his mind," of how Fred and Bill and Chris were stopped by the police as they drove along the by-pass at three o'clock in the morning and how they were taken to the nick and searched, but, phew, luckily they had dumped all the remaining gear in a hedge and so nothing came of it. It is a distinction to have brushed with the law.

The group will continue in this way until a key figure gets "busted"; until they get regular girl friends who disapprove (the weekend group may include girls who get "blocked up," but they are not usually the ones with whom more stable relationships are later formed). Or until they consider themselves too old. One boy states categorically: "I've got four years, until I'm 21, and then I'm stopping. Well, you're too old then, aren't you?"

Within the group, however, there are always one or two for whom the whole ethos of drug-taking holds a special appeal, and these are the ones who come to regard it rather more seriously than their mates. These, I would suggest, are probably young people with personality problems or severe domestic problems.

"Terry" began his flirtation with drugs in much the same way as his contemporaries. He began as a weekend junkie, simply using the pills as a means of enabling him to keep awake all night on Saturday and listen to the music. They made the music sound so much better too. But Terry is a very highly intelligent boy, who, as the result of having a criminal record, finds it difficult to get the sort of job he thinks he would like.

It didn't take him long to discover that the pills could be used as a means of escape from his problems and his sense of frustration. Gradually he found that the usual amount had ceased to be effective; he had to increase the dose in order to get any sensation at all. Soon he began experimenting with stronger drugs and was soon running the real risk of becoming addicted to a hard drug.

It would seem that once one is accepted within the charmed circle of drug takers, it is possible to obtain practically any preparation, from cannabis to heroin, within a few hours. Consequently, young people who may think that they have their drug taking perfectly under control, and who categorically state that they would never touch the "hard stuff," are, in fact, constantly at risk through being in contact with the drug scene. Also it is clear, that, while under the influence of the pills, the sense of responsibility and proportion tends to become blurred and the temptation to experiment, in a congenial setting, becomes great.

Members of the group will lie and exaggerate the extent of their involvement to achieve status in the group. Yet many of them are undoubtedly constantly dabbling with all the paraphernalia of real addiction. They will "jack up" pills, they will boil up concoctions of heroin and morphine, which they then use for "skin-popping," they will even inject themselves with "pro-Plus" pills readily available over the counter at any chemist. They are *playing* at being junkies. Yet, for Terry, and others like him, the game can easily become a harsh reality.

The real tragedy is that the youngster can pass from being a weekend junkie to being a full-time one so imperceptibly that not even he is aware of the transition.

He'll begin by being absent from work on Monday, one week, two weeks, three weeks running. This will stretch to more and more days off until he gets the sack. Once out of work, he'll find it difficult to make the effort to find fresh employment. With more free time, he'll spend more and more days playing around with drugs, only now it's rather less of a game. Perhaps sometime about now, his mother will find a syringe under his socks in a drawer and he'll have a lot of explaining to do. The pressure's on, and there's only one way he's found of relieving pressure. Short of cash, which he now desperately needs to buy his own gear, he'll begin "pushing" to pay for his own, or he may steal or attempt to obtain forged prescriptions. In fact, he's beginning to lead the life of a real live junkie.

The interesting aspect of all this is that the group which encourages and fosters the light-hearted use of drugs tends to reject its member who becomes more seriously involved. Terry becomes the scapegoat for all their fears. They will refer to his increased consumption with morbid fascination, will express the belief that he's "gone too far," will conjecture as to how he can be helped to "get off the stuff." Yet he is only doing now what they all, in theory at least, ran an equal risk of doing themselves.

As a youth worker, I have met, and dealt with, a large number of young people who have taken drugs in the "social" way I describe. Yet only a very small percentage of these have been led into more serious involvement. These were all boys with problems in relation to their environment or in coming to terms with their own personal situation. Perhaps they would once have run the risk of becoming alcoholics. Now they run the risk of becoming drug addicts.

While I would in no way wish to justify or condone their abuse of drugs, there is little doubt, that to these particular youngsters, they represented the key to a different kind, a different quality of life. I have met boys, who, under the influence of the pills, expressed, probably for the first time, their

317

deepest feelings about life, who discovered an appreciation of art and music, who realised—and, more miraculously, could discuss—the subtleties of relationships. These may seem to be irrelevancies, but, to the young people of Greytown, perhaps they hold a special significance. Without these stimuli they felt dead, or at least, permanently half-alive.

Everybody knows the beats and the weirdies in Greytown. Their rebellion is apparent; and their separateness is obvious. But the weekend junkies and their more seriously involved friends merge into the landscape with ease. They are a product of it and they remain a part of it.

[*19 February 1970*]

HOW CHILDREN USE TELEVISION

P. W. Musgrave

How far can parents control their children's use of television? Some of the work done in the United States, particularly in the early 1950s, tended to show television as a "family medium." The stereotype was of a family integrated into the home, happily gathered round the television set. More recent studies question this and so does research of my own in a project now in its first stages at Aberdeen University.

We are investigating how a sample of children use the various mass media, including television, during early adolescence—ie, between 11 and 15. The sample totals about 600. It is divided almost equally between boys and girls, and it also contains about equal numbers of children with working class and middle class parents.

During May and June 1967, we interviewed all these children individually in their schools for about three quarters of an hour. They were then aged between eleven and twelve and were in their last term at primary school. (Transfer to secondary school takes place a year later in Scotland than in England.) The children also completed a short questionnaire in their classrooms. Then, between November 1967 and January 1968, most of these children's mothers (87 per cent) were interviewed in their homes. This article is mainly based on our interviews with the children and their mothers.

There is a large sociological literature about how parents of different social classes discipline their children (the sex of the child also is relevant). There are not only formal rewards and punishments but also informal ways by which parents try to achieve control. For example, they try to ensure that their children come to hold the same values as themselves, so that they will govern their behaviour automatically by the same code as their parents. Often parents hope to achieve this by the example that they set in front of their children. We had both means of control in mind during our research.

Almost all of the children (97 per cent) lived in homes with television sets. There was no real difference between social classes in this, or between boys and girls. Only one of the children who had no set at home claimed that he had no access whatsoever to a television set: all the others without a set were fairly regular viewers outside their own homes. Television was to all intents and purposes available to the whole of our sample. But how popular was the watching of television among these children? When we asked the children which of six competing media they would prefer to use on a winter's evening (film, television, comics, book, radio, records), 28 per cent gave television as their *first* choice. Even when we asked them during June to rank their first three preferences out of 18 ways of spending their spare time, 25 per cent put television as *one* of their first three choices.

What, then, about formal control by parents? Take outright prohibition, first. We asked mothers if there were any programmes that they did not allow their children to watch: 53 per cent said that there were none; mothers of girls were slightly stricter than mothers of boys (56 per cent, as against 50 per cent); middle class mothers were very slightly stricter than working class mothers (54 per cent, as against 52 per cent). This finding replicates that of Hilde Himmelweit's survey, *Television and the Child*, twelve years ago. The mothers in her sample— even when they were teachers—"insisted that they did not direct their children's viewing." The prohibitions in Aberdeen related mainly to plays, films and programmes like z *Cars* (22 per cent) to programmes which emphasised sex (10 per cent), and to those where violence or horrors were expected (8 per cent).

As few mothers said they forbade such things, it is not surprising that when we asked the children if there was any programme they watched just because everyone else was watching it, about 7 per cent named programmes of the aggressive-hero type and 11 per cent mentioned films or plays some of which we know some of the mothers thought unsuitable.

Any look at the formal control of viewing must take account of positive encouragement as well as prohibition. So we asked the mothers whether they encouraged their children to watch any particular programmes. About 40 per cent said there were no programmes that they encouraged; there were no important differences between the working class and middle class mothers;

nor between the mothers of boys and of girls. Of the 60 per cent that did encourage their children to watch some particular programme 16 per cent named animal programmes (mainly *Daktari*), 13 per cent quiz programmes and 7 per cent *Top of the Form*. The main difference between the social classes was that, following a Scottish tradition, slightly more of the working class mothers said their reason for encouragement was educational or to help the children with their work at school. There was one difference between the sexes: the mothers of girls mentioned animal programmes rather more often than the mothers of boys.

For informal controls, there are three types of evidence: the example set by the parents; the way in which the family as a whole chooses television programmes; and the favourite programmes of the mothers and their children.

What was the example set by the parents, and how effective was it? We asked the children to say which of four categories best described how much television they watched. Some 25 per cent said they watched "several hours every night," 52 per cent said "most nights," 17 per cent said "just a few times a week," and 6 per cent said "not much at all." We asked the mothers the same question and also asked them to indicate what category they would put their husbands in. If there were any tendency for children to follow the parents' example, the parents of the children who viewed a great deal would also be heavy viewers, and so on for each of the four categories. This was not the case. (There was, however, a very slight tendency for children who did not view much at all to have mothers and fathers who also did not view much at all.) Parental example appeared to have no effect on television watching.

The second type of informal control could be the way in which choices of what will be watched are made within the family. A popular view is that television sets are switched on each evening without any thought about the programme. If this were so, one could understand parents who neither encourage nor prohibit the watching of specific programmes by their children. However, the facts are as follows.

We asked mothers: who chooses which channel will be watched? Almost a quarter (23 per cent) replied that it depended on the programme; in 19 per cent of cases the mother claimed that she chose, and in 17 per cent of cases the father did; 8 per cent of the children were said to choose; and in 21 per cent of cases the choice was by agreement. In middle class families the mother and the father both chose more often than in working class families (mothers 20 per cent, as against 19 per cent; and fathers 19 per cent, as against 15 per cent). In working class families the children chose slightly more often (9 per cent, as against 8 per cent); and agreement was more frequently named as the method of decision (22 per cent, as against 19 per cent) than in middle class families. The process of choosing what will be watched on television is rather less haphazard than is often thought. This impression is further supported by the answer we were given by the mothers when we asked how they themselves decided what to watch. Almost half said they used published programmes of one sort or another; a further quarter answered, "By knowing what's on," or some similar phrase. There was little difference between the social classes in this.

Was there finally any relationship between the nature of the programmes watched by the children and their mothers? If parents can influence the viewing habits of their children, one would expect that, despite differences in taste between the generations, there would be some overlap between the programmes named as favourites by mothers and children. We found no such coincidence. (On this subject there was more difference between the social classes and between boys and girls than in the other data.)

The four categories most mentioned by the mothers were: plays (22 per cent middle class, 14 per cent working class); serials (8 per cent, as against 19 per cent); news, documentaries or current affairs (15 per cent, as against 8 per cent). The children chose a totally different range of programmes. By far the most popular were pop (24 per cent middle class, 22 per cent working class) and programmes about aggressive heroes (27 per cent, as against 21 per cent). Pop programmes, which did not even appear as a category in the days of Hilde Himmelweit's study, were named as favourite by 25 per cent of the girls and 18 per cent of the boys. Programmes about aggressive heroes—like *The Avengers, Man from* UNCLE and *Batman*—were named by 26 per cent of the boys, as against 21 per cent of the girls. The next two categories in order of preference were magazine programmes like *Blue Peter* (7 per cent middle class, 10 per cent working

322

class) and sports programmes (5 per cent, as against 9 per cent). Our data on the programmes most *disliked* by mothers and children confirms that in this respect the children are not being influenced by their mothers.

Altogether, the situation in these families resembles that in the American high school reported by James Coleman in his study, *The Adolescent Society.* Coleman found that though those running the high school aimed to produce an academic ethos, the prevailing climate was "a fun culture." Despite the wishes, plans and efforts of the teachers who were seemingly in power, their pupils were importing into the school values and attitudes from outside. A somewhat similar process seems to be revealed by our research and it can probably be generalised beyond Aberdeen.

In spite of the overt efforts by some mothers, children are largely out of detailed parental control in this respect by the age of twelve. They are imposing the patterns that they learn outside the family onto their use of television within the family.

Even if parents were entirely successful in controlling (by whatever means) their children's viewing we have evidence to make us doubt whether such control would necessarily bring about the result the parents desire. This is because, as my colleague David Smith has recently said in a paper to the British Association, "It is not the media content itself, but the way in which it is used by the children which appears to be important." As an illustration of this point, let me quote some answers to our questions about violence. When we asked children to name "a programme where there is a lot of fighting" (in the context of a number of questions about violence), several children answered "The News" or gave the name of some current affairs programme. Which parent will ban a child of his (or hers) from watching the news?

But which of us knows the use to which his child is putting that programme of news as he or she watches it? Is our child learning what seems to us worthwhile knowledge about the geography of the Far East or is he using this programme for the violence in the war scenes?

What remains uncertain in all this—and I have brought no evidence to bear here—is what effect this comparative freedom from control has on children.

[20 February 1969]

NEIGHBOURHOOD SCHOOL

Robin Guthrie

Fifty-odd members of staff are squeezed into the library on tiny chairs. The headmaster is speaking.

"Now, gentlemen. There are three main problems associated with this school which we are now facing in acute form. The first is the fact that we have to work in separate buildings. The second is the low standard of the entry. The third is the discipline of the boys and, it must be said, gentlemen, of the staff."

It was said afterwards that he had never spoken so frankly in all his 15 years as headmaster; yet somehow he always manages to just miss the point.

The school is a boys' comprehensive school, 900 pupils, in an inner urban area. It occupies two buildings of unequal size, situated in different neighbourhoods three quarters of a mile apart, with a trunk route running down the middle. A third building, as far away again from the others, is used for some technical classes.

I am a very junior master there, in my second year of teaching, and I know of school policy only what I can see from its results or gain from judicious questions. This is simply a worm's eye view, and must be judged as such, but it is typical of the view that any worm would get in a good many of our schools.

The head was certainly right that the starting point of some of our problems is the physical separation of our buildings. The best of the equipment and of the staff tend to be concentrated in the larger building. This means that if the boys whose base is the annexe are not to miss some of the best things the school has to offer, they must have some sessions in the main building. This itself involves the movement of a considerable number of boys back and forth in the dinner hour and under their own steam; it also means that they have to report on different mornings of the week at any one of three different buildings, widely scattered. One group of eleven year olds in my first year class were caught setting light to a rag soaked in petrol underneath a lorry parked on their route; another group called in on Woolworth's for some

324

quiet shoplifting. Undoubtedly a great deal more goes on than we know about, and the possibilities of evasion and petty delinquency open to older boys of 14–15 are even greater.

I am not alone in placing some store by the corporate atmosphere generated by a school. A sense of unity, a sense of loyalty, and a feeling of common purpose can be over-emphasised at the expense of the individuality and self-expression of the individual members of the school. But where the sense of corporate life is fragmented almost to vanishing point the school's tasks, particularly in a difficult neighbourhood, become almost impossible to perform.

This is not, however, the chief among our difficulties. It was a ludicrous administrative decision to amalgamate the separate buildings of separate schools in separate neighbourhoods into one "school," and it leaves us with a lot of problems, some of them insurmountable. Nevertheless the educational short-comings of the school cannot be blamed on it alone; there are more vital factors still.

My job when I first arrived at the school was to teach all subjects except science, woodwork and games to an "experimental" first year class of mixed ability. This experiment had in fact three variables and no standard of measurement. The boys were selected by neighbourhood, not by ability or achievement; the head had a problem with those eleven year olds who lived on the far side of the annexe from the main building and who therefore had a long way to walk, including the crossing of the main road, to school unless they were based on the annexe. It had one master to teach virtually everything, like a primary school. Thirdly, the boys formed a random selection of abilities (this is different from a deliberate mixing of abilities): 16 per cent were totally illiterate; some were quite bright, or seemed so by contrast. I could never get complete records for the class, but they seemed to range from average to well below average in achievement, and possibly from well above average downwards in ability.

Thanks to the help of the art master, the PE master and the speech and drama master I was able to vary their timetable and to see that their first year of secondary education was not too lopsided. Other members of staff were also very helpful, and gave me all the help they could, when I asked. Together we

325

salvaged for the class a year of some educational value; since we started the year with no timetable, no classroom (I had to oust senior masters myself in order to achieve a majority of time in one place) and no directives, this was something of an achievement. We had some good outings, too, including a day trip to France (we got them all back in the end, though one boy lost his trousers to the tides of France), and I tried to link them with local organisations with whom I was in contact; every Wednesday, too, we went swimming—it seemed essential to have some regular form of contact outside the classroom.

I did not feel, however, that anybody could feel proud of the year's work, educationally speaking, and I was puzzled by the praise we received from the authorities. Some of my colleagues this year have congratulated me. "They're a joy to teach—so keen to learn"; others have simply said "That class of yours: noisy lot" (I dream sometimes about the reaction of some of my colleagues to the noise we sometimes make). But the authorities (the head, the master in charge of the annexe, the inspector) seem to have been entirely satisfied. Out of the shambles we started with, and in view of my unlikely qualifications and other inadequacies, such praise is unlikely to be deserved, and was not. The fact is, I kept them quiet enough; they were successfully contained, so I must be doing a good job. It might have been different if we had made more noise still.

The parents of my boys are unlikely to read this article. Some of them are living in new council flats and only just feeling their way; I hope they will gradually become more involved in and knowledgeable about their children's education. Others are waiting in slums until they are pulled down about their ears; a whole area round the building I teach in is at present being demolished. I have a delightful, dreamy West Indian boy whose house was the last in the street to remain, both intact and inhabited; he is now in the happy position of "being transferred," and I doubt if either school will catch up on his attendance (one session out of 30 since Easter). Contact with parents by staff, however, and parental contact with the school, are officially discouraged by the school. The analysis that follows is what I would like the parents to know.

The "low standard of the intake" has become the catchword in frequent use to excuse all our failings. In 1964 our entry had

326

been divided into five grades. We had no grade As, no Bs, 18 Cs and the rest of the intake were Ds and Es—in achievement. This year, seven grades were divided into three groups, and we were supposed to have an even spread from each of the three groups. We had none from the top group, one from the big middle section, and all the rest from the bottom: 93 per cent of the intake was classed as below average.

There is some doubt in my mind as to whether these gradings give a true picture. A longitudinal study is at present being conducted in our neighbourhood in which a number of our first and second year boys are involved. This study suggests that in native ability the boys of our neighbourhood are as good as their contemporaries anywhere in the country, but that in reading achievement 38 per cent of them have failed to achieve a minimal standard exceeded by all their contemporaries apart from the bottom 5 per cent. In other words, they are not stupid, but the grading system makes them look so.

The causes of this disparity between ability and achievement are unlikely to be found only in the school, nor even only in the primary schools; many aspects of the subcultures which make up the neighbourhood militate against education. It must surely, however, be the schools which mount the counter-attack. Ours does not.

Instead we concentrate our efforts on those few boys who may at some time pass an outside examination. To this end there is a rigid structure of streamed classes and subject teaching modelled on the grammar school and more distantly on the public schools. In 1964 one boy achieved one A level pass; in 1965 there were six A level passes in four different subjects. In that year also there were 50 O level passes achieved by rather fewer boys. At the moment there is alarm and disgust because the "low standard of the intake" will make it difficult or impossible to maintain this improvement; indeed it will.

The investment, which is now paying a few dividends, will turn out to be a dud—yet we hang on to it grimly, as though there were no alternative. It has been costly. The major educational effort of the school has been concentrated on less than a tenth of the school population; some favoured masters rarely see any boy outside that tenth, and heads of departments tend to concentrate almost exclusively on them. The rest of us, 90 per

327

cent and more of boys and staff, are left to contain and occupy each other till blessed release comes at the age of 15.

It is, inevitably, in these lower reaches of the school, where the educational effort should be concentrated, that there is waste and suffering. First and second year boys are often a pleasure to teach, and respond well to the variations in curriculum and method which are possible in view of the lack of any kind of academic pressures. By the time they are third year, however, they become dimly aware of their true position; educationally speaking, they have been sold down the river.

Although they could not possibly explain themselves verbally, they respond to their situation as though they understood it perfectly; discipline becomes a serious problem. All that stuff they hear about school being a waste of time was true; they are living examples of it, and cannot escape. "What *is* the point of our coming here?", asked a fourth former, sincerely, in a class I was trying to teach. There is no honest and constructive reply to give; the truth is too harsh.

This aspect of the school's failure is seen at its worse in the so-called remedial classes. There is one remedial class in each year; each contains about 25 boys, few of whom can read. The first and second years are treated like inadequate children. The third year is transitional, as they begin to realise their true position. By the time they reach the fourth year, 14 turning 15, only the toughest available master can cope with them. If we ever have a compulsory fifth year, the logic of our present system will suggest simply that we must find a tougher master still.

The staff of the remedial department, some of whom have a genuine interest in the tasks of remedial education, have no training beyond what they have been able to gain from short courses after they started work in the field. Certainly no remedies are produced. Few boys, if any, are transferred upwards from the remedial classes; many leave illiterate, or with so weak a grasp of reading and writing that they revert to illiteracy shortly after leaving. These classes are simply the bottom stream, the dregs of the dregs; and the secret is not kept from them.

This situation is the result of the headmaster's preoccupation with those who have already achieved most when they arrive and are accordingly graded comparatively high. It is a preoccupation which is becoming increasingly irrelevant, and which

328

may be losing him, from the point of view of examination successes, much of the dormant talent in the school.

The head's approach brings clearly to the surface two important elements in the school's organisation: rigid streaming, and rigid subject teaching, whereby a master is allocated to a subject rather than to a group or groups of boys.

Streaming is done on the basis of reports received from the primary schools. There are six or seven streams on entry, according to the number of the intake. There is virtually no transfer between streams save for a dozen or so boys early on in their first year. The little flock of sheep are separated from the great horde of goats at the start, and kept that way.

Emphasis on subjects, rather than on groups of boys, means that a class may frequently have a form master who takes them for register (or who at least is responsible for their register: sometimes master and class will be in separate buildings, in which case another master deputises and a slip is sent across with the names of the absentees) but for nothing else. The class thus becomes a floating entity of its own, with no one taking a particular interest in the boys as individuals; and it is hardly surprising that some individuals react badly to this—particularly the ones from disturbed backgrounds, of whom there are many.

Some schools overcame this problem with a house system, which has the advantages of providing a social system parallel to that of the classroom but not based on academic achievement, and of providing a person who is actually responsible for the wellbeing of the boys in his house. We too have a house system; it is resurrected every sports day. There are, however, no housemasters and no house meetings, and the boys do not know what houses they are in. It is not surprising that only a few members of the staff, honourable exceptions, show any real interest in the boys as individual persons.

The basic pattern of the school's organisation and goals does not leap readily to the eye; a school is a confusing place. There may be things that I have yet to learn which might lead me to modify the description I have given. If, however, I am right—as I think I am—a number of other aspects of the life of the school fit the pattern as I now see it.

I remember clearly two incidents early on in my teaching career at this school. The first was when I went to the main

329

building to pick up my form on their first day at secondary school. There was a lot of sorting out to do; a lot of waiting, and a lot of reassurance needed, in the long waits between actual events like going somewhere or shyly giving one's name and being herded into another group. A record number of parents were present, many (about the right proportion) immigrant—new to Britain.

The head delivered his speech to them, that sunny autumn morning with the sun looking kindly in through the high Victorian windows. "Glad to see you," he said (I paraphrase). "Glad you take an interest in the splendid education your son is going to get at ——— School. But, remember he's growing up now: he doesn't need you hanging on to his harness straps any more. So we don't expect to see you here again . . ." The words, I know, were better chosen for his purpose, but not much, and that was certainly the message I got; to judge by the results they got it too: "We don't want you here."

The second was a little later when, in connection with an individual problem in the class I mentioned to the master in charge of the annexe that I was calling round on the parents that evening. He was kind, but firm; we don't approve of that: let the school attendance officer do the visiting (the school attendance officer becomes a kind of policeman). I have consistently disobeyed this injunction, and I reckon all parties have gained from it. But most of the staff adhere to it.

Unfortunately this exemplifies the school's attitude not only to parents but also the neighbourhood in general. The environment in which the boys live is regarded as alien, hostile, crime-producing. It certainly does produce a lot of crime, but many other things as well, and it is the environment in which the boys spend their lives. No member of the staff apart from myself lives in the catchment area, and most would strongly support the view that it is not merely unwise, but dangerous to do so. "What would happen if my wife and I met x in the street?" My wife and I do, and haven't suffered yet. Most of the staff have other profitable part-time occupations; but work in a local youth club in connection with work in the school does not occur.

The neighbourhood is in fact an essential key to the understanding of much that goes on in the school. Both neighbourhoods with which the school is primarily concerned are in

330

transition. One is almost entirely council housing, the mid-20th century's answer to the 19th century slums (what is not council housing is rapidly being pulled down). People are still adjusting, not only to the change in the quality of our environment but also to difficulties like that of bringing up a family on the 17th floor. The other is mainly private housing in various stages of decay, with a comparatively high proportion of immigrants. The school however, is officially not interested.

Immigrants form nearly 30 per cent of the school's population. It goes without saying that there is no official prejudice against immigrants at any point; the schools really are good at this. Some sensible steps have been taken recently, at the instigation of a very good West Indian teacher, to give positive help to a number of immigrant boys who have communication problems. As in so many things, however, if we were tackling the native problem effectively there would be no difficulty for immigrants and no special arrangements would be necessary; they would simply join in with the special arrangements for native boys who have communication problems and move on according to their natural abilities. At any rate, the important case of the intelligent immigrant boy who is held back by language difficulties can now be helped in the school even if he is not always, and this is all to the good.

The boys themselves reflect the prejudices of the neighbourhood. Among eleven and twelve year olds there is absolutely no evidence of prejudice. "What happens when a black man marries an eskimo?—their baby's a choc-ice!" This joke, which I would not have dared, was entirely acceptable in a first year class of mixed races. As they grow older, however, they divide. Boys of one race tend to sit together in the classroom, to play together, to go around together. This has no harmful effects unless the heat is on. Occasionally there is a bust-up in the street after school—100 boys may be involved, tension is at snapping point, noses are broken: it always so happens that whatever started the fight, it always finishes as black versus white, two clearly divided factions.

One West Indian boy wrote on the job application forms we were using for practice: "It's no use anyway; they don't want coloured boys." Interestingly enough, the fifth form (the year after the optional school-leaving age) is over-full of West

Indians, who seem to have little or no purpose in staying on; perhaps they couldn't face the outside world. They form a difficult, irresponsible group, and arouse much criticism from the staff.

It is indeed this kind of situation which brings out the latent hostility and prejudice in the staff room. The "coloured boys" are often seriously classed together as troublemakers, and even held responsible for the falling standards of the school. I tackled this view once in a heated staffroom argument, but it was earnestly defended. There is a frightening emotional logic about race prejudice, utterly irrational, and set inexorably deep. Much more significant in our school is the disproportionate number of immigrant boys who collected prizes on prize-giving day last year; I did not keep a tally, but far more Cypriots, West Indians and Indians went up than their total numbers would have led one to expect—all credit to the school, and particularly to them.

Discipline in a school of this kind, run in the way it is, is likely to be a problem; so it often is. By and large relationships between masters and boys are friendly, if superficial; a lot of amicable backchat goes on between classes. A considerable number of boys, however, "step out of line," and the reaction is invariably repressive. It could hardly be otherwise, considering the educational position of the boys, the lack of contact with their backgrounds, and the lack of personal interest in them. The instrument is the cane, applied to the seat; few days go by without a number of canings. Any member of staff apart from those doing their first, probationary year of teaching, may use the cane, and most of us do, some frequently.

Even if one disapproved of the method, it would be difficult to do anything about it in the school as it is. Order, in many classes, is almost impossible to keep, and without some kind of order teaching or constructive activity of any kind is impossible. Hence the weak master and the newcomer rely heavily on the strong-armed men who are feared by the boys. In my first year in particular (when I was not officially allowed to use the cane and never in fact did) there were situations which I could not control, and in some of them I thought quick, sharp punishment was the only answer. I was grateful to the strong-armed man down the passage, who caned at my request without question.

It helped in the short run, though not at all in the long term. Some of my fourth year boys, whom I now refuse to cane, remain on friendly terms with me but think I am being very soft with the regular miscreants of the class: "The only thing you can do with that lot, sir, is to cane 'em hard!" A dispiriting result for ten years of liberal education. And I shall never forget the look of hatred and anger and pain in the eyes of a difficult 15 year old when I caned him last term.

School ends at 4.10. By 4.15 there is nobody on the premises save the cleaners, one or two bachelor teachers in the staffroom, and perhaps a group of West Indian boys playing cricket in the playground (much discouraged). The rest have gone; the staff to beat the rush hour, and the boys home, if anybody is there, or to devilment in the streets. "Out of school activities" do not exist for the majority. There are four activities, and they depend entirely on three members of staff. They are very good examples of what can be done by individuals even in hostile circumstances. Their success, though used by the head on occasions such as speech day, does not seem to have made much impression on the head or his staff as a whole.

The debating society has built up a good tradition and won prizes at local schools' competitions. The Duke of Edinburgh's award scheme has gained three gold, 17 silver and over 50 bronze medals in the last six years. These two activities have depended entirely on one man. Another master runs the school teams, which play other schools on Saturdays; he puts a lot of work into this. The school orchestra numbers about 60 players; this seems to me an absolutely splendid solo effort by the music master.

These are considerable efforts in their own right, but they do not involve the majority of boys and still less do they involve the staff. For most of the latter, contact with the boys is confined to the classroom, the corridor, and the occasional playground and dinner duties.

Little interest is shown in modern teaching methods, and less still in research. Much is made by the head, when visitors come to the school, of the up-to-date workshops for wood and metal, the art room, and the audio-visual aids for modern languages. There is some truth in this display. We have a local authority which is in many ways excellent, and this is one of the ways.

Nothing, in some respects, is too good for a school. Unfortunately, this applies to equipment, rather than to attitudes; to materials rather than to quality of education.

Equipment undoubtedly makes a lot of difference; it gives heart to the staff who use it, and it does offer greater opportunities to some boys. But it does not change the school. Many of the staff and boys, particularly in the lower reaches, see little if anything of this equipment. Most of the work is done in ordinary classrooms, and much of it is still containment, not education; the television set and the film projector are often an acknowledged escape from the classroom, and much sought after as such.

Before I arrived at the school I had to make it clear that owing to my other commitments to local organisations (youth clubs and the like) I would not be able to play a direct part in out-of-school activities. At the same time, I offered my local contacts if they could be useful. I expected to be the exception, not the rule. I was surprised at the lack of interest in an all-round education, and the school is not interested in my local knowledge. Some of the staff are concerned, but we are rendered powerless by the overwhelming impact of the school's organisation and expressed goals. For the majority, their attitude is summed up in the remark made by the careers master in my hearing and in the hearing of several of the boys to the youth employment officer just before he spoke to them: "They're a real shower, this lot."

I nearly hit him. It eats into one, nonetheless. The cheerful cynicism of members of staff taking a quiet drag in the staff-room during assembly has its effect: gay, amusing, and utterly deadly. "I don't take public-spirited action like that nowadays." I realised to my horror I had just said that to a younger master in connection with the blowing of the whistle in the playground in the absence of the deputed master. It jolted me; I am as cynical, as lazy, and as hopeless as any.

We are caught up in a rigid system: rigid streaming, which kills the enthusiasm and opportunities of most of the boys, rigid subject teaching, which ensures that no personal interest is taken in them, and a rigid hierarchy, whereby graded posts go to favourites who accept the status quo, and where heads are older men whose attitudes kill the ideas of young teachers from training colleges in a few terms. (This has been well documented recently by John Partridge in his book *Middle School*.) And within this invisible, rigid structure the fluid and fascinating life of the school goes on.

The boys' reaction to this misconceived organisation of goals is generally hostile; among the favoured few it is favourable, and in many others the hostility is often tinged with resigned tolerance—this makes life in the school possible. We are, however, turning out unskilled workers in enormous numbers, of which the country has a decreasing need, and we are helping many on the road to delinquency.

The job that must be tackled is being tackled, difficult though it is, in a few schools with success. We must communicate academic standards (quality of work, thoroughness in doing it, application to doing it—whatever it is); we must communicate a sense of social concern and responsibility (which we can only communicate if we first show concern for them); and we must push forward every individual possibility of independent thought and action we come across to its full potential. All this, to 70 per cent of the boys and girls of the nation, now in secondary modern schools.

Yet I rarely walk down the road feeling despondent or unable to face the milling hordes, although these moments happen. Much of the day is pleasurable and interesting work. Past the prefects at the door—"Morning, Sir." "Morning"—and into the staffroom for a glance at the morning paper before register. Then up the crowded stairs to the classroom (many "good mornings" on the way). Settle the boys down, silence for register, and then a few moments of peaceful chatter before we go into assembly. Assembly is undemanding, if ghastly. The boys sit in rows uncomfortably on the floor. A few of the staff down the sides; the rest have hopped it to the staffroom.

Sometimes it goes on for 50 minutes (boys shifting uneasily on the floor): "Some boys seem to think . . ." "You can't steal; it says so in the bible!" (The school is not a religious school, but the head is a lay preacher.) On and on. Undemanding. Then the classroom. "Quiet! SMITH!! Now . . ." The milk comes round. Twenty minutes' break follows; a cup of tea and the paper, or jokes bandied about, or a problem boy or group of boys discussed, or an argument, or a discussion about cars. Then two straight, usually uninterrupted periods. Then an hour and a half for dinner ("It's more dignified," said the head. It doesn't look dignified in the playground, or in the surrounding streets.)

There is nowhere to work on the premises, so I usually go out to the local library or to a pub lunch, to work. Back again; settle down. Silence for register, then another changeover of classes before we can get down to what is left of the first period. *"Nous parlons français . . ."* Then another break—ten minutes this time, quick cup of tea, back again for two periods; less energy available; either relax and read, or give them something testing to draw out such energy and concentration as remains. Finally, "Chairs on the desks, boys!" and we're off. Another day tomorrow, and no change. No change for a long time to come, in this school.

I wish I could think that our school, and our head, were utterly exceptional, but from what I have read and from what I have heard, they are not.

[*23 June 1966*]

ST PAUL'S

Anne Corbett

The raciest line in rhetoric at present used to defend the public schools undoubtedly comes from Thomas Edward Brodie Howarth, Highmaster of St Paul's School, London. The highmaster (ie, headmaster), was one of the three members of the Public Schools Commission to dissent from the report (which advocated partial integration with the state system). He claimed in the *Daily Telegraph*, the day the report was published, that it was such a blatant compromise that even his intellectual opposites, "the Hampstead Jacobins . . . will be finding their camparis taste all the bitterer for it amid their rose-bowered patios."

Most published opinion regards the commission's report as a charter for the continuance of the public schools, with its main recommendation for state aid for 50 per cent of pupils as the way to achieve integration with the state sector. Howarth disagrees. At this week's session in Oxford of the public school headmasters' organisation, the Headmasters' Conference, he will be elaborating on what he sees as the unworkability and rigidity of the report. It would add (he says) to the problems of integrating boys with IQs of 150 and those with IQs of 90, the extra problems of integrating those with a passion for HP sauce and those who prefer decaying game. The Oxford conference will demonstrate how many of his fellow heads agree with him.

Howarth—a very charming man—is someone to be treated more respectfully than the imagery might suggest. He heads a school with one of the consistently highest tallies of open awards to Oxford and Cambridge—27 last year, 24 this, or about one to every 15 sixth form boys. His school has just demonstrated its faith in the future by moving this term to premises so lavishly equipped that the cost per pupil works out at about four times the amount for pupils in state-maintained schools.

What's the school like? Do the new CLASP buildings sited above the reservoirs at Barnes—functional, flexible and not at all imposing—tell more about its character than that redbrick

Gothic of Waterhouse, that monument to Victorian self-confidence on the road to London airport? What are the aims of the school? How does it work? Is there something distinctive to the school that one can recognise even now in the first days in the new buildings, something that one sees despite the contractors' mud, the trailing wires, the unfinished sports halls, the current shortage of cooks and cleaners?

Something does begin to emerge about the school in even the barest facts. Like the majority of public schools. St Paul's is single-sex. But unlike the majority it is mainly a day school: even the 120 boarders among the school's 700 boys mostly go home at weekends. That and the school's position in inner London mean that almost by definition it cannot be a totally enveloping institution in the boarding-school sense.

Again like other public schools—and it's one of the advantages of independence—the school has a large staff. With almost 50 masters, many young, mostly Oxbridge, it can keep class sizes to 20 at the bottom of the school, to below ten at the top. For many of the staff the choice was often between university or sixth form teaching, and not between state or public school teaching. This aids the sixth form orientation of the school. About 50 per cent of the boys are in the sixth (or in St Paul's parlance, "eighth") forms. Few leave before they are 18. A comprehensive is lucky to have 40 per cent staying on till 16.

The school is rich in its own right. John Colet, dean of St Paul's Cathedral, started the school in 1509 with various endowments. These still help subsidise *all* fees (now running at £327 a year for day boys, £531 for boarders) but they contribute heaviest towards the fees of 153 foundation scholars, whose awards (depending on parents' income) are worth at least £141 a year.

And as a result of a recent decision by the governors (predominantly from the City of London Mercers' Company), the funds will be able to provide free tuition for the sons of masters at the school. St Paul's Girls' School and Colet Court, the prep school for St Paul's, share in the endowments too. Yet the fund was still able to provide £700,000 towards the £3·3 million cost of the new site and buildings—a substantial help in outbidding local authority rivals for the site.

The school draws from the expected source, the middle class, though with possibly an unusually large proportion of sons of prosperous foreigners: American professors, West African attorney-generals, Iranian army chiefs. "Sometimes," says Howarth, "I feel my school is the first stop from London airport." Though the school is the usual Christian foundation, it has a large Jewish contingent, and proudly claims them as intellectual pacesetters (old boys include Sir Isaiah Berlin and Jonathan Miller).

Several of the masters characterise the parents (Jewish or not) as very ambitious people, people who have made their way in life aggressively. And it's obviously very much in this context that Howarth defines the aims of the school. "We exist," he says, "in response to a need felt by a metropolitan bourgeoisie which thinks that this school can do what it wants done for its chilren." It's a long way from A. S. Neill or Maria Montessori, or even the 1944 Education Act. No question of starting with the children and designing an education for their abilities and needs. Instead you provide a service: in Howarth's words again, academic success and a sense of order.

It may sound conservative, it may sound commercial. But how can it fail to work on the micro-scale of the individual school, or even on the scale of public schools generally (which between them take only 1·4 per cent of the school population)? Heads can be selective enough to assume the intellectual quality of the boys and to ensure the cooperation of the parents.

St Paul's has plenty of evidence for the success of the particular form of education which selects pupils at eight for the scholarship route to Oxford and Cambridge. St Paul's is having to modify the approach a little in face of the decline of many prep schools. It is taking in some local-authority-assisted pupils to its own prep school, Colet Court, at eleven. Besides these scholarships at eleven, Colet Court chiefly has them for fee-paying children at eight. Parents know that if their eight year olds can do long division well enough to get a Colet Court award they are likely to be good enough at Latin and French and science to get a St Paul's scholarship at 13. That in itself will almost guarantee a place at Oxford, Cambridge or London. In summer 1967, there were 150 leavers, all but 40 were going on to higher education. Over 40 went to Oxbridge, 14 to London. St Paul's doesn't seem keen on the new universities (too trendy).

To achieve this success, St Paul's streams its 13 year olds rigorously at the moment of entry. The 40 or so weakest boys go into two "fourth" forms (ie, the beginning forms). The other 100 or so new entrants join the previous year's fourth formers in eight "fifth forms," based on the boy's dominant subject (three forms with extra maths and science, a classics form, a German form, for example). There are "sets" for most subjects, including maths, science, French and Latin.

There is some changing of forms and sets for maybe 15 or 20 boys (including change between the "fourths" and "fifths") but only until the exams half way through the autumn term. o levels are taken in the "sixth"—ie, for the majority of boys after two years. Only three or four boys are likely to leave at the end of that year. A handful, who are doing o level repeats, go into a "seventh" from where they can combine o and A level work. The overwhelming majority—90 per cent—go on to work for three A levels, in the lower and middle "eighth" forms. The upper "eighth," the university entry form, is likely to contain all but about 40 of the original 13 year old entry.

There have been major changes over the last couple of years, following on the work of a curriculum committee headed by the second master ("surmaster"), F. G. Cummings. There is no longer an express scholarship stream taking o level in one year. Now all boys take at least six periods of science in their first year. All except the classics and German forms (unless these boys particularly want to) do art and music. Everyone does English history, geography, maths and divinity.

The influence of classics has decreased and will presumably decline still further after this year when Latin ceases to be a compulsory subject in public school common entrance. Science becomes more important. There's an attempt to make biology a subject that everyone takes (biology to take in the pill and germ warfare). But it was admitted to be characteristic that a master should say that they wouldn't risk their *best* boys on the Nuffield physical sciences A level course at its beginning.

St Paul's is involved in the Schools Mathematics Project, based on Westfield College and will be adopting the Nuffield Schools Council o level Latin course. But, on the whole, attempts at liberalising the curriculum at the top of the school consist mainly in bridging gaps between A level forms.

The academic approach apart—and most schools, public schools especially, claim that it is only part—what of the character of the school? What about the sense of order that Howarth talks about?

A hierarchy exists still. But organisationally it is heavily modified—at the boys' level if not the masters. Take the traditional apparatus of houses and prefects. The eight houses (known as clubs) exist for games—of which more in a moment. But "clubs" are not as meaningful as other less hierarchical groupings—forms, school societies, or even tutor groups. Those tutor groups, which contain 10 to 20 boys, meet collectively once a week. They are designed to strengthen the contact between (on the one hand) individual boys (on the other) parents, and masters.

There are prefects. But the present 18 have few special privileges and little power. There are refreshingly few pretensions about St Paul's. There's none of the nonsense of senior boys being allowed to walk round with their hands in their pockets or with their jackets done up (or is it undone?). They don't have fags. They don't beat boys (there's apparently very little beating by masters either). Their sanctions are limited to giving detentions for disobeying what they regard as their traffic warden duties—stopping boys running down corridors or rushing into lunch.

The prefects' status may be whittled away still further. With the move to Barnes there are now three common rooms for boys. And these—the first stage to democracy?—have elected committees. There's some dispute as to whether the elections are free, and where these committees have any power anyway. But they have an obvious potential importance.

Some of the other traditional trappings of the public school have gone. There's no longer a cadet corps. Some boys may opt to do community service instead, but there's no compulsion to regard it as the cadet corps' successor. Since the change to Barnes, chapel ceremonies no longer play the usual unifying part in school life. The Latin prayers of Colet's day have vanished with the removers' vans. And without a general assembly hall to take the whole school, morning prayers are divided—compulsory (except for Jews, etcetera) for the lower school, optional for the upper school (ie, the "eighth" forms).

So far, only 30 to 40 upper school boys—out of a possible 300—attend.

It's no longer compulsory to do particular games, though boys have to take some form of exercise. The choice includes fencing and basketball. It's claimed that sporting keenness isn't a passport to the top of the school hierarchy.

But games do still seem to be important to the obviously competitive spirit of the school. Of five prefects I talked to, four regularly spent their Saturdays on the games pitches, and it is notable that many staff take games as well as lessons.

What about the attitudes of staff and boys? Do they reflect the modified hierarchy of the organisation? The masters follow the pattern discovered by Graham Kalton in his survey, *The Public Schools* (Longmans, 1966), in being mostly public-school-educated themselves and in mostly having teacher-training qualifications.

One wouldn't expect them to be objective about the value of public school education. Not surprisingly they value highly the sixth form work, the high university entry, the general will to work. They are paid well above the local authority Burnham scale. When I talked to masters at St Paul's there was no necessary correlation between youth and liberalism in attitudes to reform, whether of the public school system, of the organisation of schools in general, or of coeducation.

The boys too seem to respect the underlying sense of order that Howarth feels is so important. Rebellion seems to be on a fairly minor level. A number were sorry that, with the move, the school hadn't been able to go coeducational, bringing in St Paul's girls (at the moment only allowed into school societies and the boys' magazine).

The most coherent opposition I found to school policy is on rules about appearance—the uniformity of blazers (black), trousers (grey), shoes (no suede) and hair (short). "Shave the hair and you shave the mind," one boy muttered. Successful rebellion therefore becomes measured in terms of being able to slip past the master on duty at the form door in the morning with bellbottom trousers or a John Lennon haircut.

This concern with uniformity pervades the only school slang I heard—which could, on the Royston Lambert thesis, be significant. Lambert maintains that the prime indicators of a school's character are its language and its sexual practices (as he torridly proves in *The Hothouse Society*). At St Paul's there is a group of boys desperately concerned not to end up as "sameys"—or as the "conformo-probes of the rugger pitch."

When I asked them about their ambitions, the class of ten produced only one potential gentleman farmer, one barrister, no teachers or university lecturers, but a plethora of would-be artists, poets and novelists.

Nearer home and on their attitudes to public schools the boys had less radical views.

There were few radical questions asked by the boys I met—and this in a school which claims a large proportion of left-wingers, including the head boy, and which boasts of its Grosvenor Square demonstrators. None of the boys emphasise St Paul's *social* benefits—and several find it a compliment not to be immediately taken for public school boys. But they are at this stage convinced of the academic advantages of public school. Most think of reform *within* the public school system. Among those I met, only the head boy looked at the public schools' place in the education system as a whole.

Is there any reason, in fact, why St Paul's should worry much about its place in society?

It will obviously try not to worry openly—it needs confidence in its way of life to survive. With its lack of social pretension—apart from minor aesthetic disasters like the mock cloisters around a CLASP court in front of the school—its academic reputation, its wealth of facilities, it offers an attractive form of bourgeois education.

Any cracks in its confidence must at present be infinitely small. Apart from any financial restrictions the government might impose, it would need the development of state sixth-form junior colleges to provide an academic alternative. It would also need the belief by many more parents that what the Plowden committee found about primary education applied to *them*—that it's their influence on their child which matters most and not the school's.

[*26 September 1968*]

THE BRADFORD BOLSHEVIKS

Albert Hunt

At eleven o'clock in the morning on 2 November 1967, a dozen students suddenly appeared on the steps of the Queen Victoria monument in the centre of Bradford. They were all dressed in black—black jeans, black sweaters, black polythene capes tied round their necks, and they all wore red armbands. They climbed up the steps, turned round and began to read aloud in unison from the thoughts of Chairman Mao. A policeman at the foot of the steps tried to pretend that nothing was happening.

At roughly the same time, two miles or so from the city centre, a procession of more than a hundred students, led by a chance band, came swinging through the gates of the park in which the city's main art gallery, the Cartwright Memorial Hall, is set. These students, too, were dressed in black, but with white armbands. The girls had boots and long skirts that swung round their ankles, and they carried wooden home-made rifles. Behind them, in the procession, were four huge, twelve foot puppets, made out of cardboard boxes painted black. The students carried slogans on banners: SUPPORT YOUR GOVERNMENT, DOWN WITH RED AGITATORS, NO PEACE WITH AGGRESSORS.

In the city bus station, a bus arrived from Barnsley. About 25 students, in black with white armbands, got off the bus and looked around. While they were deciding where to go, a van drove up, crudely camouflaged. Out of it leapt a student with a red armband. He picked out the four prettiest girls, told them to get in the van, and drove away. Inside the van, the girls had their white armbands exchanged for red.

Outside a bread shop, in the city centre, a queue of two dozen students formed. They wore red armbands, and carried the slogan: PEACE, LAND, BREAD. Each student bought one teacake. Then they all took their teacakes across the town to a disused post office in a working class area. In the window of the post office were placards announcing that the shop would accept anything but money. A wordless poster showed Lenin reaching out over the Italianate city hall and the mills of Bradford.

344

We described the event as an experiment in public drama. Using more than 300 students, mainly from Yorkshire art colleges, we turned Bradford into St Petersburg for a day, and tried to re-create, in the form of a dramatic game, some of the events of the 1917 October Revolution.

What were we trying to do in this experiment? And what was the educational context in which it took place? To understand the answers to these questions, one needs to look a little wider—at the general experiment in liberal education that we are carrying out at the Regional College of Art in Bradford.

The revolution was one of about 20 projects that make up this year's liberal studies programme. In this programme we are trying to break away from the pseudo-university form of liberal studies—lectures and seminars in which established culture is handed down—and to create situations which will involve students working actively together as a group.

The revolution project sprang out of a Vietnam war game we played last year. Each student in the group took a role in playing out an imaginary future crisis—a threatened American blockade of Haiphong. The students got very involved. They learnt not only about Vietnam, but about having to work with people whose aims differ from your own, about the need to use words carefully, and about the personal as well as political pressures that affect people who have to make decisions. For a week, everybody was talking about Vietnam. Could we, I wondered, extend such an event outside the college? Could we get Bradford thinking, for a day, about the Russian revolution?

We began serious work with a group of 28 students about ten days before the event. We started with background. We looked at the *Potemkin* film, had lectures from university experts on Soviet history, listened to and argued with a militant Trotskyist, We also had in college Ron Hunt's exhibition on post-revolutionary art in Russia—"Descent into the Streets"—and we had a lecture from Hunt himself. But we had too little time to come to grips with these subjects because I had underestimated the amount of practical organising we should be caught up with. We ought, I feel, to have talked in some detail, not only about the revolution, but about Meyerhold and Brecht and American street happenings. But it soon became clear that we would be

345

dealing with large numbers of students, and the problems of planning the day became central.

We divided into groups. One group worked at inventing the game. Another built the giant puppets. A third made a wall newspaper. A fourth prepared the moneyless shop.

The most interesting work was done with a group of advertising students who were preparing the poster. This led to exactly the kind of extension one is looking for in liberal education— the students were using their specialist skills, but in a context that forced them to reexamine many of their assumptions. So— we looked at propaganda posters by Mayakovsky, and at the pictures of his propaganda sweet wrappings. We discussed what he was trying to do, and how his intentions differed from those of commercial advertisers.

The game itself turned out to be difficult to plan. The problem was to keep the tension of a game while preserving the dramatic shape. We wanted the day to start white and become increasingly red. Eventually, we divided the participants into two teams and gave them four locations to capture. A location would be captured by whichever team had more bodies there—one man, one vote—on the stroke of the hour: extra votes, in the shape of red or white discs, could be won by carrying out instructions (given in envelopes) with invention and imagination.

The instructions were practical: "Find a communist and take him to the shop"; "Interview a journalist and ask him what he thinks he is doing"; "Take six bourgeois heads to an agent in the technical college canteen." Some left room for flights of the imagination: "Unite the workers of the world"; "Put down red plots."

We were a little worried as to how the visiting students would cooperate. We need not have been. All we asked them to do was to come dressed in black and ready to keep to the rules—but in fact many of them made elaborate costumes and weapons. The Leeds contingent in particular flung themselves into the experience, even after it began to rain at about one o'clock.

How far did we succeed in doing what we set out to do? I personally felt that in a number of points we failed. The rain washed out some of the most interesting activities—a group had been asked to prepare a propaganda play, but everybody was much too wet to bother. Some of the schemes, such as having red

346

and white provo bicycles, and releasing hydrogen balloons, never materialised. And the events were, perhaps, too scattered to make a total impact. We wanted events to take place all over the city—but if all you saw was a group of students building a cardboard tower, it was fairly easy to dismiss the affair as a student rag.

The moneyless shop made the biggest impact, because it was concentrated in one place, and sustained over two days. At first, people stood around cautiously, not knowing whether or not to go in. Then they began, not only taking, but bringing things. At one stage, twelve yards of Harris Tweed appeared. Money which was on offer remained untouched until some schoolchildren came in and helped themselves. Just before we closed, on the second day, a woman said, "You've made us all feel very uncomfortable refusing to take our money." A basic assumption of society had been directly challenged.

And what of the students? What was so great was the extent of their commitment. A group of first-year boys sat up half the night in a tutor's flat, working at the final plans. Another group came in at halfpast eight in the morning to finish painting the puppets. And their seriousness was answered by the seriousness of those who took part. Although it had been pouring with rain all afternoon, more than a hundred stuck it out to take part in the final two-mile march. Soaked to the skin they carried their banners and puppets through the Pakistani quarter across the city centre to a rally in a huge, derelict engine shed. The barriers between students from different colleges, and between students and teachers, had been completely destroyed.

Above all, the students seemed to enjoy themselves. And that, to my mind, is where learning begins.

[23 November 1967]

JOHN LENNON'S SCHOOLDAYS

Michael Wood

A heavy man with glasses sits on a chair looking at a green monster with four legs. Caption? "An adult looks at a Beatle." The caption is mine, but the drawing is John Lennon's. It appears in his second book, *A Spaniard in the Works*.

There are four-legged things everywhere in Lennon's drawings: sheep, cats, cows, Sherlock Holmes on his knees. The first book, *In his own Write*, has a huge Wrestling Dog ("But who would fight this wondrous beast? I wouldn't for a kick off"), and a piece called "Liddypool" is accompanied by a sketch of chatting quadropuses.

It is a child's world, or a world that Thurber might have drawn for a child. Animals and freaks have comic dignity while adults look silly and too big, bending over and crawling. A double suggestion runs through the writing in both books: adults *are* silly, they give children rubbish to read and expect them to like it; and left to themselves, adults are worse than children—they talk jabberwocky about politics and colour and religion, and they believe what they say.

So we get Enig Blyter's famous five—all ten of them taking off for Woenow Abbey—"'Gruddly Pod, Gruddly Pod,' the train seemed to say, 'Gruddly Pod, we're on our hollidays'." There is a trip to Treasure Ivan with Large John Saliver, Small Jack Hawkins, Cpt Smellit and Squire Trelorgy. But Prevalent ze Gaute also appears, and Docker Adenoid along with Harrassed MacMillion and the late Cassandle of the Mirror on the Wall. The bible, hymns, newspapers, the telly, bad films: the world shrinks to the nonsense of a book for small children.

The trick is simple, a standard schoolboy game. You retreat to baby-talk, to mock-childishness, to the linguistic pranks of Lewis Carroll and Edward Lear. This is your revenge on all the language, life and literature that people are asking you to take seriously. You bend and break what they teach you; you make their world sound like wonderland. Vile ruperts spread through a village, an old man leaves his last will and testicle, there is

348

dirty weather off Rockall and Fredastaire. A day is a red lettuce day.

The jokes are John Lennon's, but they have already seen good service in most grammar schools in this country. The grammar school is the place for this intelligent, informed and infantile humour, I think; and school may have been more important for Lennon and McCartney than either home or Liverpool, whatever sociologists and trendmen say. Grammar school pupils are alert, disciplined and frightened. Their pleasures are psychological—torturing a nervous teacher—and fairly secret.

I remember a joke that ran for months when I was at school. Whenever a teacher left the room, someone would draw a head, side view, on the blackboard. It would be a policeman in a huge helmet or a guardsman in a vast busby. At the side of this would appear a drawing of the policeman or guardsman without his helmet or busby. His head would be exactly the same shape as his hat. Another version showed a grotesque clubfoot—with or without a shoe, it looked the same.

Thinking back, I can see two things in our enjoyment of those gruesome gags. First, a hope that the world would stay simple, that our fears of mess and complication might prove to be unfounded. Just think. If the mask should fall to reveal a face just like the mask, if the truth about life, which parents and teachers hinted at so darkly, should turn out to be exactly like the façade, then they would be the fools with their conspiracy theories, and we would be right in our scared simplicity. And, secondly, I think we were fascinated by disease and deformity, which represented the future ugliness of life itself. If we could keep that at the level of a joke, if we could tame it in the safeness of school, everything would be all right.

All this is in Lennon. The adult world makes him larf, and his books are a vengeance. He has verbal forms of the clubfoot joke—Mr Borris Morris, in the story of that name, has a happy knack of being in the right place at the right place—and a splendid visual version. Two beggars stand side by side, each complete with stick, trumpet, dog and begging tin. One of them has dark glasses, and his dog has dark glasses too. The man carries a placard on his chest, saying: I am blind. The other man also has a placard. It says: I can see quite clearly. Thus does the world shed its secrets for the innocent. Although for the

349

person who can make such a joke, as for the boys who could laugh at our drawings, innocence is already a fantasy, an incipient nostalgia, no longer a state of mind.

But most strikingly Lennon sets up a gallery of deformed and violent people, a literal menagerie of creatures born on the blackboard during a break. A man clubs his wife to death. A friendly little dog ("Arf, Arf, he goes, a merry sight") is put to sleep. Eric Hearble, who has a growth on his head, loses his job teaching spastics to dance ("'We're not having a cripple teaching our lads,' said Headmaster"). Randolph is killed at Christmas by his pals ("at least he didn't *die* alone did he?") and a girl wonders about flowers for her wheelchair at her wedding—luckily her father comes home and cancels the husband. Little Bobby, 39 years old, gets a hook for his missing hand as a birthday present. Only the hook is for the wrong hand, his good left hand, and they have to chop that off to fit the hook.

It is absurd to compare Lennon to Joyce. Lennon's puns are piecemeal, scattered and unequal. Joyce's punning in *Finnegans Wake* is a system, a metaphysic for melding worlds. When Joyce writes of the flushpots of Euston and the hanging garments of Marylebone, the bible and London really collide. But Lennon has some fine effects. A pun is what Durkheim in another context called a logical scandal, it is an escape from linear meaning. It is language on holiday, and Lennon occasionally gets the authentic glee of this.

"Anything you say may be used in Everton against you." "Father Cradock turns round slowly from the book he is eating and explains that it is just a face she is going through." People dance with wild abdomen, and send stabbed, undressed envelopes.

Why is there so little of all this in the songs Lennon writes with Paul McCartney? McCartney's sobering influence? Hardly. More likely both are being tactful towards their public. They know that people are offended by nonsense, by things they can't understand; they know that people tend to take jokes that baffle them as a personal insult, a calculated exclusion. And their songs after all are a commercial enterprise—Lennon and McCartney have written well over 100 songs since 1962, and their work has been recorded by almost everyone you can think of.

Certainly there are occasional puns—"It won't be long/Till I belong to you." *A hard day's night,* the nonsense title of a film and a song, comes from a Lennon story called "Sad Michael." There are all the double meanings concerning pot and LSD on the *Sergeant Pepper* album, there is the sound play of by, buy, bye-bye in the song *She's leaving home.* And the songs have developed towards complexity.

Lennon and McCartney's early lyrics were thin and conventional: "Well my heart went zoom/When I crossed that room." There was rain in the heart, there were stars in the sky, birds were always threatening not to sing. The tunes were good, some of them as good as those of Rodgers or Leonard Bernstein. But the gap between words and music in pieces like *If I fell, And I love her, Ask me why, Not a second time,* was embarrassing for anyone who wanted to take the songs seriously. The best lyrics, which went with up-tempo numbers like *I feel fine, All my lovin', Can't buy me love,* were the ones which said the least. They said yeh, approximately. I'm not suggesting that Lennon and McCartney didn't know how conventional they were being, or that they couldn't have done better. But they didn't do better, presumably because they weren't interested.

Now they are interested. We get the sharpness of "Your day breaks/Your mind aches," where the rhyme really does something. People, characters, begin to take the place of the anonymous lover of the early songs, shouting, sobbing, missing, losing, promising his standardised love. We get Rita the meter maid, and the man who wants to be a paperback writer. We get Eleanor Rigby and all the lonely people, and the sights and sounds of Penny Lane. To say nothing of Billy Shearer, Sgt Pepper and Mr Kite. And we get the complex compassion of songs like *Wait* ("If your heart breaks/Don't wait") and *She's leaving home,* where the girl going off writes a note "that she hoped would say more," and her parents moan their incomprehension: "We gave her most of our lives. . . ." The whole work develops a sense of waste, of "tears cried for no one," as one song has it.

But still, the music has developed more than the language, and the language is not a main attraction in these songs. Lennon and McCartney's words are still less important than those of Bob Dylan, or Lorenz Hart, or Cole Porter, or Ira Gershwin. We

351

have to look elsewhere for the link between the songs and Lennon's stories.

The link is not hard to find. It takes us back to school, and Lennon and McCartney's repeated flights into the past. Think of the titles: *Yesterday, the night before.* Think of the nostalgia in songs like *Things we said today*, or *In my life*: "There are places I'll remember all my life." Think of the echoes of melodrama and music hall in the *Sergeant Pepper* album, the jaunty George Formby tone of *When I'm 64.* In *Good morning good morning* we take a walk past the old school—"Nothing has changed, it's still the same"—and *She said she said* flings a bewildered boy out of the classroom on to a hard life. The girl tells him that she knows what it's like to be dead, and he can only reply

> No no no you're wrong
> when I was a boy
> everything was right
> everything was right.

Lennon and McCartney in their songs do indeed "live in the past in the present," as Richard Poirier wrote about them in *Partisan Review.* But it is a personal and sentimental past, not a historical one—it is the specific past of good schooldays, when the world was simpler and adults looked like fools. Lennon and McCartney are not naively nostalgic, but they are nostalgic. Their songs and Lennon's stories express the *good child's* hostility to grown-ups. That is what we mean by the youth of the Beatles, an attitude not an age—after all, they were in their twenties when they began to make it around 1962. The attitude is not dangerous, at worst it deserves a detention, and this is why adults have been so keen to endorse the Beatles. This is safe play for children, mild naughtiness, and much better than breaking up Margate or digging up Paris.

The Beatles are a middle generation between the old conformers and the new rebels, between those who find it hard to believe that the world will change and those who know it's got to. Lennon and McCartney protest against the world adults have made, of course. They hate its pain and loneliness. But their protests are quiet, and their only answer so far has been escape into dope or India.

But the question remains. The Beatles have by-passed adulthood, and this links them with the revolutionary students, who are asking why they should grow up when growing up means napalm, treachery, compromise, and Porton Down. For years we have sole maturity as a virtue, we have preached the careful ethic of the status quo. But the Beatles are nearly 30 and wildly successful, on anyone's terms. If they haven't grown up yet, why should they now?

[*27 June 1968*]

THE HISTORY OF SELF HELP

R. J. Morris

When the vogue words of the sixties are dead, the participations, the productivities and devolutions no longer used, the words "self help" will still have a place in our endless debates over the way in which we shall organise our social life. *Self Help*, the book by Samuel Smiles which established the phrase in our language, was first published in 1859, and had sold over a quarter of a million copies by the end of the century. Proof of the book's continuing vitality was provided by the 1968 paperback edition, with an introduction by Lord Thomson of Fleet. Although Lord Thomson had not read the book until he came to write his introduction, he immediately recognised in it principles which had guided his own career—"the necessity of hard work," perseverance, honesty of intent, and success brought by "the energetic use of simple means and ordinary qualities."

Self Help has been translated into many foreign languages. It had an important influence on the ethical ideas of Yang Chang-chi, a teacher of the upper classes at Changsa normal school in 1913, where the young Mao Tse-tung was a student. It may be a coincidence that one of Mao's earliest published writings was *A Study of Physical Education*, in 1917, and Smiles's first book was *Physical Education*, in 1836. But Smiles, whatever he would have thought of the party and the Red Guards, would have recognised the clear-sighted determination of Mao; and both saw good health as essential to all other achievements. It is a powerful tradition, which finds its way into the lives of such different personalities as Mao and Lord Thomson. It is an idea worth closer attention, but it is an idea which can be appreciated not by the study of world figures but by following to its origins and taking a walk along the streets of Leeds, the industrial town in which the first pages of *Self Help* were written.

Samuel Smiles was born in the Scottish town of Haddington, and trained in medicine at Edinburgh University. He was one of the great stream of Scotsmen who made their way south to

354

seek careers in industrial England. He became doctor, journalist, newspaper editor, secretary to a railway company and then successful popular writer, whose books poured from the publishing house of John Murray. The formative years of his life, 1838–54, were spent in Leeds. Here he was editor of the radical *Leeds Times*, crossing editorial swords with the complacent upper middle class views of the whig *Mercury*, the Tory *Intelligencer*, and the aggressive Chartist demands of the *Northern Star*. His carefully argued leading articles on the folly of working class violence and the evils of middle class conservatism seemed to go unheeded, and in 1845 he changed his job to become secretary of the Leeds and Thirsk Railway Company, building its line north of Leeds. Until he left for Newcastle in 1854, he took an active part in the social and cultural life of Leeds, the experience which was the basis of his *Self Help* ideas.

The finest products of self help were not the spectacular careers of hard-working business men and politicians. The finest traditions of Smiles's books are found in the thousands of clubs, societies, libraries, chapels and meeting halls which the people of his England created, independent of all government aid or wealthy patronage. It is appropriate that Smiles's early ideas of self help should have been developed among just such people.

It began, he claimed, in the first edition of *Self Help*, in the following way: "Two or three young men of the humblest rank resolved to meet together in the winter evenings, for the purpose of improving themselves by exchanging knowledge with each other." The numbers increased and they used a cottage garden summer house until winter came, when they found "a large dingy apartment to let, which had been used a a temporary cholera hospital." It was in 1845 that they came to Smiles and asked him "to talk to them a bit."

With that mixture of patronising cooperation and naïve enthusiasm, common to many who sought to help working class education at this time, Smiles "felt that a few words of encouragement, honestly and sincerely uttered, might not be without some good effect ... he addressed them on more than one occasion, citing examples of what other men had done, as illustrations of what each might, in a greater or lesser degree do

355

for himself." He also gave these lectures to a Mechanics' Institute at Woodhouse, and a young men's improvement society connected to the Roman Catholic church.

The village of Woodhouse has long ago been absorbed into the built-up area of Leeds city, but like many of the settlements of that city it still retains its sense of identity as a village, with its network of loyalties—family, business, sports club and chapel. It is here that there still exists one of those three groups which first heard *Self Help in Men Illustrated with Biography.*

The Woodhouse Temperance Hall and Mechanics Institute stands in Institution Street, which makes its way from the open space of Woodhouse Moor to the mills and factories of the Meanwood Valley. It is a red brick building of simple classical lines. The few stone facings, door lintels, and window sills, are in yellow sandstone, as is the tablet on the front that bears the name, the date of building, 1850, and the clasped hands of friendship carved out. The hall served the people who lived in the back-to-backs, the terraces and the yarded-through houses of the streets and courts of Woodhouse. It is still in active use, although many of the people have been moved from nearby houses which are boarded up ready for clearance to make way for the new blocks of flats.

This hall is the nearest we can get to the beginning of self help; for when it was built, Samuel Smiles was the president of the Woodhouse Temperance Hall and Mechanics' Institute joint committee; Smiles laid the foundation stone; Smiles put his name to the mortgage deed; Smiles took the chair at the opening meeting; and the traditions of the building and using of the hall reflect the ideals of *Self Help, Character, Thrift, Duty,* and the many other books of their first president.

Local tradition, which I heard from Mr Hartney, now caretaker of the building, records that the hall was built entirely by the people of Woodhouse, mainly unskilled men, with only three craftsmen among them, a joiner, a plumber and a master mason. The money for materials was subscribed in small amounts by local working class men, and they took on the management of the hall. When the newspapers of the time reported the laying of the foundation stone on a site between the Wesleyan chapel and St Mark's church, the *Mercury* said, "Messrs Wood and Whitely are the architects and Mr John

Bailey is the contractor for the new buildings, the foundations of which have been dug out and prepared by a number of the working men of Woodhouse. The size of the new building will be 22 yards long by 14 wide, and is estimated to cost £800, which amount, with the exception of about £150, has been raised principally by subscriptions collected by the working classes themselves. On Tuesday evening, a procession was formed in front of the premises at present occupied as a reading room and library, and after walking to the site of the new building, where a large number of persons were found assembled together, the foundation stone was laid by Dr Smiles, secretary to the Leeds and Thirsk Railway."

Smiles praised the spontaneous efforts of the working class in collecting subscriptions and digging the foundations, and the meeting was closed with a hymn sung by the Woodhouse Band of Hope. When the building was publicly opened, on New Year's Eve 1851, over 700 people took tea together, and the paper could give a fuller description of the building, a description which is still a good guide today:

"The new building is a very commodious one with a handsome front, and contains a spacious lecture room capable of holding without seats, about 1,000 persons, having a gallery at one end and a raised platform at the other; eight classrooms and two rooms to be used as a dwelling. The land on which it was erected cost about £80, the building £720, the heating apparatus £50, and the furnishing about £50, making a total of £900. Towards this amount £500 has been raised by subscription. James Brown, Esq. of Harehills, having generously subscribed the sum of £100." Besides this, £300 was to be borrowed, and £100 more collected at the opening meeting. "We understand that this great acquisition to Woodhouse is the result of the self-denying efforts of a few working men, who, in the face of many difficulties and much undeserved opposition, have succeeded in this great object." If this is not quite the picture which tradition has left, it is near to it.

Here are a few of the inscriptions put on the walls with the flowers and laurels on that opening day:

For lack of knowledge the people perish
One of Heaven's choicest gifts is water
Elevation of the labourer

> The pen shall supersede the sword
> Self respect is worth a lot of fame
> Temperance and Education
> Union is strength

The "union" was that of the joint committee of the Temperance Society and the Mechanics' Institute, which was to run the building for the use of the two societies. In all other respects each was to run its own affairs. The Temperance Society was founded about 1840 and with it a Band of Hope for the younger people. This was soon after Jabez Tunnicliffe of Leeds had founded the original Band of Hope in Leeds in 1838. The society still has a banner with the figure of Tunnicliffe and the date 1838, that was copied from the original. There is no record of the Mechanics until 1847, when Smiles and others started lectures to them including "Self-education" and "The principles of mechanics."

The Temperance appeared to come first, and after a slow start it turned attention to "the agency which a Mechanics' Institute afforded where in place of gin or beer they could give instruction by books or lectures." The cooperation of the two societies began; and the grand, rolling mid-century Victorian prose of Samuel Smiles at the opening meeting described their work:

"A room in a tumbledown tenement was taken, and fitted up at a cost ot £90 collected from philanthropic ladies and gentlemen in the neighbourhood. Evening classes were formed and gratuitously taught by the best informed members, and though at first few attended, after some superior specimens of writing had been produced, the thing began to be talked about, and so many applied for admission that further accommodation was indispensably necessary. Three to four hundred were taught. As well as the elementary classes for teaching reading, writing, grammar, arithmetic, geography, etcetera, other agencies sprang up, and there were added a discussion class, a class for reading poetry and finally a reading room and library. All these agencies had been found to work admirably and not fewer than one third of the male members had been gathered from the public houses, from dog fighting, from gambling, and other low vices, and were now amongst the most industrious, sober and intelligent men in the district."

Smiles was soon to leave Leeds, but he left an institute which had a stability and permanence which lasted until its centenary celebrations in 1950, and still lasts in the building in Institution Street, a visible element of continuity with the traditions of the prosperous artisans, operatives and labourers of the Victorian working class.

I have talked to two trustees of the hall whose memories went back to the Edwardian years. These are years of violence and luxury: Tom Mann breathing defiance at the employers, the troops firing on the people at Tonypandy, gun running at Larne, the hysterical imperialism of Mafeking night, the arrogant wealth of the card tables at Biarritz and the house parties before Ascot. But these years, which we picture as high spending and grinding poverty, were, to Walter Thackray, the best years of his life, when he was carried in his father's arms to his first Band of Hope meeting, and learnt enough to make his first temperance speech at the age of 15.

He and Joseph Robinson told me how their life in Woodhouse centred upon the hall in the days when meetings were always "packed out." They were both Temperance people, but they knew much that happened on the Mechanics side. The main work was done by the Woodhouse Trades School. Here there was a day school for the children and a night school which taught science—chemistry in a long room lined with bunsen burners. Coopers, silversmiths, cobblers, blacksmiths and butchers learnt their trade there. The hooks still hang on the thick metal pole in the room where the boys were taught the butcher's trade so that the cuts could be demonstrated to them.

Much of the teaching was done free of charge, specially at the night school. Thackray's father and uncle taught the building science classes, after the day's work in their own businesses. The school was taken over by the council about 1906, under the new education act, but the building still has a part in the technical education in the city, for the education committee hires a room for the woodworking classes of the nearby Central High School.

But it is really the Temperance activities that Walter Thackray and Joseph Robinson can tell you about. The most important point of the week was always the gospel Temperance meeting on Sunday. The hall with the platform, and balcony on the top floor, would be filled with the songs from Sankey's hymn book, to the accompaniment of the harmonium. There would be prayers and readings, and the service would finish with a temperance lecture. There was no formal sermon. Instead, the service was often illustrated by lantern slides. Robinson's father operated these, carefully controlling the hissing gas cylinders which supplied the limelight. The slides were bible scenes or pictures illustrating the moral lessons of temperance, thrift, hard work, honesty and charity which the members preached and endeavoured to practise.

Earlier in the day there had been the Band of Hope Sunday school for the children. They were mainly children of members following their parents in the pledge not to use alcohol. The great day for the Band of Hope was the Good Friday procession. Then they would parade from the hall, round the village and down Woodhouse Lane to the town hall in Leeds. The magnificent silk banner was brought out for the parade.

At the town hall they met the processions of the other Bands of Hope in Leeds; Hunslet and Armley had the other two big ones. The children stood on the steps of the town hall to hear Temperance addresses and sing with the aid of a local brass band—Temperance if possible, like Rothwell and Morley. Then they would return with their banners to the hall, the streets closed and kept clear specially for the parade. At the hall the children had a special treat, tea in a bag, with a large hot cross bun as the central item.

On Easter Sunday the children would recite and sing before a visiting adjudicator. The winner was announced at the end, and he received his prize after reading the lesson in the service. The memories of these men, like the writings of many Temperance people, suggest that it was Easter, the season of renewed hope, rather than Christmas, the celebration of God's gift of a Saviour to men, that formed the most important feast of their religious year.

The gospel meeting was an integral part of a week which included work and leisure. Every Saturday night there was the "free an' easy," with dancing to the music of Will Parsons and his Band from Burley; traditional dances like the military two-step, a night of entertainment that was a direct challenge to the nearby pubs. Both men remember with enjoyment, and an impressive exactness, that every Saturday, for a sixpenny ticket, you got tea, half a pie and two buns, which was good value even then.

But there was also hard work done on Saturday night. As the pubs began to close, members of the Temperance would stand outside the doors and invite the drunks down to the hall for a cup of coffee to help them sober up. It was a way of recruiting people, of course; and those who accepted the invitation were soon told of the benefits of Temperance to health and prosperity. It was a tough way to spend an evening. It was not the occasional violence of the drunks that Thackray remembered but the grim squalor of it all, in which his father, uncle and others calmly persisted, in the hope of bringing more to take the pledge.

There was another way of approaching the public of Wood-house at this time, by taking advantage of a custom associated with the High Moor, where a number of solid square stones, three by three, had been placed, and anyone had a right to use them as speaking platforms. The biggest crowd came on Sundays to hear and to heckle all types of subjects. The Temperance people would tow their harmonium up there, on the summer afternoons, to preach and sing and counter the shouts and shoving of those who had been primed with beer in the pubs to come and upset them. Not that they resented this, for a quick exchange between a Temperance-speaker and a beery heckler was entertainment which would draw the sporting instinct of any crowd. And the speaker didn't know his job if the laugh didn't end on beer.

One thing is clear. The Temperance movement of this age didn't seem to restrict these men's lives. They didn't sit solemnly behind lace curtains, at home every Sunday, but were quite prepared to enter the fray for signatures to the pledge, because Sunday was the working man's holiday, and the day he might have time to listen. Temperance didn't stop them enjoying life. "It's no kill-joy," was the phrase they used; and it does seem that there is nothing like Temperance people for telling jokes about rolling out of pubs. There was the sad tale of the two who came out of the Swan with Two Necks in Woodhouse. (Note the care-ful exactness again.) "One says, 'Lovely red sun.' 'Nay,' says t'other, 'that's moon.' 'Bet you fourpence it's t'sun.' 'Done.' says t'other, when his friend stops and asks, 'but how are we going to decide which of us is right?' 'Don't worry,' the other man replied, 'we'll ask this chap coming down the street, intellectual looking chap, happen 'e can help.' The man walking down the street was asked, 'Sorry,' he replied, 'I'm a stranger round here meself.' Such then are the evils of drink."

Temperance people condemned drink without reservation. But this didn't mean they couldn't appreciate the attractions of the public house, its company, its newspapers and conversation, sports and entertainment. Some knew this only too well from their pre-pledge days, and all set about giving a real alternative to these leisure activities. There was the Woodhouse Temperance association football club which won many championships in its league, and the Woodhouse Temperance cricket club which played with equal success in the Leeds Amateur League. It is still an active cricket club associated with the hall, though perhaps they cannot insist on all members taking the pledge in the way that used to be possible.

In the winter the hall was a fine place for music, with the cantatas, and performances of Elijah, Samson, and at Christmas the Messiah. The fame of West Riding choral music is based on the success and enjoyment of people like this. Members supplied the chorus and singers themselves, but they were prosperous enough to hire someone from outside if they hadn't the right voice for one of the solos. The sheets of music for these performances are still stacked away in the cupboards of the hall, the parts unused for many years.

To Walter Thackray, his father, Ben, represents all that was best in the Temperance when its activities were still at their fullest. His sound health and his long and successful life was proof enough of the value of the pledge to many who knew him. When he was rising 70, the newspapers reported that Ben took four wickets with four successive balls for the Woodhouse Temperance eleven in a league match. His career, and that of his brother William, are part of the heroic age of self help, when the master craftsman could make his small business a success with little fear of the big corporation, and be content that what mattered was not amassing a large fortune but the personal freedom and integrity such modest success could bring.

William had taken the pledge as a boy after attending a Band of Hope lecture at the Friends' Meeting House in Blackman Lane. He set up in business as a master builder. In the early days his reputation as a steady man was a great gain, for his partner left him with a load of debt. Still, the creditors trusted him to work it off and he survived without being bankrupt, or banked as local terminology had it. As his fortunes rose, he began a career in which he and Ben built half of Woodhouse between St Mark's Church and the Ridge.

It was soon obvious that the Thackrays were not building any public houses on their land, and the brewers, sometime in the sixties, stepped in and offered William a blank cheque and the clearance of his mortgage debts if he would build a pub for them. He refused and neither man ever built or repaired a pub, although to show they were not vindictive they would help a publican with the rooms he lived in.

Most of the houses were back-to-backs, the sort condemned now but then built carefully to bye-law standards. Ben himself never moved away from Woodhouse, and built himself a through-house, sometime in the 1880s, in Midgely Place just off Institution Street. His support for the Temperance and his generosity to others gained him the title of "Uncle Ben" in Woodhouse, and the strong face of the man in the mason's yard above Woodhouse suggests something of the character which supported this reputation. Most years the banner of the Band of Hope procession carried black tapes in memory of some dead Temperance member; but it never carried them for Uncle Ben, for he lived to see the last procession in 1939, since they called at his door during his last illness as they were making their way round Woodhouse.

Ben was a careful and successful builder, an employer of men who owned land and houses—but he never left the working class community in which he lived. Instead he chose to lead and influence those who would follow him in Temperance. Of course, he was one of the most prosperous members of that community. The difference between prosperity and poverty in Edwardian Woodhouse would appear on a wet winter afternoon, when the school visitor came round and found a large number of children absent. Few were ill, but they had their shoes in the pawn shop until next pay day. The visitors at Quarry Mount council school would offer a book to any boy who would run home and bring a pair of spare shoes for the absent. It was one of young Walter Thackray's privileges to be able to do this many times.

One of the qualities which kept Ben a part of the working class Woodhouse was summed up by his son: "He was a humble man, a very humble man." It's not a compliment that would come easily to modern lips, for we see it only as a Dickensian caricature. But Ben's humility was not that of the down-trodden or obsequious, its mood still survived in the centenary service of 1950. Listen to the hymns chosen for that meeting. If this is deference, it is deference with a sting in it. First came that ever vigilant hymn, the jewel of Sankey and Moody Protestantism. *Onward Christian soldiers,* then came the verses of the old Sheffield Corn Law Rhymer, Ebeneezer Elliott, written even before the hall was built:

> When wilt Thou save the people
> O God of Mercy when,
> The people Lord the people,
> Not crowns and thrones but men.
> Flowers of Thy heart O God are they,
> Let them not pass like weeds away
> Their heritage, a sunless day;
> God save the people.

> When wilt Thou save the people,
> O God of mercy when,
> The people Lord the people,
> Not thrones and crowns but men.
> God save the people Thine they are
> Thy children as Thine Angels fair
> From vice, oppression and despair,
> God save the people.

Such humility recognised the duty or worship, but it also made clear demands for the decent life due to each human being in God's creation. By temperance and hard work, that congregation could claim to be doing their bit.

That meeting in 1950 was probably the last time the hall was packed out in the old manner. The cricket club still meets there, as do the Rechabites and the Good Templars, but the annex of the day school is the main use the building has. The numbers had been declining even before 1939. Where did self help go wrong? Is it that the brewers and the advertising agencies have lured the young away from the hall, or has Temperance done its job, and total abstinence is no longer needed to keep us from the abuse of alcohol? Certainly, street drunkenness and brawling are less common now, though the impersonal translation of such aggression to the motor car seems to remain. Do public libraries and free schooling mean that the Mechanics and the library are no longer needed? It is hard to think that these are the only reasons, for the conversation of both trustees brings the historian sharply against one of the greatest discontinuities of British history. Between 1914 and 1918, the Woodhouse Band of Hope sent 40 away to the war. At the end, three came back. After that, says Joseph Robinson, "It never really got on its feet again."

There were the processions: league championships were won; but the old life never returned to the hall. To Joseph Robinson and to Thackray, 1939–45 was just—"another war came." It finished off the processions, but that was just the working out of the long process which the Great War began. The hall still survives because the committee took care to appoint members of the old families as trustees, men like the Mitchells, Thackrays and Robinsons, who had the interests of the hall bred into them, however far they moved from Woodhouse. The greater mobility of families as businesses and people move from Woodhouse has steadily taken people away. The clearance of the old houses will dislodge a few more.

The Woodhouse Temperance Hall and Mechanics Institute is still there—a fine building, as yet not threatened by clearance. It has its problems. It needs a good damp proof course and an exit, to satisfy fire regulations; but the careful management of self help has maintained healthy finances to deal with any such claims. What self help could not do was resist the social pressures which since the Great War have taken away the people.

[*3 December 1970*]

ILLUSTRATIONS

The illustrations which decorate the section title pages all originally appeared in *New Society* and accompanied the articles listed below.

All diagrams are by Richard Nathiel.